ariaready

THE BUSINESS OF SINGING
SECOND EDITION

ADVANCE PRAISE FOR
ariaready

"Carol Kirkpatrick's ARIA READY: *The Business of Singing* is a remarkable book filled with tremendous insight, humor, and real world advice that is easily accessible, immediately practical, and frankly indispensable. I consider it to be essential reading for all singers, and I am thankful that Carol's voice continues to be such a prominent one in our industry."

— JAMES MARVEL, STAGE DIRECTOR

"At last! Here is a book that offers real and practical advice on navigating the business of singing, focused towards singers, but with valuable information for all those who care about the art and business of singing! Carol Kirkpatrick's words and sage advice aim to bridge the gap between academic studies and real-world career savvy, and to do so through words of wisdom delivered in a conversational style. This is essential information for a career in singing for which there isn't time to address in the voice studio, and that many academic programs do not attempt to address. It is a must-have for singers and teachers of singing alike!"

— MICHAEL EGEL, ARTISTIC DIRECTOR, DES MOINES METRO OPERA

Just like building anything, if the foundation isn't sound, it might look pretty and stable, but with the right conditions it will fall apart in an instant. With Carol's wonderful breakdown of the building blocks in ARIA READY: *The Business of Singing*, even the most seasoned professional can find something useful. It's always a good idea to come back to basics. Be open to a new way of thinking and prepare yourself for the ride you chose instead of the ride you just hop on. Make notes, break the binding and make this not just a book you read but a part of your daily life. Even if you take only one thing at a time you'll still be going someplace. Enjoy the journey.

— ALEXANDRA LO BIANCO, SOPRANO, 2011 LIEDERKRANZ VOCAL COMPETITION WINNER, 2011 IRENE DALIS COMPETITION WINNER

ARIA READY: *The Business of Singing* is an invaluable addition to the young professional singer's tool box. Carol brings a wealth of detail and knowledge of the obstacles that face singers—both those each of us create for ourselves, and those which the profession puts in front of us. The greatest strength of this book is that it is so wonderfully supportive. Carol never forgets for a minute that each of us is different, and encourages us to find creative ways to use our strengths and the materials she offers to find our way to success.

— DAVID OSTWALD, STAGE DIRECTOR 2011, AUTHOR, ACTING FOR SINGERS

"This book will be an excellent tool in any singer's arsenal. I have learned skills that informed not only my professional life as a singer, but the rest of my life as well. ARIA READY: *The Business of Singing*, along with Carol's teachings and workshops, have helped me cope with the inevitable rejection involved in this career, study music more effectively, create 360-degree, full-dimensional characters, and perhaps most importantly, communicate more effectively with others. I feel these skills are incredibly necessary to survive and thrive as a singer, an artist, and an individual. They say you can't learn these things from a book. But Carol gives exercises, questions to challenge oneself, and the invaluable opportunity and encouragement to follow-up with her. Do yourself a favor, and truly study this book—and yourself. You'll be glad that you did."

— MICHELLE TROVATO, SOPRANO, 2011 LIEDERKRANZ VOCAL COMPETITION WINNER

"Carol Kirkpatrick's book, ARIA READY: *The Business of Singing*, should be required reading for aspiring young singers making the transition from university life to a career on the stage. Not only is her advice inspirational, but it lays out the joys and dangers of a singer's life.On page after page, she gives advice and techniques for everything from managing finances to rehearsal etiquette to contracts. Most importantly, she guides the reader through the process of creating a personal brand that reflects one's true self. Although I am a director, not a singer, I really wish that this book had been available to me at the beginning of my career!"

— ELIZABETH BACHMAN, ARTISTIC DIRECTOR, TYROLEAN OPERA PROGRAM

"I found the 2nd edition of Carol Kirkpatrick's book, ARIA READY: *The Business of Singing,* a fascinating read. As much as we all think we know about the world of auditioning and building a singer's career, that world is always changing and evolving. There are always new ideas and concepts. That is the reason that this new edition is so valuable. It has much new information, a blend of the fiercely practical balanced by more abstract concepts for each singer to apply individually. It's possible that after reading this book, one might feel that he or she has had a particularly rewarding breakthrough, as one might with an expert therapist. Carol deals with both the core values that make a singer successful, as well as ideas that may well also lead to a happier, more fulfilled life, both onstage and off."

— KEN BENSON, ARTISTS MANAGER, CONSULTANT, FORMER VICE-PRESIDENT AT CAMI

"I know firsthand the wonderful energy, verve for opera and the positive influence Carol can have on ones career. Her insightful observations, and uncanny knack at having you look at who you truly are, will resonate not only in opera, but in your everyday life. Carol continues to be an inspiration to me, and if you use this book as a tool to further your vocation and life, you won't be sorry. Brava Carol, in this business we need more people like you! Keep up the great work."

— BRANDON JOVANOVICH, TENOR, METROPOLITAN OPERA, LA SCALA, SAN FRANCISCO OPERA, CHICAGO LYRIC OPERA, BASTILLE OPERA

"One of the many things I appreciate about the 2nd edition of Carol's book, ARIA READY: *The Business of Singing*, is the great advice and preparatory work she suggests in learning the music and managing the comprehensive study of a complete role. If every singer did this it would help make my job as conductor much more fun and enjoyable because the performer, having already done the tedious and careful preparation of preparing their music and character, is then confident and free enough to try different musical suggestions that then bring their character even further to life. This is just one small part of what this all-encompassing book has offer the emerging artist interested in becoming a professional."

— VALERY RYVKIN, CONDUCTOR, FORMER ARTISTIC DIRECTOR, GREENSBORO OPERA, OPERA SANTA BARBARA

"As a teacher of numerous established artists as well as emerging professionals, I am forever searching out resources that might be helpful for them as they strive to live their lives and realize their professional goals.

GOT IT! Carol's ARIA READY: *The Business of Singing* is the one! Perhaps because Carol and I are, as they say, of 'a certain age' and the same generation, I believe that she hits the nail squarely on the head. She offers practical, realistic, and fully achievable methodology, along with a depth of wisdom, sage advice, and canny insight that is possible only in those who have 'been there and done that.' Through the years, we have observed and learned from our mentors, teachers, colleagues, friends, and family—mostly, however, we have arrived at 'who' we are because of what life itself and personal experience have taught us. The value of this kind of knowledge is incalculable—the desire and ability to share it with others is, in my opinion, inestimable. Brava Carol! Rarely have I seen a book of this sort with which I so strongly agree—we are so much on the same page (no pun intended), it jolts me to read exactly the same thoughts and philosophy in the same words that I myself believe, use, and live by.

Many music schools and conservatories now offer courses in business and career management for performers—life as a professional. What an ideal text this would be for singers. I cannot imagine that anyone in the vocal music world could fail to benefit from reading this book and employing those principles that are appropriate, for themselves personally or for their students. It is written with astute perception, great integrity, and profound respect for singers and the Vocal Art."

— BILL NEIL, 2008 *CLASSICAL SINGER MAGAZINE* TEACHER OF THE YEAR, 2003 OPERA CANADA RUBY AWARD FOR LIFETIME ACHIEVEMENT, THIRTY-YEAR INTERNATIONAL OPERA AND CONCERT CAREER

CAROL KIRKPATRICK

ariaready

THE BUSINESS OF SINGING

SECOND EDITION

*Personal and Business Strategies for Making the Transition
from Aspiring Artist to Prepared Professional*

BANCROFT PUBLICATIONS

NEW YORK • DENVER

BANCROFT PUBLICATIONS
10732 West Florida Avenue, Suite A, Denver, CO 80232
www.ariaready.net

© 2012 by Carol Kirkpatrick

All rights reserved. No part of this work covered by the copyright hereon may be reproduced or used in any form or by any means graphic, electronic, or mechanical, including photocopying, recording, taping, or information storage and retrieval systems without the written permission of the publisher. This publication is designed to provide accurate and authoritative information in regard to the subject matter covered. It is sold with the understanding that the publisher is not engaged in rendering professional services. If professional advice or other expert assistance is required, the services of a competent professional person should be sought.

LIBRARY OF CONGRESS CATALOGING-IN-PUBLICATION DATA
Cataloging-in-publication data for this title is on file with the Library of Congress.
ISBN 978-0-97705-240-0

Manufactured in the United States of America on acid-free paper

*In fond memory of Herbert Grossman,
my musical mentor and friend.
Thanks for giving me a firm foundation
on which to build my career and life.
It's paid off!*

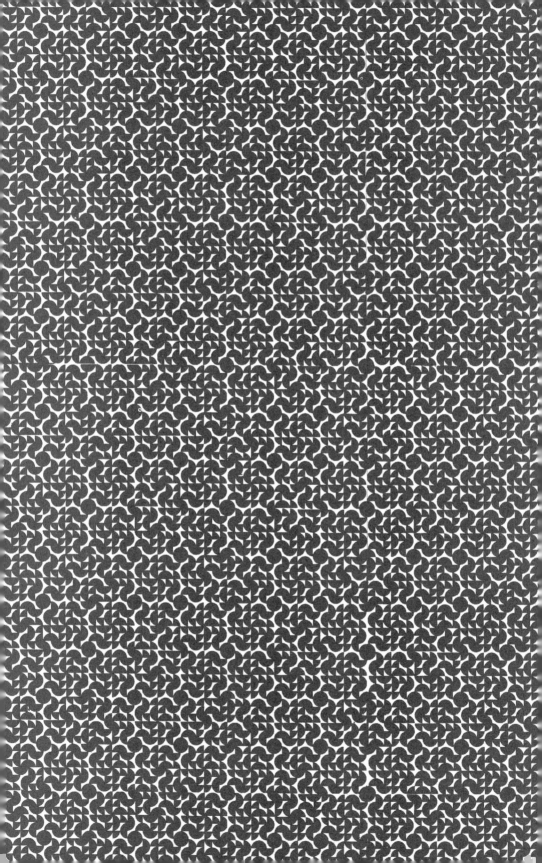

FOREWORD

THIS IS THE BOOK we have needed for years in the world of classical singing! *Aria Ready* will be a necessary tool for every aspiring opera singer, as they exit the conservatory or university and begin their journey to a professional singing career. Dealing with very serious inner and outer issues, both in performance and preparation, Carol Kirkpatrick boldly dares to face up to the universally unspoken "fear factor" so urgently in need of an open discussion in our field.

The vocal study, artistic decisions, self-discipline, teaching, marketing, and audition process are all carefully analyzed, and detailed advice is given on a wide range of crucial matters, in the complex and often confusing progression needed to arrive at a professional career in classical singing. Our field is very old-fashioned in its personal requirements, not, surely, a path of instant gratification, and this book shows very powerfully the needs of patience, hard work, and self-assessment required for the beginning of a career.

God-given talent and strong ambition are not enough to make an important career, but the need shared with other professions, to be "Chairman of Your Own Board" while still maintaining a strong sense of team work, consideration, and openness to advice, is excellently covered in the book. Given the utterly collaborative nature of this art form, this is central to the message of *Aria Ready*.

Brava for a big job, superbly well done!

— **MATTHEW EPSTEIN**

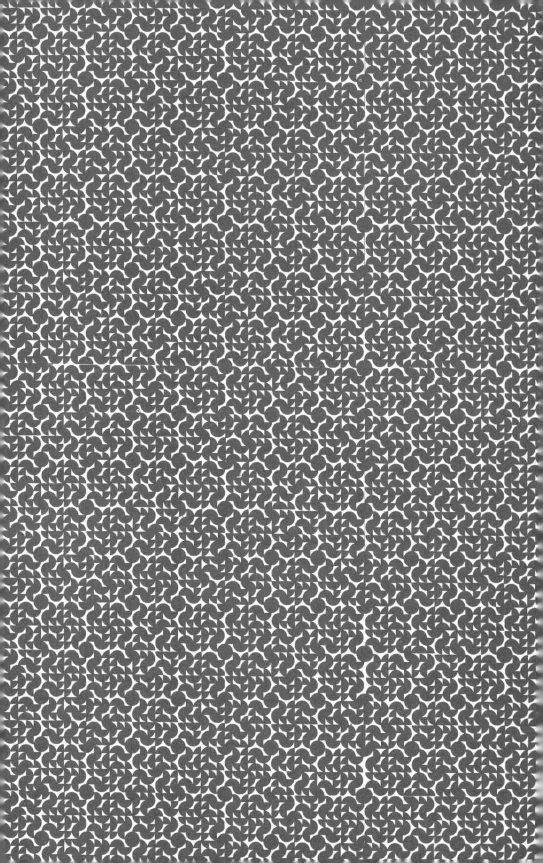

contents

Foreword xi
Acknowledgments xv
Introduction xvii

PROLOGUE
A Singer's Profile   4

ACT I
LAYING THE GROUNDWORK:
Getting Your Act Together   7

Voice Teacher, 8 • Alexander Technique, 15 • Systems of Practice, 17 • How to Practice and Prepare for a Performance, 21 • Fach/Voice Category, 23 • Language Tools, 25 • How to Work Your Music, 28 • Character Comprehension, 32 • Musical Style, 38 • Repetiteur/Accompanist/Pianist, 39 • Coach, 42 • Drama Coach/Classes, 45 • Polishing/Finishing Touches, 49 • Getting Experience, 50

ACT II
INSIDE OUT:
Inner Systems and Patterns   55

Getting To Know the Person Inside the Singer (Personal Branding), 57 • Individual Belief Systems, 63 • Tools and Skills for Keeping You On Your Path, 72 • The Gate Keeper, 85 • Rapport Skills, 89

ACT III

BUSINESS BASICS:

User-Friendly Business Skills and Tools   111

Skills, Tools, and Other Practical Business Information, 116 • Office Manager, 140 • Manager, 147 • Marketing/PR Director, 176 • Financial Officer, 188 • The Client—You, the Singer, 208

EPILOGUE

Looking Ahead   247

APPENDICES

Inner Language Systems Sample Words   255

Recommended Reading   256

Weekly Professional Expenses   260

Audition Journal Example from *Velvet Singer*   261

Goal Flow Chart   262

Goal Flow Chart Example   263

Sample Résumé   264

Short Bio Sample   265

Sample Cover Letters   266

How to Mark Your Music   268

Character Chart   270

About the Author   273
Index   275

ACKNOWLEDGMENTS

I WANT TO TAKE THIS opportunity to thank all of my students over the years, my colleagues, aspiring artists, and emerging professional singers, for urging me on and inspiring me to write this dramatically revised and updated second edition of *Aria Ready*. Thanks for your much valued input and encouragement.

A very special thanks to Kevin Hanek, for your discerning eye, and your layout and design skills. Your inspiration and guidance throughout this process were invaluable, and the outcome is more than I could have ever wished for. Kathy Geary, your eyes and ears have been a welcome addition through this process as well. Thanks to you both for your continued support, I could not have done it without you.

Last but not least, I want to thank my husband, David Anderson, for being my sounding board, always offering your well thought out suggestions specifically from a business and spiritual point of view. Thank you for your cherished love and support throughout this long process.

— **CAROL KIRKPATRICK**

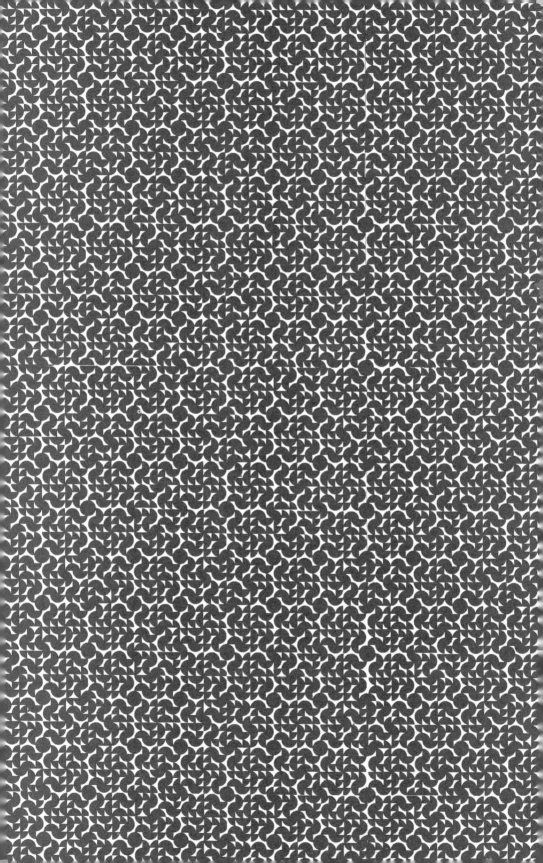

INTRODUCTION

PREPARING FOR A CAREER in any specialized field is an important process, and the industry you are considering stepping into is no exception. The transition from aspiring artist to the professional world of singing is often filled with doubts and insecurities. It can become a daunting task that might even create stumbling blocks for you along the way. The information, knowledge, skills and tools needed for this journey may have been peripherally studied and talked about during your schooling, but the actual acquisition of this working knowledge based on your firsthand experience and combined with a solid understanding of the basic rules of our industry is another story. There are three things that are essential in any endeavor: Know the name of the game you want to play. Know the rules of that game. And most importantly, you have to know how the game is actually played. And this is especially true as you face the challenges of preparing for a career as an opera singer. Not only will you likely have to secure a regular job to pay for the day to day bills, but you must also find the extra time, energy, money and commitment to support and sustain your continued preparation; development and reinforcement of the necessary vocal, artistic, and business skills and tools necessary in establishing a professional singing career.

Knowing what lies ahead and how to better prepare for this adventure is key to counteracting some of the fears

The journey of a thousand miles begins with a single step.

– LAO TZU

Life was meant to be lived, and curiosity must be kept alive. One must never, for whatever reason, turn his back on life.

– ELEANOR ROOSEVELT

COMMITMENT

"Until one is committed, there is hesitancy, the chance to draw back, always ineffective, concerning all acts of initiative (and creation). There is one elementary truth, the ignorance of which kills countless ideas and splendid plans: that the moment one definitely commits oneself, the providence moves, too. All sorts of things occur to help one that would never otherwise have occurred. A whole stream of events issues from the decision, raising in one's favor all manner of unforeseen incidents and meetings and material assistance which no man could have dreamed would have come his way. Whatever you do, or dream you can, begin it. Boldness has genius, power, and magic in it. Begin it now."

– WILLIAM HUTCHINSON MURRAY, *THE SCOTTISH HIMALAYAN EXPEDITION* (THE LAST 3 SENTENCES ARE BY GOETHE)

one may have when stepping out of the college or university comfort zone and transitioning into the real world. *Aria Ready* does more than tell you what needs to be done—it offers a detailed, how-to, step-by-step guide towards building a solid career foundation, and understanding why that is important.

You will learn that no two people are internally wired in the same way. Therefore there is no one particular method or specific path for accomplishing any task, activity or job. You are a unique individual that deserves to create and represent your own authentic Personal Brand. You get to be more of who you are at that deep core level and feel more comfortable there than you ever thought possible. By going through this process of getting to know and like the legitimate person inside the singer, you liberate the artist.

Once you recognize the value of who you are through your Personal Brand and feel ready to establish the Business aspects of your career, as I said above, it's important to know what the game is, what the rules are and most importantly how the game is played. Then and only then can you make a thoughtful choice about playing or not. Even when you know where you are going, you may still feel a bit afraid, but because you have all of these tools, skills and information and know how to use them, you will find that you have more courage as you challenge yourself on this exhilarating and fulfilling journey. The amount of improvement you experience will depend on how much you are willing to participate in each activity. So give yourself a winning chance for success by using the tools and skills offered in this book. "*ARIA READY*"?

HOW TO USE THIS BOOK

While this book is mainly structured to aid the emerging professional artist in planning his or her career, the table of contents clearly outlines topics for easy reference to specific subjects important throughout the life of a singer's career. *Aria Ready* is a workbook, informational resource, tool, and guide. I have tried to cover most of the subjects that compile a professional singer's career track. Not every subject has been discussed in depth; sometimes ideas are presented in the hopes of stimulating and inspiring you to seek further guidance pertinent to your specific needs.

I hope that my book helps inspire you to make a commitment to begin the process of knowing the person inside the singer, so that you will be ready to start your journey with confidence. My personal philosophy is that each of us is responsible for passing on to the next generation of singers, the accumulated information, skills, and tools that we have learned from our own experiences, as well as from those who came before us. First you are the apprentice, then the mentor. The insights and experiences gained from actively performing and pursuing a singing career are not readily available in any virtual world, book, or class. I hope that you will continue this tradition of passing on the knowledge that you have had the privilege of gaining from those who came before you, along with the lessons you have learned from personal experience, to those coming after you.

"If you don't know who you are at the core, it's almost impossible to succeed at anything."

– OPRAH WINFREY

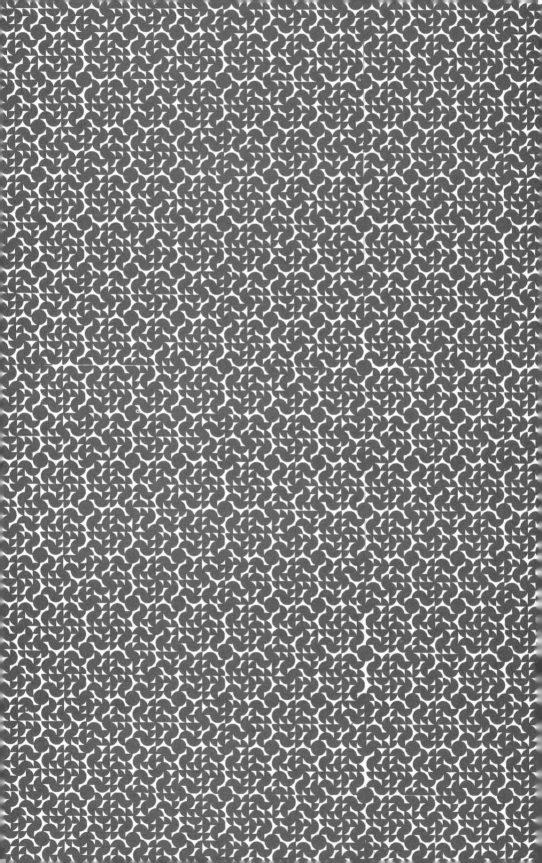

PROLOGUE:

a singer's profile

MANY YOUNG SINGERS, PRIMED only with their dreams, idealistically set out on their journey to become professionals, unaware of the sacrifices and commitment it takes. One may have an idealized, romantic notion of what ones daily life in the world of performance entails. Some of these ideals might come from your own experience at High School and University level where your performance context from year to year is familiar and feels supported and safe. However, once you make the transition out into the real world of performance, you will find it is a matter of hard work, commitment, and persistence with little to no support other than your desire to follow your dream. You are now a participant on a much larger platform for getting that job, role, winning a competition, or being chosen for an apprenticeship.

The biggest shock for most singers making that transition from university to the real world of performance is that they are once again, even if they have completed a masters or doctoral degree, viewed as a freshman who must learn what the new game is, what the new rules are and most importantly how the new game is played. The more you pay attention with intention, the shorter the time needed to pay your dues. So stay awake and be con-

> *I really haven't had that exciting of a life. There are a lot of things I wish I would have done, instead of just sitting around and complaining about having a boring life.*
>
> **–KURT COBAIN**

scious as you gain experience each and every day on your journey.

The following questions and your answers will give you an honest evaluation of whether or not this is the career path for you. This book is designed to enlighten and inform those of you whose essence demands that you follow your passion for building a solid platform from which to establish your singing career. It will help clarify and demystify some of the doubts you may have as you start the complex, demanding and challenging process. If you feel this is not the career path for you, you can still satisfy your need to perform and at the same time make a significant contribution to your community by participating on a more local level. That is after all, how performing started. Each community would provide their own excellent entertainment. You might want to also take a look at the section on Career Transition in the Epilogue to help you understand how to better move from pursuing a singing career to finding the thing you feel you are truly meant to do. You might find that it still involves the arts, but from a different prospective. *"ARIA READY"?*

What is put before you here is real and gleaned from years of experience. It can be an overwhelming and risky trip. Please consider these questions carefully:

- Do you remember when you made the transition from high school, where you may have been at the top of the food chain, to university, where you were surprised to find yourself at the bottom of it once again? Well this next stage of preparing for a singing career is very similar. Once you are out of university, no matter your level of degrees, most times you have to be willing to start at square one of the learning process needed to prepare you for becoming a young professional. Are you willing to commit to spending this similar amount of time, energy and money, once again at this juncture in your life and at your age?

- Are you exceptionally talented and who says so?
- Are you innately musical and who says so?
- Do you have dramatic instincts and who says so?
- Is the person or the persons advising you honestly qualified to give you trustworthy advice in this new and larger arena?
- Do you love the classical art form and learning all you can about it whether it is music, drama, literature or art?
- Are you willing to forgo the social life style most of your non singing friends have, so you can spend most of your extra time, energy and money on preparing for your musical career?
- Once out of University, preparing for a singing career, especially in the beginning, requires you to focus almost exclusively on yourself and your preparation for that career. As a result, are you ready to deal with the emotional toll that a singing career can take on your personal relationships?
- Do you know the building blocks required in creating a singing career? How are your business and networking skills?
- Have you created a realistic plan of action to reach your goals and with whom have you collaborated on putting this plan in place? Is it someone who has already been through this process or understands it well? Do you realize that most times you will be your own manager, the one who gets you jobs?
- How well will you be able to balance and manage a full or part time job while dealing with the demands of studying, practicing and managing your career?
- Are you lucky; do you believe in fate? This is true to some extent, but your luck increases proportionally with your level of knowledge, preparation and focus. In this state, it is easier to be aware of the opportunities.

Alas for those that never sing, But die with all their music in them!

– OLIVER WENDELL HOLMES

- Are you bright, intelligent, clever and fast at learning music, grasping the concepts of singing and business?
- Are you linguistically gifted? If not, are you willing to spend the time, energy and money necessary to become proficient in foreign languages?
- Is the process of learning and making a piece "your own" enough satisfaction? Do you enjoy the process: rehearsals, absorbing information, listening, learning, practicing, etc.?
- Do you feel comfortable with constant change in your life, traveling, living out of your suitcase for weeks at a time and spending a lot of time alone as you continually focus on your singing career?
- Are you comfortable in foreign countries? Do you speak other languages? Is it easy for you to assimilate into a new culture?
- Are you self-motivated?
- Do you enjoy your own company? Can you productively spend much time alone?
- Can you stay healthy? Do you have a health condition such as allergies that are a constant battle?
- Do you have severe PMS? Do your periods put you out of commission for a couple of days or weeks every month?
- Are you responsible? Are you independent? Are you committed?
- How well do you deal with rejection?
- Are you looking for a career to give you an identity? Having a singing career is, when all said and done, just another job that comes with all its own particular ups and downs; the usual baggage.
- Can you create boundaries, and learn to say "no" to doing too much, too soon along the path towards a successful career?

- Can you accept delayed gratification? The career payoff may or may not come until after completing school followed by further years of study and polish.

- Do you enjoy spending time with your musical colleagues, conductors, stage directors, etc., or does their behavior and company annoy you?

- Do you understand that very few professional singers make the whole of their living as a singer? Is that OK with you? Will you mind having that second temp job to make ends meet, to be able to pay your bills so that you can sing?

- Do you really know what the game is? Do you know what the rules are? Do you know how the game is played, which is usually completely different from what the rules are? Do you want to play?

Understand that there are many levels of performance. Singing is something everyone should learn to do well, whether singing professionally as a vocation or for pleasure giving service to your community as an avocation.

You can have lots of fun and give lots of joy and service performing in less demanding and stressful circumstances. There is no disgrace in changing directions and you don't have to feel guilty if you find you are not willing to pay the price of having a career as a professional performer. Know that we are all internally wired and programmed differently, we all have many differing talents so it's up to you to make sure you discover and use all that you have been given. The most important point is to be happy in and with your life and to continue to evolve. If after answering these questions you are still passionate about becoming a professional singer, this book will give you the essential, down to earth, step-by-step materials, skills, tools and information you will need to help build your career.

Don't ask yourself what the world needs. Ask yourself what makes you come alive, and then go do that. Because what the world needs is people who have come alive.

– HOWARD THURMAN

ACT I

laying the groundwork: getting your act together

YOU ARE THE PRODUCT, the company, and the person who manages your business, so it is your responsibity to learn how to weave these parts together into a successful venture. This process involves learning how best to utilize your time, energy, and money in building your career. Developing a solid foundation, beginning with the product—you, the performer—is the first and most important part of the process, and this chapter is intended to help you maximize the effectiveness of how you do what you do, the steps you take in the construction of that foundation.

No more spinning your wheels, no more playing at having a career. Now is the time to begin this process, one step at a time, in a smart and practical way that is custom tailored to you and your own unique manner of working. This helps keep you motivated and excited about the possibilities.

One thing you can be sure about in this profession is, no matter where you are in your career, there is always something new and interesting to learn. This learning comes in part from gaining your own experience, as well as from working with others who have already had that experience, and eventually, from teaching others what you have learned.

Everyone wants to live at the top of the mountain, forgetting that how we climb is all that matters.

– GABRIEL GARCIA MARQUEZ

Assuming you have the necessary vocal gifts, here are the fundamental building blocks essential for having a profitable, secure, and solid performance career:

- Find the right voice teacher for you
- Familiarize yourself with Alexander Technique or a similar practice to get in touch with the physical aspect of singing
- Know what and how to practice
- Determine your correct voice category (fach)
- Develop proficiency in the core operatic languages and utilize the International Phonetic Alphabet (IPA) in preparing your music
- Know how to efficiently work on your music, both individually and when working with a répétiteur or coach
- Learn how to create, develop and work a character into your voice and physical actions.
- Get comfortable with acting techniques and stagecraft
- Seek out performance experiences to further polish and refine your product

VOICE TEACHER

A bird doesn't sing because it has an answer, it sings because it has a song.

– MAYA ANGELOU

Finding the right voice teacher is of paramount importance. A great voice teacher, in addition to being able to teach vocal technique, should be trustworthy, responsible, knowledgeable, imaginative, inspirational, and a great communicator. I cannot stress this point enough: acquiring and maintaining a solid vocal technique is arguably the single most important element necessary in establishing any kind of successful singing career. Singers must learn how to properly manage their instrument like any other musician. Just because it is built into your body doesn't mean you automatically know how to use it. Raw talent is not enough to sustain the vocal demands of a professional career. You need to learn how best to use and maintain your instrument, both now and over the course of your career as your voice continues to mature. It is essential during the course of this process that you discover and embrace your own individual and unique sound.

What distinguishes opera from any other form of music is that with few exceptions, the entire dialogue is sung rather than spoken. Your job as a singer is to produce a beautiful, authentic, and individualistic sound which carries all of the emotion of the story, words, music, and character through the sound of your voice. Because there is a mind-body connection, you will discover that the physicality of the character you are portraying (physical gestures, facial expressions) will more easily emerge from what the mind is thinking.

Every teacher will have a different style of teaching, and for every style of teacher there are dozens of students who swear by them. But that doesn't mean that *their* teacher is necessarily right for you. Your job is to find a teacher with whom you have rapport.

Some teachers teach using imagery, some are pure pedagogues, others help you learn technique while also showing you how to use that technique to put the drama into the sound of your voice. Some may go even further, assisting you in understanding and effectively dealing with the rigors of establishing a singing career. Teachers are usually able to recommend good coaches, and often have connections that could be useful later as you begin to develop a more polished product.

There is no right or wrong to this process; your job in the beginning is to find a teacher with whom you have great rapport, absolute trust, someone who has the ability to communicate effectively what is needed to help you accomplish the necessary technical work and with whom you are

It's very easy, with the instant gratification of today's technology, to spend too much time listening to and imitating the timber, quality, and character of other singers' voices and sounds, rather than taking the time to discover, accept, and develop your own authentic sound. Once you have a career going, you will want others to be able to recognize and associate your unique and particular voice and sound with your name—not someone else's.

able to notice tangible results vocally. You must also learn to trust your own instincts, as well as listen to what others are saying about your progress. This will help guide your choice. If after several lessons you feel you are not communicating well or are not making progress vocally, it may be time to look elsewhere.

In most of the larger cities there are a plethora of voice teachers. Remember, you are looking for a teacher who will not only help you to build a reliable vocal technique, but will also encourage you to break new ground, strive toward your career goals, and develop all the potential of your instrument. You also want a teacher who will appreciate your unique qualities as a singer. You shouldn't end up sounding like a clone of your voice teacher, cheating you out of your own authentic and individual voice. So, how do you find a teacher who will keep what is unique about your voice, while still giving you the tools you need to make it better?

One great way to start your search for a teacher is to listen to fellow singers in the profession. When you hear someone who sings well, find out who they study with. If it's possible, ask if you could sit in on a lesson. This will allow you to observe the teaching process in action, to determine initially if this is a teacher you'd wish to consider further. If you feel comfortable with the process and language that the teacher uses to communicate, and feel rapport with that individual, schedule a lesson. If the first lesson is still a positive experience, give yourself a month or two of working with this teacher, to get a better perspective as to whether this teacher can lead you where you want to go. If not, thank the teacher for what you have learned and continue your quest. You are paying for this process, so don't waste your time, energy, or money to work with someone who is not assisting you in accomplishing your goals. Remember, this is business, not personal, so take a step back from your emotions as you attempt to determine the right choice for you.

> *Music is one of the ways we can achieve a kind of shorthand to understand each other.*
>
> — YO YO MA

Here are some other items to consider when choosing a voice teacher. Take your time in choosing a teacher: this will be one of the biggest investments of time, energy and money you will make in the course of your career, so make sure it is the right choice for you. Remember that you are paying a voice teacher for a service—your teacher is employed by you—so make sure you get what you are paying for:

- Does this teacher have a good reputation?
- Is this teacher interested in you as an Individual and believe that you have the potential for having a professional career?
- Does this teacher have adequate time for you in order to accomplish the work that needs to be done?
- Is this individual in touch with what is happening currently in the profession?
- Is this teacher knowledgeable about the voice categories (fachs) and their corresponding repertoires?
- Does this teacher work well with your particular voice type?
- Does this teacher have the patience to see you through the process of developing a technique?
- Is this teacher able to help guide you through the vocal changes you may undergo as your voice matures, and direct you to the appropriate level of competitions and auditions for where you are in that process?
- Is this teacher overly possessive, not wanting you to try other teachers or insisting you only work with certain coaches? No one teacher has all the answers.

Stay away from teachers who:

- Tell you you'll become the next great star at the Met
- Claim they can have you ready for major auditions and jobs in a very short period of time

> *So many people walk around with a meaningless life. They seem half-asleep, even when they're busy doing things they think are important. This is because they're chasing the wrong things. The way you get meaning into your life is to devote yourself to loving others, devote yourself to your community around you, and devote yourself to creating something that gives you purpose and meaning.*
>
> — FENDERX MORRIE SCHWARTZ

- Insist they are the only one who can teach you what you need to know
- Speak ill of other voice teachers or other individuals in the industry
- Intimidate or abuse you vocally or psychologically into believing you will never succeed without them.

Once you have chosen a voice teacher, what do you need to know in order to be prepared for your lessons?

In the beginning, go to your lessons with an open mind and a willingness to try what is being asked of you, even if you make mistakes or fail to get it right away. Remember that what you hear in your own ears is not necessarily what is heard by those listening to you, so ask yourself if you feel you can trust how it feels, rather than how it sounds.

As you progress, go to your lesson with an agenda in mind. Know what you want to accomplish at each lesson to avoid wasting your precious time, energy and money. You might need to work on some difficult passages from several different pieces that you're finding technically challenging, or perhaps you want assistance in working a new piece into your voice.

I'm not suggesting that you try to control the lesson, but it helps your teacher know how better to help you when you ask questions or request further clarification, so speak up. Sometimes you just need to ask for a different example or verbiage.

Record your lessons if you're able to, and listen to the recording as soon after your lesson as possible, to reinforce what you have just learned. Use a designated notebook to write out exercises and any pertinent vocal instruction. This will give you a permanent record of the process of your technical development. These can be great and useful resources once you are out having a career, especially if you run into any vocal trouble. If you're going to spend the money taking lessons, take the additional time and effort to practice regularly in a focused and conscious manner, and come to lessons and coachings in an equally focused and receptive state for the work you need to accomplish.

Don't be embarrassed in your beginning lessons if you make mistakes or can't immediately grasp the new exercises. You are there to learn, not to impress. If you don't understand something or have questions, ask as many times as it takes until you truly understand the information that is being presented to you.

Don't try to fit new technique or ideas into your old habits and manner of singing—that doesn't work. Start with an open mind and clean slate. Have the courage to allow your real voice to come out, and make a sincere effort to attempt what is being requested of you. And remember, trust the physical sensations of singing, and not what you hear in your own head. As I said before, you will never develop a reliable singing technique by listening to yourself, because what you hear is never what is heard by others. If you start to use that as the benchmark, you will find yourself adjusting what you are doing technically for every venue you sing in, rather than using one technique for everything. It's better to become familiar with and focus on how it feels rather than how it sounds.

If you are hoarse, have excessive phlegm, or your throat hurts following a lesson, beware! This can be a warning sign that you are either not properly understanding what is being taught, or that what is being taught is harmful to your vocal cords and throat. Singing should be a natural, organic process. If this happens consistently, look for a new teacher.

Don't fall into the trap of spending your hard-earned money to study with the most famous "name" teachers. Some of the best voice teachers are neither famous nor cost a fortune to work with. Rather, find a teacher who has the

> *Make it a rule of life never to regret and never to look back. Regret is an appalling waste of energy. You can't build on it—it's only good for wallowing in.*
>
> – KATHERINE MANSFIELD

> *Alas for those that never sing, But die with all their music in them!*
>
> – OLIVER WENDELL HOLMES

> *Practice isn't the thing you do once you're good. It's the thing you do that makes you good.*
>
> – MALCOLM GLADWELL

necessary technical knowledge, one with whom you have amazing rapport and respect, and can therefore develop an unshakable foundation on which to build your vocal strengths. Save working with the famous teachers until you are at a stage where you can take advantage of what they have to offer, or at a point where they might be helpful in furthering your career.

In any case, don't become so attached to any one teacher that, if the time comes to move on you can't, either because you are afraid you will hurt his or her feelings or fear some form of retribution. This is professional, not personal. Most good teachers understand that there might come a time when you want to move on, and that should be okay with them. Most good teachers want you to do in the end what is best for your vocal technique and career.

Be prepared and efficient in your lessons. Don't waste time by making your lesson a therapy session or social event. If you need some advice or help with a problem or situation, find out if your teacher might have extra time to discuss it with you. Otherwise, it might be better to discuss the situation with family or friends, or make an appointment with an appropriate professional.

If you are having financial difficulties, let your teacher know immediately prior to your next lesson to see if you can work something out. That's behaving professionally. Don't be afraid to take a short hiatus as you work your financial situation out—you can still practice. If you really like what you are learning from this teacher, you might be able to sit in on others' lessons, where you can observe and continue gaining knowledge, using what you learn as you work on your own. Perhaps you could afford to take one lesson a month, to ensure that you remain on the right path as you continue to practice what you have already learned. Ideally, you'll be able to resume lessons on a regular basis when things are resolved.

Do not rush on to the successive steps mentioned in this section of the book until you have a very firm grasp on your technique. Having a solid vocal technique gives you confidence and ease as you pursue a singing career, and is what all the other areas of study are based upon. Your singing should feel effortless, fluid, and connected to your body. Because of the mind/body connection, your body will respond to what you are feeling emotionally. Your voice must be anchored to a secure, well grounded technique that is second nature to you. Knowing how to develop a specific agenda for the work you want to accomplish and becoming comfortable with what to expect in your lessons, will help you to work efficiently and be able to take full advantage of what your voice teacher has to offer.

Having a solid vocal technique can be compared to an anchored boat. It has the freedom to be moved within its confined area by the elements. A dramatic song or operatic role can be like a stormy sea with its great waves and winds; a love song can be like the calm, placid sea. Neither is rigid or tied tightly to one spot, nor are they completely loose, able to be tossed about by whatever is encountered.

ALEXANDER TECHNIQUE

In the 1890s, the Australian Shakespearean recitalist, Frederick Matthias Alexander, often became hoarse while performing. He sought the help of medical doctors, who found nothing physically wrong. Resting his voice worked only temporarily. His determination to find a solution came following a nine-year observation of his own actions and reactions using a three-way mirror. What he discovered was a pattern of tension called the "startle response"—our reaction, for example, to a door slamming.

This physical response is universal. Our head, which weighs from eight to twelve pounds, reflexively moves back and down, compressing the small vertebrae in the neck. This position affects our whole body. We often continue to hold ourselves in this physical state after the door-slamming experience has passed. It becomes a habit, creating unnecessary muscular tension throughout our entire body.

The Alexander Technique, developed from Frederick Alexander's observations and conclusions, works to change and free us from these unnecessary tensions or harm-

Anything unattempted remains impossible.
– UNKNOWN AUTHOR

ful habitual movements in our everyday activities. If the muscles of our bodies are habitually over-tightened, they become distorted, unbalanced, and compressed. Unfortunately, this condition becomes habitual and therefore feels "normal." The Alexander Technique teaches the use of an appropriate amount of effort for a particular activity. By learning to release these unnecessary tensions while re-educating our mind and body, we discover a new balance, new support, new poise, and increased ease of movement in our bodies.

What does a teacher of this technique do? During a lesson, which usually lasts from 30 to 45 minutes, the teacher will observe your posture and movement patterns. Gently placing their hands on your neck, shoulders, back, and so on, the teacher will be gathering information about your patterns of breathing and moving. You will be asked to perform some simple movements such as walking, standing, and sitting. Their hands will be in easy contact with your body, sometimes gathering information, other times gently guiding your body to release these restrictive muscular tensions.

Just like finding the right voice teacher or coach, take the time to find an Alexander Technique teacher with whom you feel comfortable, safe, can communicate, and have rapport. Lessons should be more frequent initially, 2 to 3 times a week if you can afford it, to insure that this new approach to movement and the thinking about it become firmly established. As this process proceeds, pupils find they can do the work with only one lesson a week or every other week. Alexander Technique is also taught in group sessions, which might be a more financially feasible way to try out this technique.

If you want to improve what you are already accomplishing, or if you are having a vocal problem you can't seem to get beyond, this technique might be worth looking into. Prices vary from teacher to teacher and place to place. The best way to look for reputable teachers is to check their references through the NASTAT (North American Society of Teachers of the Alexander Technique) or STAT (Society of Teachers of the Alexander Technique). Another good source of information for finding a teacher of this technique is through colleges or universities in your area or online. There are also many books and web sites on this subject. Find what works for you.

SYSTEMS OF PRACTICE

Working with your teacher and coach will help you to gain an objective view of your technique and its application. The feedback they give you will help you to make the adjustments necessary to create a more functional and solid technique. As a result, you will learn to work more within your imagination, your feelings, and by visualization, rather than listening to yourself.

The goal of practicing is for you to be awake, conscious, objective, mindful, and focused on what you are doing while you are doing it, as well as *how* you are doing it, the same way as you are when working with your teachers and coaches. When you practice singing, you reinforce habits physically and mentally, so before you begin, consciously choose what you want to accomplish—what your present objective and specific agenda for this particular practice session will be.

Here is an interesting exercise to try that will allow you to leave the day's activities behind and focus on practicing:

Create two imaginary circles on the floor, out in front of you about 2 feet apart. Make them big enough to stand in comfortably with your arms outstretched. Make the field of each circle a different color. Stand in circle 1 and, as you do, allow all of the day's unwanted thoughts and activities to fall off you, physically and mentally, into the circle you are standing in. See, hear, and feel them falling to the

I set a simple goal for this season, just to come to practice every single day. It kind of sounds funny, but I feel like, when I'm out there practicing and getting better every single day, the games will take care of themselves. If I can practice every day, that means I am staying healthy and good things will happen for me.

— CHRIS GBANDI

ground and lying there in the circle. When that is accomplished, take a step outside that circle, leaving all your day's "stuff" over there. Notice that you are disassociated from your emotions as you look at and observe the "stuff" you left in that circle. Take a few deep breaths.

Now notice circle 2. It is the same size as circle 1 but is empty. Notice that it looks, sounds, and feels fresh, light, and airy. Take a step into circle 2. Be aware as you do so that your energy level is high, you are smiling from the inside out, and are present, focused, and ready to commit to your planned agenda for practicing. When you are done practicing, step out of circle 2 and get on with whatever is next on your to-do list.

Here are some other suggestions that might help you improve the results of your practicing:

- If you live in an apartment, being a good neighbor is important. I have found that it pays to go to your neighbors on both sides, across the hall, over and under you, introduce yourself, and let them know you are a singer who needs to practice every day. Let them know that you will respect the rules already in place for the time "noise" is allowed in the building, which is usually between 9 a.m. and 9 p.m. If your practicing disturbs them, ask them to please knock on your door and say so, and you will respect their request. Knowing at what times practicing will be the least disturbing for your neighbors also allows you to feel more comfortable when you are doing so. Remember, it's all about creating and maintaining relationships. It shows that you respect them and their needs as well as your own.

- Practicing "on purpose" with a well thought-out agenda allows you to get more done in a shorter period of time. Singing for hours in an indulgent, mindless matter is also not productive technically. All you are doing is reinforcing bad habits and wallowing in your emotions.

- By knowing exactly what you want to work on in each practice session, you are free to experiment, to make discoveries or connections to what you and your teacher or coach have worked on recently—which up to this point, may have only been understood intellectually. Devise a regimen that will help strengthen and focus your attention in this area.

- If your mind keeps wandering off to other things, keep a paper and pencil handy, and take a moment to write down these thoughts. This will get them off your mind until you are ready to pick them up again, allowing you to be present and focused when practicing.

- It is impossible for anyone to really hear themselves while singing. What you hear on the inside is not what others hear on the outside. If listening to yourself is genuinely the only way you can work successfully while practicing, record yourself as you work. Recording your practice sessions gives you that extra dimension, and helps create an objective view of what you are doing. Make sure to stop often during your practice session to play back what you have just done, so you can hear what the differences are when applying new vocal techniques or trying different emotional interpretations.

- If you are too tired to practice vocally, you can practice in the same focused manner, without using your voice, by simply visualizing yourself doing the exercises or singing the music you are presently working on without making a sound. Be present and focused, mentally and physically. The imagination is a great tool. Notice that if you mouth the words and imagine you are singing the vocal line, your jaw, throat, tongue, and vocal chords all move as if you were actually singing—they don't know the difference between actual singing and imagining this function.

Use your practice time to listen to what you have recorded during a lesson or coaching. Jot down any questions or concerns you may want to discuss at your next lesson regarding what you have learned up to this point.

For some, keeping a notebook to help reinforce any new ideas or discoveries you have made—in your technique, or your understanding of an aria or song, or opera role—will be very helpful. Write out any new vocal exercises and a description of what they address.

Here are some useful ideas about how to approach a new piece of music:

- Copy the words onto a separate piece of paper, translate them into your native language, then practice speaking the foreign words as if you were learning the dialogue of a play, without the added constraints of the music.

- Make a noticeable but light pencil mark through the strong beats of the measure, and through the part of the word that is to be sung on that strong beat. This will help keep your focus moving forward to the next strong beat, rather than getting stuck on trying to figure out the rhythm and what the next part of the word is.

- If there is a tricky or difficult rhythm, try slowing down the tempo and beating time, while you simply speak the rhythm on some nondescript syllable like "di, di" or "la, la." Do this several times, then try adding the actual words to the rhythm, while you continue to beat out the strong beats and gradually speed up the tempo to where it needs to be.

Don't rely on learning a role or piece by listening to a recording. Often times there can be wrong notes, words, or rhythms, which you will learn wrong as well. Learn your music the old-fashioned way: Get the melody in your ear, before you ever try to sing it or add words, by plunking it out on the piano.

Once the piece is vocally in place, memorized and dramatically prepared, find a recording of a singer with whom

> *All of the top achievers I know are life-long learners... looking for new skills, insights, and ideas. If they're not learning, they're not growing... not moving toward excellence.*
>
> — DENIS WAITLEY

you have vocal rapport (similarity of voice type and technique) performing the aria, song, or role that you are working on for possible further refinement. Again, make sure the performance is musically accurate, so that you don't learn wrong words, rhythms, cuts, etc.

Know something about the composer, the time in which the piece was written, and the style of the music. Learn something about the period of time in which the opera takes place, which is often different from the time period in which it was written.

If this piece is from an opera, know the entire story, what your relationship is to the rest of the characters, if you are singing to yourself, having a sort of internal conversation, or a conversation with someone else, and how this piece fits into the story as a whole. Educate yourself.

HOW TO PRACTICE AND PREPARE FOR A PERFORMANCE

After your program, aria, or role is technically prepared, focus on visualizing or imagining yourself performing the entire role, song, aria, or program successfully, with all the emotion of the storytelling, just the way you want it to be. See yourself up on a movie screen as you sit in the audience watching. This is a great tool for preparing for any audition or performance. Do this over and over again for several days, several times a day.

If you are in rehearsals for a production, know what the shorthand symbols are for marking the staging in your score (see pages 228 and 269), to make it easier to quickly notate directions as the stage director gives them to you. Following the day's rehearsals, use your imagination to practice and memorize the staging you have been given, in preparation for the next day's rehearsals.

Creating a performance routine is a matter of experimentation and experience:

Having even a rudimentary understanding of how to play the piano gives you, the singer, the ability to understand the harmonies of a piece and a better sense of the rhythm. Being able to play the line or chords that come before your entrance allows you to find your entry pitch more securely. As you feel more secure in the music, you can start incorporating the dynamics and tempo markings the composer has given you to work with, then finally the words. This method of working helps you to memorize not only the music and words, but the emotional impact and intentions of the character as well. After working with the music alone in this manner, put the words and music together. You will be surprised to find that the piece will be nearly memorized.

- Make sure you know when and what to eat before a performance.

- Both before and during their menstrual cycle, women often have different energy levels; know how best to deal with this issue for yourself.

- Know your energy needs on the day of a performance. Perhaps rest and no talking works best for you, or perhaps physical exercise of some type works better, while others may find keeping to a normal, everyday routine is best. It's about experimenting and finding just the right habits and routine for you.

- What is the right amount of time for you to get to the theater before it's time to go on?

- What kind of time period do you need after you are in costume, make-up, and wig to put yourself in the performance zone?

- What is your *modus operandi* (from the Latin, literally "way of operating") just before going onstage?

> There is a saying among professional singers: If you miss one day of singing, you know it. If you miss two days of singing, God knows it. If you miss three days of singing, everyone knows it.

Practicing anything, so long as you are awake, mindful, and focused while you are doing it, will eventually become habit over time. That is why it is so important for you to know the very best method for activating that tool, so you can achieve your goals. There are many different approaches to practicing. You need to figure out what the best system is for you and stick to it, adding to or altering your routine as you gain more experience. You will move ahead much faster and with more accuracy. Knowing your music, words, translation, and interpretation absolutely cold, will give you great confidence as you move from the practice room and voice studio to auditions and performance opportunities. You will not only feel more professional, but will be perceived as an artist who management would like to ask back.

FACH/VOICE CATEGORY

"Fach" is the German word meaning "compartment" or "subject," and is the term used in most European opera houses to refer to voice categories and their associated repertoire. These categories are mainly used as tools to help identify and classify different voice types and the repertoire appropriate for them, which is especially important information for European repertory opera houses. The repertoire lists for each fach can be found online or in various books aimed at foreign singers coming to audition in Europe. In North America, the term "voice category" is used most times to define and classify the different voice types and their appropriate repertoire, which can sometimes differ significantly from the repertoire associated with the corresponding European fach.

Once you have identified your correct fach or voice category, it will steer you in the appropriate direction concerning which roles, arias, or songs would be best for you. Your voice teacher and coach will be among your best guides in helping you with the process of determining your correct voice category. They should have a pretty good understanding of your voice as it is now, as well as an idea of what your voice will eventually mature into, as you gain a solid vocal technique and more performance experience over time.

Another tool which can assist in this process is listening to recordings of different types of voices and the repertoires they sing. Listen to both current singers and singers of the past, to help you develop a good understanding of what kind of voice performs what vocal literature best. The orchestration of a piece also helps to denote a particular fach or voice category. Notice if the orchestration is lighter or heavier for the roles you are interested in singing. The orchestration for larger voices is usually heavier and more lush, often with large brass sections or lots of violins

If you're planning an audition trip to one of the German-speaking countries, be sure to look up the repertoire for your fach in a current German reference work. The selections for each voice category are often different from those we use in North America, so become acquainted with how the system works in those countries, and be prepared to sing the arias and roles that they consider pertinent to each fach. Because many European opera houses are smaller than those in North America, the roles within a particular fach will include roles that would be considered on the more dramatic side in North American theaters, and therefore sung by larger voices.

> *Those who admire the massive, rigid bone structures of dinosaurs should remember that jellyfish still enjoy their very secure ecological niche.*
>
> — BEAU SHEIL

doubling the vocal line, like in the operas of Puccini, Verdi, Strauss, and Wagner.

In your beginning professional studies, it may be difficult for your teacher or coach to define your voice category or fach, other than in very general terms: you are a soprano, mezzo-soprano, contralto, tenor, baritone, or bass. As your vocal technique becomes more secure, unleashing your authentic sound, you will come to know what pieces fit your voice best, and be able to settle into a particular and more defined vocal category: lyric soprano or tenor, dramatic mezzo-soprano, contralto, Verdi baritone, bass-baritone, etc. As your voice continues to mature, the eventual range, color, and size of your instrument will further help to define your voice category.

You must settle on a fach or voice category before you can decide on the appropriate operatic repertoire to sing. This takes the time it takes, so don't become impatient. It is important that you understand what repertoire your particular voice category contains and what demands that repertoire will place on your voice and singing.

Often, if a singer has a really large range and a large voice, they will feel that they can cross over into many different voice categories, and sing just about anything to prove their versatility. That may be your thinking, but when it comes time for auditions, it will put you on the "no" list, because the adjudicators do not have the time or interest in figuring out what to do with you, and will assume that you have not yet settled into a voice category. They are looking for more than just potential.

If you do not feel comfortable with those advising you on this matter, don't be afraid to sing for and ask the opinion of others whose knowledge of this industry you trust. This will give you a better and more informed overview, so you will feel more comfortable with the decision you all make together. Also, as you gain performance and life experience, and your voice continues to mature, your voice category might change. This can and does happen. Do not be surprised or alarmed; it is part of the process.

Here are some resources for finding appropriate repertoire for each voice category or fach:

- Kagen, Sergius. *Music for the Voice: A Descriptive List of Concert and Teaching Material*, 2nd edition, Indiana University Press, Bloomington, 1968.
- Coffin, Berton. *Singers Repertoire*, 2nd edition, The Scarecrow Press, Lanham, MD (four volumes).

Settling into a voice category or fach is an important part of career preparation. There are many different resources available to help you find what music you should be concentrating on, but in the long run, it is best to trust the input of your voice teacher and coaches to help you make that determination.

LANGUAGE TOOLS

The better you are able to articulate, pronounce, speak, understand, and emote, the better your performance will be. Being able to capture the flavor and color of a language not only benefits the accurate pronunciation when sung, but helps vocal production as well. Here are some suggestions on how to find and work with a language or lyric diction coach, as well some tools that can serve you in that work.

In most major cities, there are many wonderful resources for learning languages. Check with university language departments, private teachers, language schools, high schools, etc. There are also a variety of courses available on CD or as software, as well as others that can be accessed directly over the Internet.

With the many resources available to you, there is no excuse for you not to know how to pronounce words in the

Those who know nothing of foreign languages know nothing of their own.

– JOHANN WOLFGANG VON GOETHE

languages you sing in, or to do a literal translation of any piece you are working on. Familiarize yourself with the IPA (International Phonetic Alphabet) and how to use it. While spelling varies greatly from language to language, the phonetic symbols of the IPA always represent a specific sound, regardless of the language you are working with. It is an invaluable tool for learning the correct pronunciation of all the languages in which you need to be proficient.

Music and diction coaches will use these symbols to clarify the correct sounds in a language when they work with you. It is an international language in and of itself. Ideally, go to a lyric diction coach and ask them to listen to your pronunciation. Let them check your literal translation. If there is a phrase or word you don't understand, ask for help or clarification. Find out how to discover this information for yourself, so you can do the necessary work on your own.

The important thing to remember is that lyric diction (the diction involved in singing) often differs from the diction used when speaking. There can be important differences between learning to speak the words of a piece of music and learning to sing them. For example, in French, individual vowels are often silent when spoken, but sounded when sung. Guttural r's are flipped in sung German and French, unlike their spoken counterparts.

It is imperative that you learn to pronounce the words of your music correctly, sounding as much as possible like a native speaker of that language, and this is what a lyric diction coach will help you accomplish. Often there are combinations of sounds in foreign languages that we do not have in English. While the English language has many dipthongs, other languages have pure vowel sounds with no diphthongs, which help you sing a long, fluid line. Don't underestimate the importance of good diction in your singing: Pronunciation and diction can often make or break your chances of employment, or winning first prize in a competition.

Listen to recordings of great singers singing in their native language. Listen to the arias and songs you are preparing, sung by several different singers from several different time periods. You will start to get a very good sense of the style and flavor of the language through this process.

Here is a partial list of resources for translations and transcriptions that will be helpful:

- Castel, Nico. *Opera Libretti Series.* Leyerle Publications
- Castel, Nico. *A Singer's Manual of Spanish Lyric Diction.* New York: Excaliber Publishing, 1994
- Glass, Beaumount. *Schumann, Schubert, Brahms, and Wolf: Complete Song Texts.* Leyerle Publications
- Colorni, Evelina. *Singers' Italian: A Manual of Diction and Phonetics.* New York: Schirmer, Inc., 1970
- Odom, William. *German for Singers: A Textbook of Diction and Phonetics.* New York: Schirmer Books, 1981
- Grubb, Thomas. *Singing in French: A Manual of French Diction and French Vocal Repertoire.* New York: Schirmer Books, 1979
- Marshall, Madeleine. *The Singer's Manual of English Diction.* New York: Schirmer Books, 1953
- Moriaty, John. *Diction: Italian, Latin, French, German, the Sounds and 81 Exercises for Singing Them.* E.C. Schimer Music Co., Boston, 1975
- *www.musacom.com.* This is a great web site. It has lyric diction and translation, accompaniments, melody alone, and much more, which can be custom-designed by you to prepare a song.
- Coffin, Berton. *Singers Repertoire Books,* (four volumes). This will also give you information about music for your particular voice category.

They spell it "vinci" and pronounce it "vinchy"— foreigners always spell better than they pronounce.

— MARK TWAIN

- Check the classified ads in Classical Singer magazine for language teachers and lyric diction coaches.

Taking the time to properly enunciate, translate, and understand the meaning of each word in a song or aria takes effort on your part. But the rewards outweigh any sacrifices you have to make to do so. As you become better at successfully applying all the different components of your craft to your work, your chances for getting hired, winning a competition, or getting into that apprentice or summer program improve exponentially. Most importantly, the smarter you work, the quicker you become a more complete and professional performer.

HOW TO WORK YOUR MUSIC

Habits are at first cobwebs, then cables.
— SPANISH PROVERB

Creating smart and productive working habits at the beginning of your professional study period is essential to maximize the effectiveness of your efforts. Knowing how to work your music efficiently requires an understanding of how this process will work best for you.

Once you are comfortably settled in your fach/voice category, your voice teacher and coaches will be able to help you select appropriate pieces to sing. If you are still in the academic world, your choices will no doubt be dictated by what that particular institution requires. Once you are out in the real world, the rules change, because what is expected of you as an aspiring artist is different.

I have already presented this concept for learning music, but it bears repeating:

- You must do a literal translation, word for word, of each piece, writing the English word above the appropriate note and corresponding foreign word, so you can see it peripherally each time you sing through the piece. Almost by osmosis, your eye will take in the English word, even though you are concentrating on the foreign words. Soon you will realize that you are understanding what is being said with almost no effort. It is amazing how well this works. (See the appendix for an example.)

- Make sure you learn and practice exactly what the composer wrote—the exact musical values, the correct dynamic markings, etc. If you are true to the composer when learning a piece, you will have a head start on understanding the musical style and dramatic content of the piece and your role. It is then a lot easier to add or subtract to that foundation if requested by a conductor or stage director.

- It might also be helpful to write the lyrics, with the translation above the foreign words, on an index card. You can study it wherever you go. It is a great way to memorize a piece.

- Draw a light, vertical pencil line through the vocal line, text, and piano part for each strong beat of the measure. Then your eye can easily see where the next beat is and is drawn forward to the following strong beat, always moving you forward. This is especially helpful with learning recitative, coloratura passages, or syncopated rhythmic lines. (see appendix)

- Mark any cuts given by the conductor or coach in the traditional way, using brackets and the syllables "Vi-" and "-De." (see appendix)

- Mark where you plan to take all of your breaths. Ask your teacher and coach for help. This not only helps you prepare your breath as you sing, but will help your accompanist move more easily with you.

- Make sure you understand the tempi, and all the musical and dynamic markings. You can find this information in a great little book, Theodore Baker's *Schirmer Pronouncing Pocket Manual of Musical Terms*. I'm sure there are others available online these days.

- If you choose to add your own embellishments, traditional alternate notes, coloratura passages, cadenzas, or other such alteration to the music, they should be clearly marked by you in your score.

> *We all have ability. The difference is how we use it.*
> — STEVIE WONDER

If you are learning a role, make sure you know what edition of the score is most often used. When being employed by an opera company, always ask if there is a particular edition of the opera score you should have. There can be substantial differences between editions, including things like cuts or additions to phrases, and even different text. It also helps if you have the same score as the conductor and stage director, so you will literally be on the same page when working together. Be aware that there is the possibility of misprints and errors in your score.

Now you are ready to start learning the piece. Here is one example of how this might be accomplished:

- Start by highlighting your entire role by running a highlighting marker through all of your words. This will help give you a sense of how much work is going to be involved in learning this role, and will give you a sense of timing as far as your entrances and exits are concerned. When there is a break in your part, write down the page number of your next entrance. You can also tag the entrances of your part, so they will be more easily found as you work your music.

- Translate all of the text in all of your character's scenes. Also translate any of the other characters' text that is just before or after your part, or sung along with you. This is especially important in recitatives, which are nothing but sung dialogue. Your character will then know how to act or react to those around you.

- Learn the text and the music using the techniques described in the preceding section.

- First learn the arias, second the duets, then the trios, quartets, larger soloist ensembles and finally your part in the chorus scenes. This sequence expedites the learning process.

- Learn to express the words through the music, and the music through the words. Know your text as if you had written it yourself. Know the context as well. Don't just sing with your voice, sing with your eyes, face, body, heart, and soul. Understand that language and music, projected with energy, knowledge, experience, and a great vocal technique, are irresistible to the listener.

- As you start memorizing, and you stumble over a forgotten word, write that one word down. Often it is the first word of the phrase which will prove difficult. Then go through the words from the beginning again. Once you know the beginning word of the phrase, the rest somehow follows with no effort. Do this each time you stumble. It will be memorized in no time.

- With your score in hand, listen to a great recording of what you are working on. Make sure there are no mistakes or significant differences between the recording and your score, so you don't learn the piece wrong as you listen. It is helpful to listen to a singer with whom you have found great vocal rapport. Do this right before you fall asleep and just upon waking, before you get out of bed. Remember, your technique will mimic those you are listening to, so make sure you are in vocal rapport with that singer.

- Don't make the mistake of learning a part only from listening to a recording. There can be musical mistakes, different cuts, wrong words, bad diction, or just plain sloppy singing on a recording, and you do not want to have to "fix" things later once you have memorized a piece—it makes for unnecessary extra work. Be true to the music and the markings of the composer. This habit will serve you well.

I have been impressed with the urgency of doing. Knowing is not enough; we must apply. Being willing is not enough; we must do.

— **LEONARDO DA VINCI**

- It would be beneficial to look at a conductor's score with all of the orchestration, so you can see for yourself the texture, color, and density of the orchestra as you sing your part. What is played from the piano score is often not what you actually will be hearing from the orchestra. You may have to listen for a single instrument like a flute or oboe to give you your pitch on a particular entrance. Be prepared—it shows that you are a professional.

The next step is to take your music to a répétiteur, and eventually to a coach. As I said in the beginning, there is a lot of work involved in setting up all of these habits and systems. But if you are awake and do your work consciously, you will find that learning new music is much easier and can be done much more quickly once these habits are established. You will begin to enjoy the learning process, because you have created a smart, structured, focused process that works just for you. It makes sense because it is meaningful just for you, and ultimately provides you with a complete and satisfying performance. When future opportunities arise and you have to learn a role quickly in order to get the job, these habits will be an enormous asset.

CHARACTER COMPREHENSION

Your primary job as a performer is to transport the audience away from their everyday lives, into a believable, imaginary world where they can enjoy being part of a different time, place, and emotional state. This is all done through the amazing story, and the journey you are able to take them on through your character.

Here is an remarkable opportunity, if you like using your imagination and sleuthing like I do, to investigate and learn everything you can about a particular time period and place, and how life was lived there—fashion, customs, manners, behaviors, physical uniqueness, etc.—in order to put

---

For me, what makes singing exciting is the idea that you are communicating not just the composer's intentions and the emotions , but are also investing part of your own intrinsic, inner nature, gathered through your own experiences, into the role.

— LUCIANO PAVAROTTI

Actors should be overheard, not listened to, and the audience is 50 percent of the performance.

— SHIRLEY BOOTH

each specific character together. From this investigation, you begin to develop a strong personality for this character that you will inhabit when you perform the role. You will start feeling the energy that allows your character to grow and change, as you experiment with who they are through the performance experience. You get to step into a whole new person—a whole new reality.

This process is great not only for the different roles you will play in various operas, but will also be of great use when you are investigating individual arias and recital pieces.

Every piece of music tells a story. It has a beginning, a middle, and an end, even when it stands alone. The challenge is to bring it to life, by ferreting out all the complexities and interesting facets you can find within that piece, and perhaps fill in any gaps with your own intuition and cunning.

What does one need to know to do that? Because this subject could be a book unto itself, only the basic elements are covered here. It will be up to you, as a sleuth, to find the resources that spark and expand your imagination. That might include anything and everything within the virtual world, physically developing your acting skills while attending straight acting classes, or sitting on a park bench, studying people's gestures, posture, dress, walk, trying them out to see how they feel and how that might change your behavior. It's the old mind/body connection, and it works both ways: What the mind thinks influences and shapes your physical behavior, and vice versa.

Here are some of the basic elements to consider:

- A good place to start all research is with the original text, poem, story, or other source for the text or libretto. How many of you have read *La Vie de Boheme* by Henry Murger? It is what inspired the libretto for Puccini's opera, *La Boheme*. Read the original source from which the song text or opera libretto was derived. What are the differences in the story line?

I am enough of an artist to draw freely upon my imagination. Imagination is more important than knowledge. Knowledge is limited. Imagination encircles the world.

– ALBERT EINSTEIN

What are the differences in the characters? What words have been changed or omitted?

- Know something about the composer and the inspiration for composing this opera or song. Research both what was happening around the world at the time the piece was written, as well as the time or historic period in which the action takes place, to gain a deeper understanding of the complexities and situations that might have influenced each composer or character.

> *A racehorse is an animal that can take several thousand people for a ride at the same time.*
>
> – AUTHOR UNKNOWN

If you are preparing an aria, know what the opera is about, who the characters are, and how your piece fits into the opera. Know what your character is involved in dramatically before, during, and after this aria. I recommended that you memorize the music for these sections as well, even if it involves other characters in the opera. Then when you sing the aria alone, you will have a better sense of how it fits into the whole, and it will allow you to be more convincing and believable to those listening.

- Are you singing the aria to someone or reflecting to yourself how you feel? If you believe it yourself, it is easy to convince others, and helps you take them on your journey.

- Use your character portrait chart to further enhance the believability of your performance, even if it is just an aria or song (see appendix). Make sure you fill the chart out as completely as you can. It may take several days to complete, and may change as you work on it.

- Write down the similarities between you and the character:
    a. Physically
    b. Emotionally
    c. Intellectually
    d. Psychologically
    e. Spiritually

- How is your character connected to the other characters in the opera?

  a. How are you related? Are you mother, father, daughter, son, cousin, friend, enemy, or lover?

  b. What do the other characters say about you when they are with you? What do you say about them when they are with you?

  c. What do they say about you when they are not with you? What do you say about them when you are not with them?

  d. What customs of behavior are different in regards to the time frame in which the piece takes place? How do family members relate differently than they would today? How do lovers act toward each other in the time period of the piece?

- Go to an art museum and study paintings from a particular time period to gain information about modes of dress and social behavior.

- Try finding an animal, person, insect, or inanimate object that has the associated characteristics of your character. It will give you some new perspectives into your character, both physically and mentally. For example, if you are working on the role of Count Almaviva in *The Barber of Seville,* he must be able to not only be regal, like a lion, but also pious as the music teacher—perhaps a camel looking down it's nose at you), and must then play the drunken soldier (perhaps using Dudley Moore in the movie *Arthur* as a model).

- What personal situations, persons, events, etc., from your own experience will help evoke and stimulate the emotions needed in your piece or role?

- Can you glean any other pertinent information about the characters that will help you with your character study?

> *I made mistakes in drama. I thought drama was when actors cried. But drama is when the audience cries.*
>
> — FRANK CAPRA

It's very important that you learn where the edge is between portraying an emotion and becoming too involved in that emotion. The line between being at the edge, and taking one step beyond, can be the difference between allowing the audience to participate in the feeling of the emotion you are portraying, or closing it off to them by overindulging in the emotion yourself. One allows you to include and invite the audience into your personal space, and the other is pulling your personal space in close to you, effectively excluding the audience. Another effect of going over the edge is, it immediately takes you off of your vocal technique, and puts you mentally, physically, and spiritually into an entirely different inner place. Your job is to portray the emotion, so the audience can then be drawn into experiencing that emotion.

Here are some other thoughts and ideas, to help you dig deeper into both your character and the timeline involved with the particular piece of music you are working on.

- How long did it take for communication (a message or letter, telegraph, phone call, or e-mail) to reach a far-away destination during the different time periods of the pieces you are working on? How about communicating within a 20- to 50-mile radius?

- Was there electricity, gaslight, or just candles from which to work?

- What percentage of the population lived in the cities versus the country? How was life different in each place?

- How did people dress? Did the women wear many layers of undergarments that were confining, and if so, how did this impact their behavior and movements? Did men feel more confined in their suits, vests, ties, gloves and hats, thus helping them feel more formal most of the time?

- What were the social customs of the time?

- What separated the classes? What were the differences in the traditions, customs, and formalities practiced by the different classes?
- What were the differences and similarities between what men and women were permitted or not permitted to do? How did a man or woman behave differently than they might today?
- What physical movements and behaviors would be different because of customs, clothing, or social class?
- What were the customs for courting a young woman?
- At what age did women and men marry?
- What was the division of labor between men and women so far as household chores and work outside the home were concerned?
- What role did religion play in their lives?
- What were the politics of the time, and how did they influence the population and your character?

The implications of this type of holistic, historical learning provides you with an invaluable reservoir of interesting tidbits, which can happily be incorporated into conversation when networking or schmoozing. This style of learning influences each and every part of who you are. It's wonderful to have this type of never-ending self-education, with information and resources that help you continue to grow and solidify your Personal Brand.

These are just a few of the general questions that you should be asking yourself about each piece as you prepare for a performance. The purpose of this work is to give you an opportunity to immerse yourself in a different time period, a different class structure, and to use this information to your interpretive advantage.

Congratulations, you have now created a family tree for your character, a general timeline, a historical timeline, and an emotional timeline. As the character, you can see where you came from, where you are presently, and where you are going.

Remember, there is a history for your character that began before the opera begins, and oftentimes continues to unfold after the opera is over. As you understand and embody your character through the work you have done, you

> *Begin at the beginning and go on till you come to the end; then stop.*
>
> — LEWIS CARROLL, ALICE IN WONDERLAND

will begin thinking as this character, first through your singing voice, then your actions, reactions, and body will want to follow through with corresponding movements. You are integrating what you have researched, as far as your character is concerned, with your own belief system, your values and truth. This way you make the character your own, within the confines of what the composer and librettist intended.

As you already know, science tells us that the mind does not know the difference between what is real and what is imagined. Through this process, which is actually great fun, we get to become someone else in mind, body, and spirit for the duration of a performance, and take the audience on a magical journey.

MUSICAL STYLE

When you think about it, it is quite easy to notice that the music from different time periods sound different from one another, and that the composers within a particular time period can sound different from each other as well. For instance, the music of Mozart (1756–1791) reflects the country, lifestyle, fashions, and times in which he wrote his music. His music had a very different style than that of Rossini (1792–1868), whose music reflects *his* country, lifestyle, fashions, and times. The list goes on up to and including the music being written today. Each composer reflects and preserves his or her particular musical style through the composition of their music, the story they want to tell and the musical language they use to tell it.

> *Music is your own experience, your thoughts, your wisdom. If you don't live it, it won't come out of your horn.*
>
> — CHARLIE PARKER

How does a singer support a particular style of music without it seeming contrived, purely technical, or having to change their voice altogether? If you are true to what the composer wrote, paying attention to the dynamic markings and using your ability to fill the words with meaning, you can't help but represent the style of music you are singing, no matter what style that is. It is all right there on the page—the composer saw to that—so sing it with your voice, and don't try to alter your sound to match what you might hear listening to others' singing of this particular piece. Put your authentic, unique voice into whatever the musical style happens to be, to create a brand new interpretation of the piece, within the confines of what the composer and librettist wrote.

RÉPÉTITEUR/ACCOMPANIST/PIANIST

What is the difference between a coach and a répétiteur? A répétiteur is usually a pianist/accompanist who knows and can play your repertoire well. The dictionary description is that of an assistant teacher. They help prepare you musically to work with a coach.

A répétiteur gives you the opportunity to run your pieces over and over again, so that you have them in your voice technically without being stopped for any reason or suggestions. Your work with a répétiteur will give you the opportunity to experiment technically, dramatically, and musically.

This is the progression in which you should work your music: Use a répétiteur to help you better learn the notes and rhythms of your music, experiment dramatically, and work the language. Once that is down, you can take this to a coach to help with interpretation, style, phrasing, traditions, and cadenzas and ornamentation.

Répétiteurs are usually less expensive than a coach, therefore you can hopefully afford to see them several times a week for shorter periods of time. It could be that you continue to work with a répétiteur while you are coaching, to be able to practice the suggestions given by the coach. Because a répétiteur is often working toward becoming a coach, what you bring to a session from your own coachings gives the répétiteur new ideas, as well as new ways of presenting those ideas when passing them on to other singers they are working with.

If we are together nothing is impossible. If we are divided all will fail.

— WINSTON CHURCHILL

Please do not shoot the pianist. He is doing his best.

— OSCAR WILDE

Répétiteurs often play for auditions, while a coach may not. It is my strong suggestion that you work first with a répétiteur, to help you get used to simply singing and working through the music with someone. It gives you the opportunity to establish self-confidence in the pieces you have been working on, when it comes time to move on to working with a coach.

Here are some suggestions for finding a répétiteur:

- Ask your colleagues and teacher if they could give you reputable names or ask the virtual music community.

- Ask at music schools, or music departments at universities and colleges. Post a notice on their bulletin boards, advertising for a pianist who can play through whatever it is you are working on.

- If you don't live in a community that has a college, university, or music school, check with private local music teachers.

Once you have the names of several potential répétiteur/accompanists, here are some important insights into what to expect and what you will learn. Start by creating good habits right out of the gate:

- Rule #1: GO KNOWING YOUR MUSIC. Don't waste your time, energy, and money having someone else teach you your notes. Use this time to stay focused on putting the music into your voice by repetition. Don't be lazy.

- Work with several different people at the start. It is important to find a répétiteur/accompanist with whom you have rapport—someone who plays well, and helps keep you honest about singing the correct note values, someone you feel comfortable working and making music with.

- Make sure to always put what others tell you into your own inner language (see Act II). A répétiteur may use different examples or words from what you are used to; you need to translate them into the examples or words that work for you. It helps if you repeat what you think they have told you, using your language, and see if it is a match. If there is no clear understanding on your part, always ask them to say what they are saying in a different way, perhaps using different examples or words. If there is no connection, no matter their reputation or how good they are, you are working with the wrong person. It is a matter of rapport and communication.

- Don't let any répétiteur/accompanist/coach change your vocal technique. If you have a vocal challenge, you can let them know you will take it to your voice teacher or they may suggest you take it to your voice teacher to work on.

- Once you have found a répétiteur/accompanist that you are comfortable and have rapport with, try to work with them once or twice a week, if it is financially feasible.

- If you are working on new pieces, you might want to have your accompanist make a study tape of the piano accompaniment for you to work with.

- Often one can barter or exchange services, instead of paying cash for coachings. Maybe this person needs help with his or her computer; perhaps you can clean their house or walk their dog, do their laundry, etc. Be creative.

- Create two three-ring binders containing copies of your music. One is for you to use for vocal lessons and to make notes in. The other is for your répétiteur/coach/audition accompanist, and it needs to be clean and readable. Make sure all the musical notes are on each page, and that the pages are double sided (or taped back-to-back), all in numerical order with the page numbers showing. If the page numbers are not on the copies, make sure you number the pages yourself. Put protective rings on both sides of the punched holes to give your music longevity. Put the music in your three-ring binders. Even-numbered

When we think of failure, failure will be ours. If we remain undecided, nothing will ever change. All we need to do is want to achieve something great and then simply to do it. Never think of failure, for what we think, will come about.

— **MAHARISHI MAHESH YOGI**

pages should appear in the book on the left, and odd-numbered pages on the right, the same as the pagination in the printed music. (This makes for easier page turns by the répétiteur.)

- Make several copies of each aria and keep them in a file. As you audition, you will need to replace copies, because they might get torn or just simply worn from use.

- Do not put the music for your accompanists in plastic sleeves. They are too difficult to grasp for page turns, and often, the light shining on them makes the music hard to read in auditions or onstage.

- As you add music to the binder, put a tab with the name of each piece on the outside edge. This will make the pieces easier for you and your accompanist to find.

- Make sure all your music is clearly marked with only the following: Where they are to begin playing the introduction, and where they are to end the piece; breath, musical, and dynamic markings; added fermatas, rubati, and inserted or added endings, ornamentations, cuts, etc. (see appendix).

- Make all of your markings very clear and readable. When you feel you have all the notes under your belt, and can sing through each piece with vocal ease, you are ready to take your pieces to a coach.

You will continue to work with a répétiteur/accompanist even when coaching. They are an invaluable part of continually getting better at what you do. It is with them that you will learn all of the basics of the music you sing, and with them that you will begin to put in place what you have learned from your voice teacher and coach.

COACH

A coach works with singers who are ready to polish their prepared arias, roles, or recital programs. A coach works musically, stylistically, dramatically, and on diction, to get you performance-ready. They will help you prepare for working with conductors and stage directors.

When you feel your technique is secure enough and you know your music cold, you are ready to work with a coach. Coaches are more expensive than a répétiteur/accompanist. Be prepared for this.

Here are some tips for working with a coach:

- Try several coaches to find the one with whom you have the best rapport.

- KNOW YOUR MUSIC. Do not waste your time, energy, and money by scheduling a coaching when you are not totally prepared. Coaches do not like wasting their time and energy on teaching you notes, rhythms, or words. This type of behavior might start you off on the wrong foot professionally. Presenting yourself as less then prepared could brand you in a way that is incongruent with your Personal Brand, and unfortunately, news travels quickly in the professional music world.

- Record your sessions. Often you will get more information than you can work with at one time, especially during your initial few coachings. When you get home, use the recording as a tool for learning, and preparing for the next session.

- Coaches will work with language, style, musicality, drama, performance traditions, and anything else they feel is appropriate insofar as the music is concerned. Be prepared to deal with all of this at the same time. That is why it is so important to be totally prepared vocally and musically, and why it is important to record your sessions.

- Often coaches specialize or are experts in a specific style of music. Find someone who emphasizes an area that you want to polish. It might be a coach who specializes in Italian Bel Canto Opera, or Verismo Opera, or perhaps the operas of Mozart or the Wagnerian repertoire.

All coaching is, is taking a player where he can't take himself.

— BILL MCCARTNEY

Failure is only postponed success, as long as courage "coaches" ambition. The habit of persistence is the habit of victory.

— **HERBERT KAUFMAN**

- Good coaches should know the history of the composers and the music you are working on, and should be familiar with singers and voices of the past and present. You can ask them for advice and direction in what roles you should be looking at, for current and future study. They should know and understand voices, but *not* give vocal advice. They should communicate instead that this is an area you need to work out technically or bring to your voice teacher.

- Having worked and studied with many excellent conductors and stage directors, coaches should have an understanding of how and why a piece works. Use their experience to gain knowledge for yourself. Ask questions when you have them.

- While working with you on a role, a coach should be able to sing every other part in an opera to give you entrance cues and an opportunity for musical interplay with the other characters. They often play what you will actually hear from the orchestra, as opposed to what is written in the piano reduction.

- A coach should know and understand the traditional cuts and embellishments in a piece, as well as the nuances, tempos, structure, and depth of the orchestra that is going to be supporting you as you perform.

- A good coach will show you how to pace yourself in a role, alert you to where you might need to have both eyes on the conductor because of a tricky section of the music, and let you know how the beats in any part of the opera might be subdivided by a conductor.

- Often, a coach is also a conductor. By being prepared for each session, and doing the work required, you may impress a coach with your skills and abilities, and could be hired for something that they conduct in the future.

- A coach can help you safely unleash the passion you're feeling for the music, without going too far and losing vocal control.

- After your coaching session, take the time to understand what you have learned and integrate that into your own practice sessions.

- Don't make another appointment with a coach until you feel satisfied with your understanding of your last session together. When you can sing through what you have worked on with confidence, it is time for another session with your coach.

Through this work, along with gaining experience as you perform, you will begin to build your own interpretation of the role, aria, or recital material. An experienced performer is always open to new ideas and suggestions. This helps the characters that you play stay fresh and alive, no matter how many times you perform them.

DRAMA COACH/CLASSES

Until you have enough performance experience under your belt, you might find that you become self-conscious and inhibited during rehearsals, auditions, and performances. In the beginning, you have to face unfamiliar territory at every turn, meeting and interacting with others in new venues. While you might have some ideas of how things are supposed to work, if you've never really experienced anything like this before, you'll probably feel unsure.

Straight acting classes (not acting classes for singers, which are usually a totally different animal) are a great place to gain some self-confidence in these situations, because you are asked to leave the "critic-brain" behind, step out of your comfort zone, and just be present and do the work. I have to admit, it can be very intimidating in the beginning, but by committing to the process, over time you will realize that there truly *is* nothing to fear but fear itself. The rest is really quite harmless, and actually quite interesting. People rarely notice, or even care, when you make (what we tend to think of as) "a fool of yourself." Making

Don't let what you can't do interfere with what you can do.

– ANONYMOUS

> *Champions know that success is inevitable; that there is no such thing as failure, only feedback. They know that the best way to forecast the future is to create it.*
>
> **– MICHAEL J. GELB**

mistakes or failing at something is simply feedback for you; this is how we all learn things. It is only when we don't take the time to look unemotionally at those occasions as learning opportunities, that they become a problem. Instead, we keep the memory locked up in some safe place inside for our private viewing, to remind us how unworthy and what an "idiot" we are. It then becomes something the "Brat"— that incessant self-talk one hears in one's head, usually in a not very productive or solutions-oriented manner, and at all the wrong times—can use to keep you from stepping out of your comfort zone to take that risk. As you learn to free yourself of your inhibitions and anxieties while participating in these acting classes, you are more free to participate fully in all your rehearsals, auditions, and performances, and enjoy the journey.

Here are some ideas for finding a straight acting class and how it might best work for you:

- If you are in a fairly large city, finding a good acting class won't be that difficult. Search the internet, or ask for recommendations from colleagues. You can also check the drama departments of your local schools and universities. Ask any local theater groups if they offer classes, or if they can refer you to someone with whom to study.

- Make sure that it's a regular acting class, not one intended just for singers. You don't want the confines of music involved in this learning process, at least not in the beginning.

- Get your money's worth by making yourself participate. It can be intimidating and difficult to do, but well worth it. You may feel awkward and exposed with no music for support. But you need this discipline to become the best singer/actor you can be.

- Ask if you can use the text of a piece you are working on, as a monologue to work on in the class. Even if it is in a foreign language, you could give them the translation, then proceed in the foreign language, and see if you are getting your feelings and meaning across.

What are the differences between acting in opera and straight acting?

- Opera is usually performed on a grander scale, so gestures are often larger than those used in more intimate theatrical settings.
- A single sentence usually takes a longer time to sing than if you were just speaking it; words are often elongated over several beats and notes, or repeated over and over.
- In a stage drama, you don't have any time constraints in which to deliver your lines. In music, you have only the time the composer has given you to deliver a line or reaction.
- Because of the constraints of the score, the pace and timing of movements are also much different.
- The use of vocal sound and color is obviously different than in straight acting.
- Some operas, such as *Carmen*, *Fidelio*, and *The Magic Flute*, have spoken dialogue. The skills and tools learned in studying acting will make the transition between the musical framework and spoken word easier to execute.

It is risky to rely only on the emotional response of the moment when performing. It can cause serious vocal problems. You know how your throat gets tight and the pitch of your voice goes up when you cry, or yell at someone because you're angry? This is what I'm talking about.

Your job on the stage is to portray emotion that you have experienced at some other time in your life, without getting caught up in it yourself. Your job is to let the audience feel and experience that emotion, not yourself.

It is important to know where your emotional bound-

The drama may be called that part of theatrical art which lends itself most readily to intellectual discussion: what is left is theater.

– ROBERTSON DAVIES

There are specific techniques one can use to put emotion in a piece that will not cost you anything physically. This means that those days when singing becomes just a job, and you really don't want to go to work, you can rely on this technique to take your audience on the journey, so they go away with a complete, emotionally charged theatrical experience. This is an important part of a singer's technique as a performer, though it seems to be rarely used these days: many performers today self-indulgently "live" the emotion onstage, rather than using their technique to portray it. This lack of discipline has cost more than one young singer a career.

aries are when performing. How much real emotion can you allow yourself without going beyond the control you need to maintain your vocal technique? As you gain experience, you will know just how far you are able to push your emotional boundaries within a performance.

It's also important to know how much physical activity you can manage onstage without going over this edge: Can you sing while walking across stage, kneeling, getting up and down, moving on a raked stage, brandishing a sword, coming down a staircase, lying down, or falling down?

A great way to experience how emotion is portrayed on the stage is by attending as many live performances as possible. You will begin to see how the craft is woven into a piece, and how you can start applying this to your own performing experiences. Attend a variety of performance genres, not just opera. Go several times to the same production, sitting close to the stage one time, then in the back of the theater another time, to observe and ferret out different aspects of the emotion of the piece. What techniques do you see employed?

When you have incorporated all of the work you have done with your vocal and drama coaches, take your pieces or role to a dramatic vocal coach—someone in the drama field who works particularly with singers. This kind of coach can help you alchemize all that you have been working on into a finished, stage-ready product.

Try enrolling in a reputable audition class to try out what you have been working on, and to learn by watching others as they perform and are critiqued. Stay out of your own head, worrying about what will happen when it is your turn. Stay focused on your agenda of learning from others.

After this foundational work, you are ready to start getting some experience on a more professional level. All of the work you have done to prepare yourself will pay off. You will perform with greater confidence, and have the ability to take the audience on a magical adventure.

POLISHING/FINISHING TOUCHES

polish: *To make elegant or to refine; to complete or embellish; to finish or perfect.*

– WEBSTER'S NEW WORLD DICTIONARY

Here are some suggestions for this next process, which will help you further prepare for performing and auditioning, the next step in your career. Your technique should, at this point, be secure enough to work with specific people to gain specific information and advice. This is the time you want to impress those you work with.

The daily grind of hard work gets a person polished.

– UNKNOWN

To get the most detailed, insightful and meaningful information about a role, look for opportunities to study with a famous interpreter of that role, or with respected coaches or conductors who specialize in a specific style, language, or repertoire.

Usually, teachers and coaches at this level know influential conductors, managers, and others in the industry. Show how consistently you learn and make the necessary adjustments in the music as you work with them, and what a wonderful and interesting colleague you are. Impress them with your polished, professional sound, secure technique, and with what you can do dramatically. Represent and present your Personal Brand—this is the way to encourage people in the business to begin talking about you.

Once you have established rapport with a teacher or coach, you might ask if they know of anyone who would be interested in hearing you for an upcoming event or production, or if they would feel comfortable making the necessary introductions or allow you to use their name as a reference to a professional company or apprentice program. This is called networking, which is really about creating and maintaining relationships.

If you should get a job or get into a study or performance program through them, always remember to keep them abreast of your progress and on your mailing list (see more on this in Act III). Also, send them a handwritten thank-you note, even if nothing comes from the contact. People like to be appreciated.

Once your vocal technique is solid, your dramatic intention is under your command, and you have had some experience, it is time to work with those in the business that can help further your career. This is the time to show off what you can do, to impress those who work with the best in your field. You need, at this point, to be ready for any opportunity that might knock at your door.

GETTING EXPERIENCE

> *One thorn of experience is worth a whole wilderness of warning.*
>
> – JAMES RUSSELL LOWELL

Putting into practice all of the skills and tools you have learned up to this point is one way for you to figure out where your strengths and weakness lie. Performing gives you the opportunity to tie together everything you have been working on. It also gives you a place to try different methods of approaching a character, complete role, or song or aria. It brings you into contact with other singers, stage directors, and conductors. Here is a chance to further hone your people skills, and continue to build new relationships. You must now rely on yourself, and trust that all your skills and tools will kick in when needed. You are ready to become a professional performer. There are still many things that you will need to learn, but gaining experience is always the best teacher, and is the next step. How does one go about that? Here are some suggestions:

WHERE TO START?

- Start in your own backyard. Find out what your local opera companies and musical groups are planning for their upcoming season. Call for information. Ask when they will be holding auditions. If there is a role for you, schedule an audition if possible.

- If there are choral groups or orchestras within a 50 mile radius, or in your own community, see if they are planning any pieces that require vocal soloists. Schedule an audition. Suggest pieces that are right for your voice, and could work for a community orchestra and chorus.

- Get a regular church job. There is often a quartet of soloists who get paid for their work, whether singing as part of the choir or as a soloist. Through this church job, one can usually obtain extra work singing for weddings, funerals, etc. It is a great way to supplement your income, as well as have a regular opportunity to sing professionally.

- Network with other singers. Find out what their connections are in the music community. Ask if anyone knows of an upcoming audition or job that requires your voice type. Don't be bashful. Remember this is business, not emotional or personal.

- Always carry your business cards. Give them out on a regular basis. Make sure you collect one from anyone who seems interested in you, whether a singer, business person, pianist, orchestra member, etc. Jot down on the back of the card where you met them and a brief note, so you can associate the name with a face and situation later. Send them an email saying how much you enjoyed meeting them and would like to stay in touch. This is also someone you'll want to add to your mailing lists. (See the corresponding sections in Act III for more on how to set up and organize your mailing lists.)

- Check your local hospitals, nursing homes, schools, and any other community groups or organizations that have regular meetings, to see if you could perform for them. You might even find a group or organization willing to help financially sponsor a bigger project you are planning.

- Every state has an arts council. They often have artist-in-residence programs that pay, inquire if there is a spot available and set up an audition.

- Put together your own recital program. Advertise in your local paper, community bulletin boards, and church bulletins. Invite your family and friends. At the performance, put a donation basket out with your programs. Include the phrase "any donations will be gratefully appreciated" in your program. Have your audio CDs available for sale at a table near the entrance. Ask a friend or family member to man the table and help sell your CD.

- Create an operatic quartet and advertise in the same manner. Get experience—sing in public as often as you can. Are there any restaurants in your area that would pay to have you become regular performers? This might be especially successful during the holidays.

You are an entrepreneur. You are presenting and representing your Personal Brand at all times. The product you are selling is you as a performer. And you are always in the business of creating and maintaining relationships, and business is business—it is not personal or emotional.

If opportunity doesn't knock, build a door.

— MILTON BERLE

Finding work is a never-ending job for a singer. Even when you have a manager, you should be looking for work and asking those in the business for any leads. Creating and establishing a business and finding and keeping customers takes a lot of time and energy. But if you continue to do the necessary work, your business will continue to grow, while these practices eventually become habitual, enjoyable aspects of the process of maintaining a successful singing career.

SUMMARY

As you continue to build on the base of information you have gathered up to this point, you should begin noticing a pattern of how you are using the information you've already accumulated. Hopefully you have established some systems of organizing this information that work well for you. This section of the book gives you an opportunity to observe, hear, and feel the path towards creating the primary building blocks needed for succeeding as a performer. The most important element of these building blocks is securing a great vocal technique, which means finding a voice teacher that you feel has all the necessary requirements you need to reach this goal. Once you have something to practice vocally, you will find some suggestions that will help you to establish good practicing habits. Before you can enter the semi-professional or professional arena of singing, you must know what your voice category or fach is. This means being patient until your voice settles down and finds it's rightful place. It is also something that often changes as you mature.

Learning how to sound like a native when singing in all the foreign languages essential to our profession is of major importance. It is not necessary to actually speak all of these languages—although it would be to your great benefit—but knowing how to speak the text with accuracy and meaning is obligatory. This involves finding and working with a lyric diction coach with whom you have rapport and trust. Once you are secure with the pronunciation of text, you then must understand the character that is speaking the words, and breathe life into the music through the text.

Once this is accomplished, work first with a répétiteur/accompanist to put the music into your voice, then a coach to bring the music and text to life. It is worth your time and effort to study drama at this point. This will help you lose those inhibitions that keep you from expressing how you really feel about the character, music, and text. The final step is to polish the entire product, by working with a specialist in whatever field you feel is necessary to put a high gloss on the finished work.

Now you are ready to seek out the appropriate performance venues to "try your wings," making any necessary

> *When you are inspired by some great purpose, some extraordinary project, all your thoughts break their bonds; your mind transcends limitation, your consciousness expands in every direction, and you find yourself in a now, great and wonderful world. Dormant forces, faculties and talents become alive, and you discover yourself to be a greater person by far than you ever dreamed yourself to be.*
>
> – PATANJALI, C. 200 B.C.E.

adjustments as you continue to gain experience. All of the many wonderful people you have worked with along the way will become part of your support team. Keep them informed about what and how you are doing, and always thank them for the part they have played in your success.

As you begin to develop these skills, you will feel more confident about auditioning and performing. Always represent and present your Personal Brand in all that you do. And remember, the more you consciously practice anything, the better you become at it.

ACT II

inside out: inner systems and patterns

Before you can successfully map out the business strategies and tactics of building your career, you must first take the time to understand the product you will be marketing and selling. The product is, of course, you, as the singer-performer.

Why is it important for you as a singer and performer to spend your precious time, energy, and money learning about yourself, the person inside the singer?

- Learning how to feel comfortable in your own skin, and with who you are in the many roles you play within your relationships, including the one with yourself, builds confidence, compassion and self-respect.

- Knowing and asking for what you want, believing you can have it, and feeling worthy of and being ready to receive what you asked for, generates realized dreams.

- Living life on purpose, with passion and internal independence, sets you free from living a fear-based life, replacing that with internal happiness and joy, and a belief that everything is possible.

Life is so only-once, so single-chanceish! It all depends on your arranging and synchronizing it so that when opportunity knocks you're right there waiting with your hand on the doorknob.

— SYLVIA PLATH

- Knowing how to release, revitalize, and liberate your full potential creates motivation.

- Unleashing your own unique and authentic power permits you to participate more effectively in everything you do, while remaining flexible when change occurs in any area of your life.

- Becoming awake and conscious of how you do what you do, gives free rein to your imagination, curiosity, and resourcefulness.

Answer these two questions honestly:

- How would you describe your life in eight words or less?

- Is your life proof of that belief?

> *Success is the sum of small efforts, repeated day in and day out.*
>
> – ROBERT COLLIER

These personal "life skills" help you grow into a confident, whole person with a lifelong commitment to excellence. You get to become more of who you are at your core than you have ever been before. This empowers you—when presenting your company's product and "brand" (you, the singer) in auditions, while networking, in performance, and in life in general—with your own unique and authentic panache. Then this whole amazing process becomes more about appreciating and savoring each step of the journey, and less about reaching the ultimate goal.

Getting to know how you tick on the inside—which particular configuration of inner systems and patterns are yours alone—will help you better understand and celebrate who you are. As you start this amazing journey of self-discovery, know that, like all journeys, it always begins with the very first step. After that, how you choose to use this new information is totally up to you. So buckle up for the wild and crazy adventure ahead. Enjoy!

SCENE I:
Getting to Know the Person Inside the Singer

PERSONAL BRANDING

Let's start this whole project by talking a little about branding in general. As you already know, our world is saturated with commercial brand images. Each of us is exposed to between 3,000 and 30,000 brands every day, and that number is expanding exponentially. They're out there everywhere, from TV commercials and magazine ads to decals and logos on clothes, shoes, caps, and coffee mugs, and are especially prevalent in our virtual world. We see branding with personalities in every field of entertainment, sports, and business. Countries, politicians, environmental issues, even ethnicity, all have a specific brand image representing them to the world—think about it!

How many of you have a favorite recording artist? Without the PR guys creating a specific brand, it might be difficult to distinguish one group or solo star from another. Their brand includes everything from what they wear to their style of hair and makeup to how the PR firm wants them to sound as artists and behave in public. Here is how Gavan Fitzsimons, a professor of psychology and marketing at Duke University, explains it: "Every brand comes with a set of associations. When we're exposed to logos, those associations fire automatically, activating our motivational systems and leading us to behave in ways that are consistent with that brand image and our preexisting drives."

Whether you know it or not, you already have a brand—your name. Just like in any other business, others recognize the quality and value of your personal brand by knowing what they can expect from you on a consistent basis. It's about your behavior and actions, which are usually different for each of the many roles you play within your different relationships.

We are all inventors, each sailing out on a voyage of discovery, guided each by a private chart, of which there is no duplicate. The world is all gates, all opportunities.

— RALPH WALDO EMERSON

An article from the *New York Times* College section suggests that today's trend for having a career in performing is not what it used to be. One must now have great entrepreneurial and communication skills, because managers and agents don't develop young talent anymore. They only have time for, and are interested in working with and representing, the finished product.

Wouldn't it be wonderful to have just one consistent behavior that you use within *all* of your relationships? Wouldn't you like to stop playing the games, getting your "hot buttons" pushed, second-guessing, or just reacting to situations and conversations, and be able to control your emotional attachments to things, people, and stuff without trying to please everyone? This continual stream of chaotic activity distracts you and zaps your energy. Discovering "how you tick" on the inside, and feeling comfortable with sharing that unique and authentic Personal Brand with the world, is the perfect place to start this whole process—from the inside out.

Acquiring and continuing to grow your own Personal Brand comes with a warning: In becoming authentic and unique, you will stand out from the rest of the tribe, pack, or crowd, and that might feel uncomfortable. For most people there is a kind of safety in conformity and a certain "comfort factor" in being similar to those around you. Know that being part of the tribe may at times be either comfortable or uncomfortable, but it is always familiar.

> *Creative geniuses are geniuses because they know "how" to think instead of "what" to think.*
> **– KAREN POST,
> BRAIN TATTOOS**

There is no risk involved in being part of the tribe, because you know the pecking order, where you stand within it, and what is expected of you. There are no surprises, because everything is routine, so you don't have to deal with your emotional responses. You have few responsibilities, because you know your place and do your job out of habit, whether you like it or not. You don't have to take action, only react when necessary.

Presenting and representing your Personal Brand allows you to:

- Project your authentic and unique self. This may, in the beginning, make you feel a little unsure, naked, and vulnerable. With experience this goes away.

- Tolerate personal differences without feeling threatened. Not everyone will like or agree with you, and that's okay, because "what you think of me is none of my business."

- Accept differences of opinion or strategy without feeling the need to sway the other person to your side, or trying desperately to have the other person understand what you are saying, which often involves evoking unnecessary emotional involvement. Conversations become more about sharing your views, ideas, or passions.
- Have the opportunity to define who you are at your core, and be comfortable with sharing who you are from that source.
- Embark on a profound new relationship with yourself. Because you are congruent on the inside, you can be consistent on the outside.

If you are ready, willing, and able, let's get started. Here is how we are going to begin the process: I have presented you with some phrases to complete. This is not a test, and you don't have to share your answers with anyone. You do, however, need to turn your thinking brain (the left brain) off and give it a rest, as this is more of an intrinsic, right-brained activity. Don't think—that's cheating!—let this be stream of consciousness, more of a spontaneous activity. It's time to have some fun.

The process is time-sensitive, so you should set a timer or alarm for 5 minutes. This will help you stay out of your thinking brain, wondering or worrying if you are getting the job done in time. Stick with the spontaneous, stream-of-consciousness, right side of your brain, and let the alarm keep track of time.

Do not read through these incomplete phrases before you start, that's cheating too. There is no right or wrong, no better or worse, no smarter or dumber to any of this—it's a way to help get you unstuck and moving in a new direction with your thinking. Complete each phrase with the first

Here are the four strategies for a better life, as ascribed by author Jonathan Ellerby in his book, *Inspiration Deficit Disorder: The No-Pill Prescription to End Stress, Low Energy, and Bad Habits*:

Clarity: Be clear about intentions, commitment levels, and what you want.

Integrity: What you feel and know on the inside matches what you say and do on the outside.

Courage: Act on what you feel and know. Don't make decisions out of fear. Integrity would remain just a good idea without courage.

Compassion: Look for the highest good in every situation; be empowering without always trying to make people happy or to "fix" things.

> *We fear that we are inadequate, but our deepest fear is that we are powerful beyond measure. It is our light, not our darkness, that most frightens us. We ask ourselves: "Who am I to be brilliant, gorgeous, talented, fabulous?" Actually, who are you not to be these things? You are a child of God. Your playing small doesn't serve the world. There is nothing enlightening about shrinking so that other people around you won't feel insecure. We are all meant to shine as children do. We are born to manifest the glory of God that is within us. It is not just in some of us; it is in everyone. And as we let our light shine, we unconsciously give other people permission to do the same. As we are liberated from our own fear, our presence automatically releases others.*
>
> **— MARIANNE WILLIAMSON, *A RETURN TO LOVE***
> **(This quotation was used by South African president Nelson Mandela in his inaugural speech).**

thing that comes to mind as you read it. Don't take time to analyze or contemplate how you might best complete these phrases, or try to find an example in your memory banks, just put down the first thing that comes to mind as you read, even if it doesn't seem to make sense to you at that moment. It will probably be just a word or short phrase—if you try to make great sentence structure, you're in your left (thinking) brain. No, no, no! This is fun, and should be approached as if you were still a child, playing a game. Stay in the moment, and quickly write down your answers without stopping to analyze them.

Remember, this is timed—write down the first thought that comes to mind as you read the beginning words of each phrase; if nothing comes to you, move on to the next one. When time is up, look over the completed phrases; your answers might surprise you. They also might stimulate an even deeper look at the person inside you, the singer, and that's exactly what you want to happen. You have five minutes to work through these phrases, so set the timer. Ready… set… go!

QUESTIONS:

1. What I always loved as a child was _____.
2. As a child, I wanted to be _____.
3. As a child, my favorite pastime was _____.
4. Now what I love to do is _____.
5. What I love about myself now is _____.
6. I feel best about myself when _____.
7. I have a strong need for _____.
8. When presented with a new experience I _____.
9. I have a gift for _ _____.
10. I respect _____.

11. Under stress I tend to _____.

12. I am most myself when _____.

13. I am motivated by _____.

14. I ask for help when _____.

15. When change happens in my life I _____.

16. I enjoy the kind of work where I can be _____.

17. I like to have the authority and responsibility to _____.

18. Others have described me as _____.

19. I have a tendency to lose sight of my own needs when _____.

20. A big priority in my life is _____.

21. I strive to do what is _____.

22. I tend to be wary of _____.

23. I often find myself _____.

24. I base my decisions on _____.

25. My strong suit is _____.

26. I am faithful to _____.

27. I tend to judge myself harshly when _____.

28. My three top fears are _____.

29. My greatest freedom is _____.

30. My current intention is _____.

31. I have balance in my life when _____.

32. My biggest regret is _____.

33. My best memory is _____.

34. My greatest accomplishment to date is _____.

My conclusion is:

35. I am _____.

36. What I do is _____.

37. It matters because _____.

How was that? What was the hardest part of this exercise? Did you find it difficult to keep out of your thinking mind? Were you surprised by some of your answers? Did you learn something new about yourself? It's not easy to change mental gears, and keep to the way I asked you to play this game, the first time around. You are welcome to play as many times as you want, but you can't come to it with preconceived answers or intentions. It always has to be done with spontaneity, with only the intuitive and intrinsic right brain involved.

Discovering who you are, by understanding what your inner systems are and how best to use them, gives you the freedom to define, then present and represent, your authentic and unique self—your Personal Brand—all the time. Without this self-knowledge, you might occasionally hide behind fabricated beliefs, excuses, or lies told to you by others, or even by you yourself. This type of negative input gives what I like to call your "Brat" permission to be in charge. The Brat is that inner voice that we habitually encounter and have conversation with in our heads. This Brat often shows up at the most inappropriate and inconvenient times in your life. He or she keeps giving you the same old messages, usually in a demeaning voice and restrictive manner, to help keep you "stuck" where you are and afraid of taking that risk.

> *It is what we think we know already that often prevents us from learning.*
>
> **– CLAUDE BERNARD**

SCENE II:
Individual Belief Systems

The next part of this process—discovering the person inside the singer—involves looking at your belief systems. This is the place where you store memories and keep experiences organized.

You often take your beliefs for granted, automatically reinforcing the ones that keep you stuck in your comfort zone, continually embellishing the stories of your experiences as you repeat them over and over again to yourself and to others.

You can also have certain beliefs that are hidden from your conscious mind, though they can still influence your behaviors. Often these beliefs can be deeply buried in your subconscious, affecting your life in unproductive ways without your being aware of it.

Your belief systems can often repress your ability to try new ideas, or perhaps take a risk in changing some aspect of your thought process or behavior. Reaction becomes your modus operandi, seemingly your only choice in a given situation, rather than deliberately choosing to take action or not. Life seems to just run on automatic pilot, instead of your being able to choose how you want to deal with it.

Your beliefs influence how you think and feel every moment of your life and can even become self-fulfilling prophecies. Powerful aren't they? Because of this, these belief systems exert an enormous influence on your worldview. If we didn't tell ourselves particular stories over and over again to help reinforce our belief systems, nothing would have meaning. So it is you, yourself, that assigns meaning to everything you think and do in your life.

Take as an example, how we view the word "failure." It is only a word which we use to label an event or outcome. The experts tell us to expect failures to occur on occasion

What you do speaks so loud that I cannot hear what you say.

– RALPH WALDO EMERSON

as we move along the path toward success. For some, that word creates bad or unpleasant feelings that get replayed over and over again. For others, "failure" is just a word that denotes an opportunity to get some honest feedback on a particular incident or issue. Thinking of getting feedback, instead of having "failed," allows you the freedom to then take some type of purposeful action if necessary, otherwise you can choose to leave the emotionally charged and hurtful "failure" story behind, and move on.

Another often misunderstood word is "mistake." Without making mistakes and experiencing failure, we would never learn anything. It is what we choose to do with what we learn from making mistakes and having failed, that helps us to grow and change. It helps us move into a brighter and more informed future. On the other hand, if one doesn't take the time to learn from their mistakes and failures, and instead continues repeating them over and over again, one gets stuck in their habitual behavior—which is definitely familiar, though probably not really such an opportune or comfortable place to be. Know that nothing has meaning until you assign it one; the choice is yours.

Now that you have this information, start taking inventory on a conscious level of what role your belief systems play in your life.

Where do beliefs come from? Discover some of the roots of your own belief systems, by writing down examples of events that have helped to change or shape your beliefs in some way. These events may be something very simple that turned into an "aha!" moment, or perhaps a major event of some kind, either good or bad. Write down one situation for each of the following five headings:

ENVIRONMENT

These are experienced though some type of interaction with family, friends, church, community, ethnicity, physical

> *The world we see that seems so insane is the result of a belief system that is not working. To perceive the world differently, we must be willing to change our belief system, let the past slip away, expand our sense of now, and dissolve the fear in our minds.*
>
> – WILLIAM JAMES

or geographical surroundings, etc. *Example:* Susan grew up in a small town where sports and music were a big focus both in her school and community. She continues to believe to this day that the support she received during that time in her life continues to give her confidence in herself and her abilities as she matures.

_____

_____

EVENTS

Events that impacted your life and belief systems, whether happy or sad, good or bad. *Example:* Jeffery and a group of buddies were in a terrible car accident on the way home from a big weekend in Las Vegas. They were going to stay one more night, but decided even through it was really late, they would drive back to school that night. They all felt awake and alert at the time of their decision. However, it was a 6 hour drive and even though they were rotating drivers, those not driving slowly started to fall asleep. Eventually the driver did as well. Jeffery was the lucky one. He received only minor injuries. To this day, no matter who is driving, Jeffery never sleeps during a car trip.

_____

_____

KNOWLEDGE

People or things that helped shape your beliefs from school, books, TV, movies, etc. *Example:* Michael learned in one of his summer programs a great lesson that changed his life forever. He learned that if he stopped simply reacting to uncomfortable conversations or situations, and paid attention only to the reality of what was being said or happening right that minute, he could make a really rational and level-headed decision as to whether he needed to take some kind of action or not, without getting all caught up in his emotions. Using this tool gave Michael a kind of confidence and pride in himself he had never experienced before and others noticed it as well.

_____

_____

PAST RESULTS

If you believe that past experiences always get the same results simply because you believe it to be true, it usually will happen that way. Example: Laura believes she has a great, always available high C, so she does.

_____

_____

EXPERIENCING RESULTS IN ADVANCE

This is something we do all the time, and it can work for or against you. We create an emotionally charged vision of some future event and play it over and over again. When the event happens, we of course experience it the way we have envisioned or practiced it in our imaginations. Example: One week before his audition, Sam chose to create in his imagination, performing it over and over again, a minute by minute play of his upcoming audition where he represented and presented his Personal Brand, sang at his optimum and portrayed the character with panache and honesty.

On the other side of the coin, Shelley had an important audition coming up and all she could think about and remember was her last audition where everything that could go wrong did, and dwelt on that over and over again as she prepared for the impending event. Guess what her experience was at that audition?

_____

_____

One way of knowing your true beliefs is to look at how you treat not only yourself, but also your environment. That means everything around you—the way you eat, how you dress, your home, workspace—as well as the language you use—both internally, when you talk to yourself, and with others. Do you treat yourself and your environment with respect and love, or is this one of the areas in which you can punish and abuse yourself? Do your beliefs let you behave one way with the outside world, one way for your family, and yet another way internally with yourself? Tiring, isn't it?

Why is it that our beliefs are so often filled with emotion? We all have something called the mind/body connection. We all experience this.

Here's an example: Think of holding a really nice, juicy lemon in your hand. Imagine smelling the oil from the skin of the lemon as you roll it on an imaginary counter, so that you can extract more juice. Now imagine cutting it open and holding half of it up, so you can squeeze the juice into your mouth. Do you notice how much saliva you have in your mouth as you read this? Those words and thoughts created an immediate, unconscious response within your body. Your body and senses follow along with what your mind is thinking at the moment.

Remember, thoughts are things—how you choose to think affects your physical body and helps shape your life. You attract what you spend your time thinking about.

One evening, an old Cherokee told his grandson about a battle that goes on inside people. He said, "My son, the battle is between two "wolves" inside us all. One is *evil*; it is anger, envy, jealously, sorrow, regret, greed, arrogance, self-pity, guilt, resentment, inferiority, lies, false pride, and ego. The other is *good*; it is joy, peace, love, hope, serenity, humility, kindness, empathy, generosity, truth and faith. The grandson thought for a minute and then asked his grandfather: "Which wolf will win?" The old Cherokee simply replied, "The one you feed."

Another interesting observation is that science tells us our mind doesn't know the difference between what is real and what is imaginary—you just experienced this with the example of the lemon. This is a big plus for you as a performer. This is how and why we can take the audience on a journey through the characters we have embodied and portray. We create a three-dimensional character who starts living inside our mind. Our bodies, through our senses, react to this new information, then we, as the performer, portray the emotion that character feels, both through the sound of our voices and through our bodies. That is the mind/body connection, the result of which we share with the audience in performance.

Getting stuck in your comfort zone is another example of the mind/body connection. Continually telling yourself what you *do not want* attracts that to you. It is reflected in your body language, your attitude, your behavior, and even the words you use. When you state what it is you *do want*, that is also reflected in your body language, attitude, behavior, and the words you choose when you speak. Again, thoughts have tremendous power, and greatly influence our actions or reactions, or even our inaction.

How do you change your beliefs if they are no longer relevant or empowering? Let's look at some steps to take toward helping you unlock your negative beliefs and getting unstuck:

The first step is to recognize that there is a specific belief you want to change. Once you have acknowledged and recognized what it is you want to change, you will be amazed at how often you become aware and conscious of this belief when it comes to mind in differing situations. You might be surprised to find that this habitual belief is no longer even relevant, but rather something left over from your childhood that can be let go of.

If you don't like the outcome resulting from some of

> *A life without a quiet center easily becomes destructive.*
>
> – HENRI JM NOUWEN

> *A "normal" person is the sort of person that might be designed by a committee. You know, "Each person puts in a pretty color and it comes out gray.*
>
> – ALAN SHERMAN

your self-limiting beliefs, you can start making a change by simply altering the story you are telling yourself about your past, from a damaging one to one with the outcome you want. Remember, our mind doesn't know the difference between what is real and what isn't—it simply reacts to whatever story we have in place.

To make the change permanent, you have to be mindful and consistent as you repeat the new story to yourself, until this new version becomes the one that is thought of first—the default system that's on "auto pilot." Practice putting this new belief to the test often if you want to change it. And remember, there can be a lag time before you get the final results you want, so continue practicing until it becomes habit. It does work.

Create a list of words that honestly represent who you feel you are right now—the good, the bad, and the ugly. Set a timer for two minutes, and don't stop writing until the alarm goes off. Don't think, just write what truthfully comes to mind, stream of consciousness. When you are done, take an honest look at how you view yourself, and try to find the limiting beliefs that keep you stuck. Start reinforcing the positive beliefs, the ones that feel honest and come from deep in your soul.

Words hold great power over many of us. One key to letting go of old limitations is to simply change the negative words you use when your Brat is doing the talking (the internal self talk) to words that make you laugh or feel absolutely silly. Try this: Write down a short list of the words your Brat offers up when you talk to yourself, either out loud or in your head, that are not so complimentary—"you stupid idiot," "you're useless," "you're not worth it," and so on. This is one way you may try to keep yourself in check—you beat yourself up emotionally before anyone else can. This inner kind of dialogue usually shows up at the most inopportune moments and can really take you off track.

Our identity is very closely associated with our thoughts and feelings. Usually, when we feel anger, we become angry. We are anger itself. When we feel depressed, we are depression. When we feel greedy we are greed. It's easy to see ourselves in the emotional "guise du jour" and mistake this costume for who we really are beneath it.

– MARC GILSON

Find the hurtful words you most consistently use and write them down. To change the emotional impact of what you say to yourself, get out your thesaurus and look up each of those hurtful, emotionally charged words. Once you have found your word, start reading the synonyms out loud until you find one that makes you laugh, or at least seems silly and harmless. Write this "silly" word opposite the "bad" one that holds the negative emotional impact. Next, use this emotionally charged word in a sentence, noticing how it makes you feel. Now repeat the exact same sentence, replacing the "bad" word with the "silly" word. Notice how the emotional impact has changed, once you replace the harmful word with the harmless one. Continually using this "silly" word in place of the "bad" one, each time it surfaces in your thoughts. This simple but amazingly effective practice will begin the process of change within you.

When you start feeling the emotional charge from one of your harmful thoughts, you can also change your focus from what you are thinking, to how and where it is affecting your physical body. Where do you feel physical tension from this negative state? Once you locate it, focus on and intensify it for about 20 seconds, making the sensation as strong as you can. When you finally release the tension, notice that you have pretty much forgotten what it was you were just thinking about.

Often your Brat, that insistent inner voice, will quickly get your attention by saying something hurtful or emotionally damaging, usually at the precise moment when you need to be alert and focused. One of the easiest ways to gain some internal quiet is to repeat the same sentence back to the Brat, exactly as it came out in your internal dialogue. The Brat likes to argue, and if you simply pretend to agree with it by repeating back what it has said to you—either as a thought or out loud—your response will stop the Brat's relentless internal chatter, and you will have a moment of absolute quiet in your head. Example: Brat: "You're never going to get this, you stupid idiot!" Your reply: "So, you're saying that I am never going to get this, you stupid idiot!" This a powerful way in which to take control of your inner dialogue.

Digging deep to find out not only what your beliefs are, but why you believe them, is worth your best effort. This is a lifelong process that, once started, will easily become part of your routine throughout your life. And that's a good thing, because the more you recognize your authentic and unique self, the easier it is to become that person which you represent through your Personal Brand.

It's not what you do that defines who you are; instead it is who you are that defines what you do.

– AUTHOR UNKNOWN

This is a fun exercise to ask your friends to participate in. Make enough copies so you can offer one to each of your family and friends to fill out as to how they regard you in each category. You will quickly understand how others see your role through their eyes. You need to do it for yourself as well and notice if any of your answers correspond with anyone else.

Fill in the blanks with what represents how you might experience yourself if you were each of these things:

Car _____ Animal _____ Color _____

Beer/Wine _____ Department store _____

Tree _____ Flower _____ Bug _____

Breakfast Cereal _____ Clothing Brand _____

Now that you have started this process, let's dig even deeper and find out how you are wired internally, which inner systems, patterns and traits you specifically favor that help make you who you are.

SCENE III:
Tools and Skills for Keeping You On Your Path

Put your future in good hands—your own.

– AUTHOR UNKNOWN

To truly understand *why* you do what you do, as well as *how* you do it, requires a deeper level of investigation into your internal wiring system. The way you are wired internally will help you appreciate, recognize, and identify with these very individual configurations of patterns and traits, which help to make up your holistic system of being—who you are from the inside out. This is a crucial part of understanding and establishing your unique and authentic Personal Brand. There is no right or wrong to any of these patterns or traits, merely a matter of determining what your natural preferences are, so that you can embrace and use them consciously as tools.

Knowing how you function at a deeper level gives you all kinds of advantages. One of the biggest advantages is feeling confident when making decisions, whether large or small. Another advantage is being able to recognize the systems, patterns, and traits of others, which allows for clearer, more honest communication. Being comfortable in one's own skin is the greatest advantage of all, because you no longer have to be at the mercy of your emotions, play the games that others attempt to impose on you, or try to second-guess or please others. Instead, you have the power to look at a situation for exactly what it is, choose to take action if appropriate, or not, and never fall prey to trying to direct, predict, control, or live only for the outcome of your story. Rather, you spend most of your time dealing with what is important and on your plate right at this moment, and enjoying the journey. This generates yet another benefit: You don't experience feeling stressed out or anxious about all that you want to accomplish in your future. You get to focus on one step at a time—the one you are acting on right this minute.

Yes, one does need a purpose in life, goals to be reached and dreams to live. It's imperative that you know where you are right now, and where you want to go in the future. Starting this kind of a journey can be more difficult for some, because they don't know which inner systems, patterns, and traits they possess. If you don't know what drives you, it can cause you to simply spin your wheels, or stay in what appears to be your comfort zone, instead of continuing to develop by growing, adapting, and changing.

Once you have the information that helps you to figure out what motivates you, and keeps you motivated, you have the capacity to use it to your benefit. Having that kind of focus enables you to accomplish many tasks—large or small, mundane or fulfilling—always moving you closer to your goals and dreams, while using your own personal timetable for the journey.

Again I will say, there is absolutely no right or wrong, better or worse, more important or less important aspects to any of these systems, traits and patterns. It's just another piece of the puzzle of " who you are" that you can put in place to better understand and recognize yourself from the inside out. The more each of us knows the "why, how, and what" involved in our decision making, the greater opportunity we have of getting it right for us.

Nothing is more difficult, and therefore more precious, than to be able to decide.

– NAPOLEON BONAPARTE

MOTIVATIONAL TRAITS, PATTERNS, AND SYSTEMS
Motivation: The Carrot or the Stick?

Your motivational traits—your inner wiring—are the patterns that indicate what gets you motivated, and *keeps* you motivated in any given situation. Does this always stay the same? Actually, no, but it's possible to make use of both patterns, the carrot *and* the stick, in different situations. Your response to significant events in your life can change how you are motivated at that moment. Each individual circumstance can elicit its own motivational pattern.

> *We are asleep with compasses in our hands.*
> — W.S. MERWIN

Your job, then, is to become aware: Is the pattern you are using beneficial to you or not? What type of motivation works better for you? Do you know whether you are motivated mostly by the carrot—moving toward something—or the stick—moving away from it? Successful people usually know which direction motivates them, and use that information to their advantage. Though we all use both systems to some degree, we generally prefer and use one system over the other. (According to many different studies, the majority of people use the "stick" or "away from" motivational system.)

Like many of these tools, there is no right or wrong to any of this; both systems have their good and not-so-good points. Gaining as much understanding as you can about how you are naturally wired, gives you the opportunity to know how to best use your system of motivation to its fullest advantage, and at the same time, helps you better understand others.

THE CARROT

The upside of this behavior is that the carrot-oriented person moves *toward* what they want—a goal or pleasurable event—allowing you to feel motivated and excited about getting closer to your goals each day. You often feel that all things are possible, and choose to look for the opportunities that are out there, right now, that will take you closer to what you want and desire in your life. You find, know, and respect what is important to you. You choose friends that inspire and encourage you.

The downside to this behavior is that sometimes, being motivated toward a specific goal may cause what is known as "tunnel vision"—seeing nothing but your goal. As a result, you may miss other interesting or important opportunities. In some cases you may unintentionally steamroll over others who seem to be in the way, leaving you misunderstood or disliked because of this behavior. You may be perceived as naïve because you do not take potential problems into account when making decisions, which may in the end create even larger problems for you in the future. Without realizing it, you can act with little or no consideration for others by jumping into situations without thinking or analyzing what the outcome may be. (Example: You alienate a peer who becomes an important stage director, someone who, in the future, keeps you from getting any work where the two of you might become colleagues.) And lastly, you might forget to enjoy the journey—to stop and smell the roses—because all you see is your end goal. This can oftentimes create too much stress, anxiety, and even burn out.

Tips for maintaining better balance if you are motivated by the carrot:

Do make sure you take the time to smell the roses along the way. That means, stop what you are doing every once in awhile, look around, and consciously notice what is going on in your environment and within your relationships. Notice that there is a life beyond your own work and what you are presently focused on. This will help keep a sense of balance in your life.

When you have a goal, be sure to take your blinders off. Don't run over others by bulldozing your way to the finish line. When setting goals, break them down into smaller chunks where only a couple of items are on your daily "to do" list, leaving you time to remain balanced with the rest of your life. You will notice that you still feel productive and in control at the end of each week. In other words, don't put too much on your plate at one time. Learn to say "no" once in a while.

Take the time to really listen to your friends, family, and co-workers on a regular basis. Stop the noise in your head, the inner mental chatter of the Brat, and focus instead on what is being said by others. Don't start thinking of your answer while others are still expressing themselves, or talk over someone else.

Be very present as you do each task. Let your mind rest wherever the working surfaces of your project or task meet. (Example: If you are at work and putting information into a computer, allow your mind to focus on the meeting of your fingers and the keys you are pressing for a few minutes, and notice how much more calm you feel.) And before you move to the next project, pause a moment, leaving what you've been working on "over there," so that you can give your full attention to whatever comes next.

Don't just focus on the future. Embrace each present moment. This will make the journey more enjoyable as well as less stressful.

> *The beginning of all wisdom is to look fixedly on clothes, or even with armed eyesight, till they become transparent.*
>
> – THOMAS CARLYL

THE STICK

The behavior of moving *away from* a situation as your motivator can also be a good thing. You are good at troubleshooting, solving problems, and pinpointing possible obstacles during planning. You automatically pick up on what is or could be going wrong within a situation, project, or relationship, which makes you a good analyst. You usually have several alternatives in mind when attempting to solve a problem, and can be very creative in doing so. (Example: Your audition accompanist almost always shows up just before you have to walk into your audition, causing you some unnecessary anxiety, which can affect your focus. Solution: Seek out a new accompanist, one who understands how you want things done, and who respects your need to have them be on time. At an audition, you might talk with the accompanist of the singer before or after you, to see if they might be willing to play for you if your own accompanist doesn't show up in time.)

The downside of this behavior is that the stick-oriented person notices what should be avoided, gotten rid of, or not happen. You are energized by threats, fear, and pain. Deadlines get you to take action. Before you buy something, it seems like you are waiting for something to happen that will influence you to do so. You often wait for others to initiate, or wait until the situation is "right" before you act. You have a tendency to consider and analyze without taking action. You operate with extra caution, and can study the situation endlessly. You also have trouble maintaining focus on your goals because you are easily distracted by and compelled to respond to negative situations. You do a lot of crisis management, and are often stressed out because you need to get to a deep level of pain, distress, discomfort, and worry before you are motivated to move on. You lose this motivation when these threats move further away, but the motivation returns when the problem reappears. This means motivation for you is cyclical—it runs in "hot" and "cold" cycles. When you do move, often you don't pay attention to *where* you are moving, and therefore tend to move from the frying pan into the fire. Your attention is on what you don't want, not what you do want. As a result, you may have some difficulty managing priorities. Others may perceive you as being jaded or cynical.

Tips for maintaining better balance if you are motivated by the stick:

Always talk to your internal self by first stating what you do *not* want—the negative thought—followed by what you really want to accomplish or get done. Our minds tend to remember more strongly what was mentioned last. (Example: "If I don't learn this music now, I will never get that job, so I will begin right now by spending the next half-hour working on the translation of the piece," is an example of good internal dialogue. Then set the timer for half

Confidence comes not from always being right but from not fearing to be wrong.

– PETER T. MCINTYRE

an hour, and stop when it rings. If you still have the energy to continue further, decide on another exact time period and set your alarm, stopping when it rings.) This kind of internal dialogue, along with setting a specific time period in which to accomplish the task at hand, will bring you more into balance, and give you a better sense of how and for how long you can successfully stay focused on a particular project.

Start noticing when anxiety and stress are beginning to build up, rather than waiting for the breaking point to suddenly appear. Before leaving the uncomfortable spot, know where you want to go. In other words, teach yourself to look before you leap. This allows you the opportunity to make a thoughtful choice about taking action if necessary or not, and begins a new habit of running toward something, rather than away from it.

When you notice that you are starting to give your power away to someone or something, or are stuck in an emotion, stop and take back your power by simply acknowledging and recognizing that you gave it away in the first place—that's pretty much it. To get out of that powerful, negative, emotional state of mind, first you have to notice that it is starting to happen; once you do, physically take a giant step back, out of the emotion, leaving it "over there," so that you can actually look at the situation for what it really is, without being entangled emotionally, then take action or not.

Consciously take some quiet time to just sit with your eyes closed and think about what you want in life, what your dreams are. Look at them, hear them, feel them, smell and taste them, so they become real to you. Do this often. By encouraging this type of positive habit, your thinking mind will return to this spot, and help you move closer to where you want to be. When any negative emotions come up, notice what's happening, step out of the emotion, and stay focused on the good stuff. This allows you to move sooner,

> *Aerodynamically the bumblebee shouldn't be able to fly, but the bumblebee doesn't know that so it goes on flying anyway.*
>
> – MARY KAY ASH

rather than later, to the more appealing outcome, not just in any old direction in order to get out of the hot pan.

Most people want to either gain a benefit or avoid a problem. Ask anyone why an issue is important to them, and see if their answer includes either to "take the initiative and get it done" or "avoid or solve a problem."

SCENARIO

Think about having a stage director that likes to motivate you by constantly changing the staging and yells at you when you can't remember which version of the blocking you are supposed to be doing.

Conversely, what if you had a stage director that seemed to want to share more time, energy, knowledge and encouragement with you because you understood what he wanted and could deliver quickly and add your own personality to the character right away as well.

Notice which story resonates more strongly within you. Then figure out how you would handle whichever situation seemed the most foreign to you using what you just gleaned from the information above about the carrot and the stick motivational styles.

- What happens to your confidence if you do not recognize the pattern they are using?
- With this new information, what would you know about how each is motivated?
- How will this new knowledge and understanding of the carrot and the stick motivation help you figure out how to better respond to each scenario?
- How will this new knowledge and understanding help you keep a more balanced perspective about how you are wired and how to recognize when you are starting to initiate the habitual responses so you can make the choice to change your mind?

Activators (Motivational Provokers):
Things That Drive You to Action.

> *Giving up doesn't always mean you are weak; sometimes it means that you are strong enough to let go.*
>
> **– AUTHOR UNKNOWN**

One of the triggers that provokes motivation is how you are hard-wired for making decisions, taking action, or making judgments. Again, there is no right or wrong, better or worse to any of this, it's only another piece of information to help you understand yourself better. You begin to recognize that you have a choice as to how you get where you want to go in life, more comfortably, without all the drama and beating yourself up. It is also a wonderful tool to better understand others, and will help improve your relationships. Remember, knowledge is power.

INTERNAL

Motivation, for those who are hard wired with the "internal" pattern, is triggered when they get to gather information from the outside, process it against their own standards, and make judgments about and decisions from it:

- You decide about the quality of your work and have difficulty accepting others' opinions and outside direction.
- When you get negative feedback on work you feel has been well done you tend to question the opinion or judge the person giving the feedback, not your own action.
- Orders from others are taken as information so you can be hard to supervise.
- You do not need external praise and tend not to give much feedback.

EXTERNAL

For those who are hard wired with the "external" pattern, getting and staying motivated means seeking outside sources, references, and direction, conducting research, and asking for others' opinions, standards, and feedback before taking action, or making decisions or judgments. Feedback from an external source is an important element if you want to start or continue any activity successfully:

- Most times you take information as orders, and question yourself when you receive criticism or negative feedback.
- Often when you are reaching for a goal or buying something, it will be done as much for effect as for your personal satisfaction.

If you still are having trouble discovering which pattern you use, here are some questions that might help make it clearer:

- How do you know that you have done a good job?
- How would you react to regular feedback from peers in some specific situation?
- Whom do you involve when you make a decision?
- If you felt you had done good work and someone you respect criticized your work, how would you react?
- Do you have an internal knowing of what you want when you see it, or would it be more comfortable to confirm the information with outside resources before making the decision?

How We Reason: Possibility or Process

How we reason is the second trigger that provokes our motivation. We either love the possibilities or alternatives, or we have a preference for following established procedures. As before, there is no right or wrong, better or worse.

> *A bend in the road is not the end of the road... unless you fail to make the turn.*
>
> **– AUTHOR UNKNOWN**

OPTIONS

The hard-wired patterns of those that prefer "options" allow them to feel thrilled by unlimited possibilities, choices, and ideas.

- You are often more motivated when you can do something in a different and interesting way, and love creating procedures and systems, but have great difficulty following them through, and don't feel compelled to do so.

- You tend to bend the rules, always examining the reasons why you should get involved in a project or buy a product. This might cause a negative effect, because you want to find ways to reinvent the wheel by trying to improve on what already works.

- Because you love options, you might have difficulty committing yourself to any project. You are always experimenting, which may make you wonder why your method is not working in your favor.

PROCEDURES

Those whose preferred pattern is to follow "procedures" like to see that a project has a beginning, middle, and end to it, and are compelled to finish whatever they start.

- You are more interested in how something is done, the process. You like knowing what lies ahead so you can plan for it and want to know who else has already had success with it and how that was accomplished.

- If you are learning something new it is important that you are told step-by-step how it is going to work or is done and love it when there is some kind of follow through regarding how the project is going to work from beginning to end.

- You will be more interested in how to buy or use something rather than why you should buy or use it. You like knowing that whatever you are going to do or buy is tried and true backed by research and testing.

If after reading the above descriptions, you are not sure which reasoning system you use to motivate yourself, answer these questions:

- Why did you choose your present career, job, city to live in, vacation, teacher?

There comes a point in many people's lives when they can no longer play the role they have chosen for themselves. When that happens, we are like actors finding that someone has changed the play.

— BRIAN MOORE

- What do you like best about learning anything new?

Internal Timetable for Change

Knowing about one's internal time clock, and how often that bell for change rings, will assist you in finding where the comfort zone is when it comes time to make an important decision or move. Do you search for something different, or are you more comfortable with something that is the same? Are you motivated by evolution, revolution, both of these things, or do you prefer stability? This is an interesting system; experts have found that most people can and do use different patterns in different situations or contexts. Here are the four patterns.

You've got to go out on a limb sometimes because that is where the fruit is.

– WILL ROGERS

SAMENESS

People using this pattern want the situation within a known environment to stay the same:

- You do not like change and may refuse to adapt.
- You may accept major change once every ten years, but you only will initiate change once every 15–25 years.

SAMENESS WITH EXCEPTION

People who use this pattern like their environment to stay mainly the same, but will accept change once a year, if the change is not too drastic. This applies to most people:

- You prefer situations to evolve slowly over time and tend to resist major changes except when they are perceived to be progressive or gradual.
- You need major change every 5–7 years.

DIFFERENCE

The people using this pattern love change. They thrive on it, and want it to be both constant and major:

- You will resist static or stable situations.
- You need drastic change about every 1–2 years, and if you don't get it, you may leave.
- You like change to be revolutionary, dramatically different.

SAMENESS WITH EXCEPTION AND DIFFERENCE (DOUBLE PATTERN)

People using this system are happy with both evolution and revolution, but are also comfortable where things are evolving. They need major change every three to four years on average.

- The people using this system like change and revolutionary development but are also comfortable where things are evolving.
- You are happy with both revolution and evolution.
- You need major change every 3–5 years, on average.

SUMMARY

It's irrelevant which motivational patterns and associated systems you use—one is not better or worse than another. All you need to be interested in is recognizing, acknowledging, and understanding which systems, patterns, and traits you utilize, so that you can start being more comfortable, resourceful, and effective within your own skin. The advantage is always being able to solicit more useful and successful choices.

This kind of inner knowledge gives you more tools with which to help build a solid Personal Brand, when pursuing your career and expanding your relationships. Being consciously aware of what it takes to get you motivated, and *keep* you motivated, is a major step forward toward getting what you want out of life. Besides understanding yourself, it

> *Let your working ideas go for a picnic—sometimes the fresh air and ant bites are just what they need. Many great ideas were bitten a little at the beginning.*
>
> – CARRIE LATET

allows you to know how to persuade and influence others, to get motivated on their own behalf or even on your behalf. No matter your preferred patterns, knowledge is power, so value and start using this new information to help keep yourself and others motivated, whether it is for business or for improving your personal relationships.

Now that we have talked about your motivations traits, patterns and systems, let me introduce you to your mental and emotional gate keeper, the Brat.

SCENE IV:
The Gate Keeper

I have referred to the "Brat" several times already. Getting to know your own personal Brat is without a doubt an interesting process. Have you had the pleasure of meeting yours yet? It's that inner voice, the internal conversation we often have with ourselves. The conversation is usually not very complimentary, and is often done to distract us. The Brat seems to need your attention at the most inappropriate times, often leaving you feeling helpless and unworthy. Notice that when you feel stuck, you are probably listening to or having a dialogue with your inner "Brat."

According to Marice Tobias, coach, consultant and director of Tobias Entertainment Group, "The Brat (as she also calls it) is the part of all of us that has an opinion about everything, and thinks it should be in charge. It's the five-year-old egomaniac who resides in our brain and gut, running the show whether we want it to or not. The Brat's agenda is that it must always 'tell the truth,' usually a good idea, except that the Brat doesn't know the difference between feelings and facts. It doesn't know about appropriateness or diplomacy. It can and will needlessly destroy an opportunity simply because it feels, at that moment, that it

It takes courage to push yourself to places that you have never been before... to test your limits... to break through barriers. And the day came when the risk to remain tight in a bud was more painful than the risk it took to blossom.

— ANAIS NIN

is being abridged, threatened, dismissed, or undervalued, no matter the cost. Despite talent and potential, if left unchecked, the Brat can, and will, eventually drive any career irrevocably into the ground."

Recognizing and acknowledging the Brat is the first step in learning how best to deal with it. We may only hear the Brat when it chastises or berates us, trying to keep us in line. And you might be aware of and familiar with the kind of white noise which runs incessantly, way, way in the background of your thinking mind, almost never stopping. That is where the Brat resides. We have turned the volume down so low that we don't actually hear its words most of the time.

I believe we created our Brat when we were young, and first became conscious that there were societal rules. The Brat was there to help remind us of how to fit into society as we grew and matured, repeating back to us the warnings of others or those that we ourselves put in place. Over time we discovered other sources for learning how to fit in, and that inner voice became just the white noise in the background, usually coming forward when we felt we had made a faux pas of some kind, or to remind us that we needed to shape up if we wanted to fit in.

Believe me when I say, the Brat is really our friend and wants the best for us. The Brat is always looking out for us, even in the midst of those short, hurtful shots it delivers every so often. It's only because we haven't had a meaningful dialogue with our Brat in a very long time, bringing him or her up to speed with new ideas of how best to be of service to us, now that we are grown up, that it seems like a curse instead of a helper.

Here are a couple of techniques for reconnecting with your Brat. They may at first seem odd, and you may feel a bit awkward when trying them. But if you want to change the message the Brat is responsible for, give this exercise a try.

> *We like Batman—we understand him, we suffer with him. On the other hand, we want to be Superman. But they're conflicting philosophies. Let's bring them together in one movie and see how we, as an audience, wrestle with our inner demons.*
>
> **– WOLFGANG PETERSEN**

It may take several sessions to get comfortable with this, so don't give in or give up.

The first step is to recognize that your Brat exists. Listen to and observe what it has to say and when it is most active. By listening, you learn to monitor this inner voice and not just get caught up in it. If you think of this voice as a five-year-old child throwing a tantrum every time it does not get its way, you realize that the Brat just wants your attention, and gets it by distracting you from whatever needs your conscious attention and absolute focus, right this minute, so it can keep you in line.

Now try this: Put two chairs close together, facing each other, with you in one of them. Imagine the Brat in the other chair. Focus on what your Brat looks like. Be very specific in describing him or her—notice how old he or she is, what color it's hair, eyes, skin are, how tall he or she is, etc. Once you have a clear picture, ask your Brat these pertinent questions, one at a time, switching seats from you asking the questions to assuming all the characteristic and personality of the "Brat" giving the answers as you go back and forth each time. Don't move to the Brat's chair with a conscious, predetermined answer or concept already formed. Let the Brat answer each question for him- or herself through you:

- "What is it you want?"
- "What do you need from me?"
- "How will you feel when your needs are met?"

You might be very surprised at what comes up. This is a great way for the two of you to get reacquainted. It may take a few times to get the hang of this kind of work, and to stay out of your thinking brain so that you don't presuppose the Brat's answers. But the more you get to know and understand what it is the Brat wants and needs, the quicker you can start setting up a new and improved program for your

If you had a friend who talked to you like you sometimes talk to yourself, would you continue to hang around with that person?

– ROB BREMER

Brat to run, one that will benefit you both. The Brat wants to be your friend and work on your behalf, eventually becoming integrated into who you are by working in tandem on only the good stuff.

You are in charge, and can treat the Brat like a child if he or she is not minding. Simply demand, out loud, that they go to the "time out" corner until you are done with your work. You might have to repeat the command a few times, but it works, and you will notice and feel the difference!

Another way to quiet the Brat is what I described earlier, to simply repeat back to the Brat exactly what it is saying. It doesn't mean you are agreeing, but it is a way to quiet the thinking mind. The Brat likes to argue and if you agree, there is no argument. You will experience a few seconds of absolute blessed silence.

You're only as sick as your secrets.

– AUTHOR UNKNOWN

As you get to know and understand your Brat, you can begin to suggest some changes you might want it to make to help keep you on track as an adult. You will need to get the Brat's agreement to these changes before they will stick, and you need to thank the Brat for having done the job you asked it to do up to this point. The Brat *does* have your best interest at heart, and just needs to be brought up to speed as to what its job is now. Once you have an understanding with your Brat, you might want to have a sit down with it a few times a year, just to make sure you are both on the same page and working in tandem. In ending a session with your Brat, always thank it for showing up, and for its input, understanding, and willingness to change.

Remember, the Brat is a program you put in place years ago when you were growing up, and it was useful then because it helped you remember how to successfully become part of the society you lived in. Over time, and because you had other resources to keep you in check, the Brat has for the most part become just some distracting, static noise running incessantly in the back of your mind. Maybe it only shows up once in awhile, but it quickly gains your attention. It is, in essence, just a mind game, so the more you can stay in the moment, representing and presenting your Personal Brand, the more you and your Brat will want to work as a team to create your success. The Brat wants to be part of the solution once again, and your friend.

SCENE V:
Rapport Skills

Rapport consists of body language, communication skills, and our use of personal space. These phenomena are all things that we utilize hundreds of times, each and every day. However, we usually do all of this unconsciously, and I want to show you how to bring these actions to your conscious mind, so you can start using them as tools to improve your ability to be understood, maximize the effectiveness of all of your relationships (including the one with yourself), and activate your personal space.

Bad human communication leaves us less room to grow.

– ROWAN D. WILLIAMS

Rapport is the prerequisite for great communication. We have this kind of experience daily. You can even have rapport with a piece of land, a tree or garden, a book, or a piece of music. The Greeks called it *aesthesis,* which means, "to breath in." It's the moment your soul-essence inside and the soul-essence from something outside meet and mingle. It's a kind of intimacy we have no words for. It is the ultimate good feeling.

Rapport is also your capacity to see another's point of view without necessarily agreeing with it. You remain on the same wavelength, and are able to appreciate and respect the other person's feeling, without needing to sway them to your point of view. When you become conscious of being in rapport and can start using it as a tool, it allows you to enter another's model of *their* world on *their* terms, because you have helped to create a climate of understanding and trust.

Rapport is another part of our inner systems that help make us who we are. Have you ever watched Fred Astair and Ginger Rodgers dancing together, or checked out the amazing connection shared by the musicians in an orchestra? These are both great examples of the art of rapport. They give and take, and are in sync with one another, mind, body, and spirit. Whether it is with one person or a whole audience, rapport is always a goal worth attaining.

BODY LANGUAGE

I think there's a natural chemistry between us as friends; and there's really no separation between the rapport that we feel when we're in conversation and when we're playing music, it's one in the same.

— BENNY GREEN

Think of someone you have an amazing relationship with. Think about the particular aspects of this relationship that make it more comfortable than some of your other relationships. You might notice that you like this person because they seem to speak your language—you don't have to try to figure out what they are trying to say to you. You are comfortable being with them, and feel safe in sharing your innermost thoughts with them. You look to them for advice and support, and are there for them in the same capacity. You might even have similar interests and tastes.

When you get right down to it, you often seem to adopt the same body posture, use the same gestures, laugh together at the same time at the same things, have a similar sense of style, and perhaps also have the same rhythm in your movements and speech. You often become very aware when something has changed emotionally with this kind of friend without a word having to be spoken, because their body language has changed. You will most times be in sync with one another, no matter what the emotional state. This kind of rapport creates a true bond of trust, and feels comfortable and safe.

Using body language in a similar fashion with others is a big part of being in rapport. When you become conscious of how the process of rapport works, it can become a very useful tool when networking, or meeting new colleagues at the beginning of a new production. It makes you and those around you feel comfortable.

Try this: When you are at a gathering, look around the room and notice the interactions among the people there. There might be a twosome, or perhaps there are larger groups. Notice the difference between what body language looks like when people are either in or out of rapport. Also notice how it is that you know that.

Try introducing yourself to a stranger at this gathering, being aware of their body language. In a very subtle way, try moving, repositioning yourself in a similar fashion with your own hands, arm gestures, head tilting, crossing of ankles or legs if sitting, etc. Know that you don't have to mimic them exactly in either their movements or in their timing of their movements, because that becomes too obvious and may alienate them. Notice that as you enter into this process, you are both feeling more comfortable with each other immediately. It becomes an elegant, sensitive, and even tantalizing dance.

Remember the mind/body connection? This is a perfect example of how that occurs. When someone adopts a similar or matching body language, it creates similar feelings in both people. Example: In order for you to be of help to someone who is venting in a dramatic way and needs to be brought back to a place of rational thinking, start your conversation at their same volume and tonal pitch. As you do this, your body language will automatically respond in a similar way to theirs. As you continue this conversation, slowly start the process of bringing your own voice out of the dramatic mode in volume and pitch, and you will notice that the other person will follow your lead. Once you have brought them down to a normal conversational level, you can then continue your conversation in a more sensible and

I have figured for you the distance between the horns of a dilemma, night and day, and A and Z. I have computed how far is Up, how long it takes to get Away, and what becomes of Gone. I have discovered the length of the sea serpent, the price of priceless, and the square of the hippopotamus. I know where you are when you are at Sixes and Sevens, how much Is you have to have to make an Are, and how many birds you can catch with the salt in the ocean—187,796,132, if it would interest you.

– JAMES THURBER

beneficial way. The other person will not have noticed this transition. Conversely, if you are feeling down and forced to be with an individual or group of people that is in a celebratory mood—up, happy, and laughing—you will have a very hard time staying down, because you automatically change to their vocal pitches and body posture.

An important note: Remember, you are looking to establish great rapport. Don't simply mimic the exact movements and the timing of those movements with someone else. That is too obvious, and in fact will move the situation in the exact opposite direction, perhaps even making the other person think you are making fun of them. In order to become a master of rapport—especially if you want it become part your new Personal Brand behavior—you have to practice doing it on purpose often and check the response of those with whom you are practicing. It's also great to start observing others who use or are instinctually good at this process.

Body rapport is a large part of learning to read another person and respond with similar movements. It's a conscious effort to help all involved in the situation feel comfortable, interested and experience an honest sense of trust. It will become a very useful tool in establishing and maintaining relationships.

COMMUNICATION SKILLS

Inner Language Systems

How many of you had a teacher in school with whom you didn't get along or just didn't connect with, or felt as if they were speaking some strange language that you just couldn't understand? That's because you literally *didn't* speak the same language. I want to give you the key, the secret to understanding all of these other inner language systems.

It is the inner language system that we each use—and particularly, the dominant one that we prefer to use—that often keeps us from understanding, being understood, or

The real art of conversation is not only to say the right thing at the right time, but also to leave unsaid the wrong thing at the tempting moment.

– AUTHOR UNKNOWN

being in rapport with others. Communicating any of your thoughts to others is done through the use of words, whether written, sung, or spoken. That is why it is important to first know which primary inner language system *you* prefer, and then have the ability to quickly establish which inner language system is used by others. For example, if you were asked by a visitor to your town how to find a specific place, and you could tell from their accent that English wasn't their first language, if you happened to speak their native language, you would give them directions in that language, to make sure they understood clearly how to get where they were going.

Everyone uses their inner language system to express themselves, as well as to "translate" or interpret what others are saying to us. In other words, some people will use mostly *seeing* words to describe something: "I see what you mean;" some will mostly use *hearing* words to describe things: "I hear what are saying;" while still others will use *feeling* words for their description: "It feels right to me." Paying close attention to the types of words someone uses when speaking will let you know which of these is their primary system. We use *all three systems*—visual, auditory, *and* kinesthetic—*all the time,* but we each have *one* system we prefer over the others.

To help you identify your own preferred style of thinking—your inner language system—circle the letter of the choice that fits your sensibility best:

• I make my most important decisions based on:

  a. My "gut" feelings.

  b. What sounds good to me.

  c. What looks best to me.

• During an argument, I am most likely to be influenced by:

  a. How I feel about what's being said.

  b. Tone of voice.

  c. Whether or not I can see the other person's point of view.

- I most easily communicate what is going on with me by:
    a. The feelings I share.
    b. Choosing the right words and voice inflection when I speak.
    c. Allowing others to see how I look at the situation.
- Things I do well or have trouble with:
    a. Being with others and sharing.
    b. Look someone in the eye when having a conversation with them.
    c. Notice when things are out of place.
- I am:
    a. Sensitive to the way music pulls on my heartstrings.
    b. Very tuned into and in harmony with the sounds in the environment.
    c. Good at discerning the overview and scope of a project.

If you circled mostly A's, your primary inner language system is *kinesthetic;* how things feel helps you to understand your world.

If you circled mostly B's, your primary inner language system is *auditory;* how something sounds helps you to understand your world.

If you circled mostly C's, your primary inner language system is *visual;* how something looks helps you to understand your world.

There is no right or wrong to any of this. It's like fingerprints; each person's is very different. Everyone uses all three of these inner language systems all the time, but has a primary one that unlocks the thinking process.

This may give you better insight as to why you do or do not communicate as well with some people. This also explains why certain conflicts may arise, or why you sometimes may feel misunderstood. You are *literally* not speaking the same language. However, with this new knowledge, you can learn to be a better communicator (see the appendix for more examples of inner language words).

Following is a more detailed description of these three basic inner language systems, to help differentiate and clarify some of the specific characteristics of your preferred way of communicating:

VISUAL (SEEING)

Most people use the visual inner language system. They deal with the world on a visual level. Books with pictures are easier than books with only words to understand. You notice when something is out of place. You can usually remember how and where to find things by relating to the pictures you see in your head. You can write down what you see when someone describes it verbally. You like everything in order and well organized. You can sit still for long periods of time. The words "I see what you mean, I'll take a look at it, I can visualize that" help you to feel comfortable and understood.

Tips for learning:

You are a fast learner, but forget just as fast. Outlining any project will help strengthen recall. Deal with one aspect of learning at a time and give yourself a specific set time to do so. Memorize your words by really looking at them over and over, and then see them in your head just as they are on the page. Do the same with the musical notes. However, do not overload yourself. See what you are working on in your imagination. Make it into a movie or video. When you are studying your staging, see yourself move on stage with the sets and the other characters present, in costume, with lights, etc.

> Look. This is your world! You can't not look. There is no other world. This is your world; it is your feast. You inherited this; you inherited these eyeballs; you inherited this world of color. Look at the greatness of the whole thing. Look! Don't hesitate. Open your eyes. Don't blink.
>
> **– CHOGYAM TRUNGPA**

> *I promise to make you so alive that the fall of dust on furniture will deafen you.*
>
> — NINA CASSIAN

AUDITORY (HEARING)

Words, sounds and intonation are most important to you. You love to talk and are a great storyteller. You can remember words to songs and are usually good at rhythms. You have the ability to write what you hear when someone describes it verbally. You are very good a mimicking accents and voices in general. The words, "I hear you, it sounds right to me, tell me the truth," make you feel comfortable and understood.

Tips for learning:

Work with a tape recorder. The more you hear, the easier recall is. Try writing in the air, high and up to your right in a bright, fluorescent color any important thing you want to remember, like the beginning word to a phrase you are having trouble memorizing. Then look up and to your right to gain recall. It is hard for you to look someone in the eyes when speaking because it distracts you from being able to really listen to what they have to say.

> *It's often just enough to be with someone. I don't need to touch them. Not even talk. A feeling passes between you both. You're not alone.*
>
> — MARILYN MONROE

KINESTHETIC (FEELING)

If you can feel it either by touch or by physically doing it, you understand it. Everything is an emotional experience for you. Taking things apart and putting them back together, whether thoughts or things, is how you best learn about them. You have the ability to write with great feeling what someone describes verbally. It is easy for you to become the character in an opera, play, or musical once you understand who that is. You are generally a good actor, and are good at expressing how you feel through your voice. You find it hard to sit still for long periods of time. The words, "It feels right to me, keep in touch, I can't put my finger on it," make you feel comfortable and understood.

Tips for learning:

Write how you feel about any subject you are studying. Talk

out loud as you study. Say your words over and over again out loud as you memorize and do it with passion. Recall will come more easily if you translate all the information you have received from differing sources into your own words and then speak them out loud. Move around physically as you practice anything. Understanding what the words mean if you are singing in a foreign language is crucial to you, so translating your text is of great importance. Find the congruence between you and the character you are portraying and use that emotion to drive your character. Feel the emotion behind the words.

In addition to learning what your inner language system is, you can use this skill to help identify other people's inner language systems, thereby becoming a better communicator by knowing how to enter their world using their identified inner language system.

First, listen to the key words they use, i.e., see, feel, hear (see the word list in the appendix). Then try using several of these words back to them, even if it feels foreign to you—and it will. You will make them feel understood, which is what everyone really wants. It creates trust, which is fundamental to every good relationship. Only when you have trust can there be rapport, which is the natural process of matching and being in alignment with another person. It allows you to enter another person's model of their world on their terms. And since we regularly use all three inner language systems, they are *all* available to us as tools. When you are having trouble making a serious decision, or trying to solve a problem, sit quietly with that decision or problem in mind. Allow yourself to search through all three inner language systems, one by one, to perhaps see, hear, or feel a better way to a successful outcome. This may help you discover many different resources and ways of thinking to make the best decision or solve that problem.

Remember that we all use all three styles of these inner language systems, all the time; we just have one we prefer over the others. When you gain the ability to create genuine rapport, by understanding and using another's inner language system, you gain confidence in your capacity as a communicator, and that will become an intricate part of your networking and business skills. Like learning anything else new, it does take consistent practice if you want to get good at it.

BEING UNDERSTOOD AND UNDERSTANDING OTHERS

I know you believe you understand what you think I said, but I am not sure you realize that what you heard is not what I meant.

– RICHARD M. NIXON

You, as the speaker (in whatever form that may take, including emails, voicemails, internet posts, instant messaging, or any other spoken or written communication), are responsible for letting others know what you want and, if possible, how you would like things to happen. You can't expect others to second-guess what you want or mean. You are responsible for the information you give and your views being understood. In other words, you are responsible for how you say what you say.

Everyone wants to be understood—that is a universal truth. So, as you engage in conversation and are truly listening, every once in a while, paraphrase back to the person with whom you are speaking what they have just said using their preferred inner language system, if you were able to figure that out. This way they will know that the message given by them was the message received by you, with its intent intact and if it isn't the message they gave, they have an opportunity to rectify it. Example: "What I heard you say was..." "Is that really how you feel?" or "How interesting," etc.

Information in a conversation may be correct or incorrect; however, when that information becomes emotional, conflicts can arise. Try to stay focused only on the message (facts) not the messenger (emotional meanings insinuated through the sound of the voice). If you feel yourself being pulled into the heat of the messenger's emotion, physically take one step back out of that emotional feeling, leaving the emotion where you were standing, so that you can deal with just the facts, and not be encumbered by the emotion of *how* the message was given. It puts you in the driver's seat.

LISTENING

Giving someone else your full attention while listening to their part of a conversation is becoming a lost art—particularly in today's world, where so much of our conversation is conducted by way of virtual media. We often don't even use real words anymore (or at least no longer spell them out), using emoticons, or internet shorthand like LOL or OMG instead. As a result, face-to-face communication—which is really a huge mixture of the exchange of words, attitudes, feelings, emotions, body language and ideas—often becomes awkward, as we become less and less accustomed to the simple act of listening attentively to what someone is saying and responding accordingly. We are often "off in our heads," trying to come up with that witty comeback or clever answer, rather than just listening to what the other person is saying. The phrase, "You know what I mean?" has become a big part of our modern lexicon, in part because we're not entirely convinced that those listening have really heard what we have to say. You don't have to like the other person or agree with their opinions, but you should respect them and allow them the opportunity to express themselves.

We have two ears and one mouth so that we can listen twice as much as we speak.

– EPICTETUS

Want to get better at listening? Here are some ideas for you to try:

- Do not be threatened by someone else's opinion. Practice listening to others and giving them your full attention, rather than starting to form your own answers or opinions while they are still talking. Really engage and listen to their views, their particular inner language, ideas, feelings, and attitudes. Stay in the moment; don't let your thoughts wander off.

- If you are feeling emotion in a conversation, odds are good you are reacting not to *what* is being said, but to *how* it is being said. In other words, you are listening to the messenger, not the message. Even if you feel passionate about a subject, let the other person finish speaking before you respond. Don't try to rush them by finishing their sentence, or overwhelm them with your own opinion. Let it be an exercise in patience.

- Everyone has a right to his or her own perspective, including you. You don't have to sway anyone to your point of view or vice versa; you can simply state your opinion, then listen with an open, attentive mind to others.

- Listen closely to find out what inner language system they are using in their speech. Is it visual, hearing or feeling? Then try feeding that same language back to them as you converse.

- If you have trouble paying attention to what others are saying, try listening for the key ideas. Most people repeat the important item in a conversation back to the speaker, to make sure they understand correctly what is being said. Review in your mind what the speaker is saying, and paraphrase it back to them. This will also let them know that you are interested in what they are saying. They will feel comfortable talking with you.

- Being a well-read and well-rounded person gives you the opportunity to engage with others on a wide range of subjects, which can be easily introduced into a conversation. Being well informed also gives you the conversational tools needed to be able to enter another person's world on their terms.

- Asking questions is another good way to facilitate conversation. I would strongly suggest using "how," "what," or "when" questions, rather than "why" questions, which can often

> *The most important thing in communication is to hear what isn't being said.*
>
> **— PETER F. DRUCKER**

result in a defensive response from the person being questioned.

- Withhold judgment. Comparing yourself or competing with others, or trying to make a point in an aggressive or argumentative manner can create a grim conversational situation. Judgments only give a single snapshot of others at a particular point in time. And because of that you don't know what went on before or what will go on after your brief encounter, so stay focused on the moment of communication.

Knowing what your inner language system is, as well as understanding better how to communicate and be in rapport, will give you more of an opportunity to participate effectively in your own life. It will help you identify and recognize your own uniqueness—reflected in your Personal Brand—which in turn allows and encourages others to express themselves, and feel safe in demonstrating who they are at their core.

Our industry is filled with strong personalities that often come accompanied by equally strong egos. Using all these new skills when communicating will help you stay centered, relevant, and focused when surrounded by these varied personalities, and will allow you to function alongside them in a harmonious and uncompromising manner.

YOUR PERSONAL SPACE

space: *A quantity or portion of extension; the distance from one thing to another; an interval between any two or more points or objects.*

– *WEBSTER'S NEW WORLD DICTIONARY*

Using your personal space is something you do unconsciously hundreds of times each day. However, the conscious use of your personal space becomes another tool that you can use to your advantage. Most people don't even recognize its existence, let alone understand that it can become

The trouble with having a body is that people know it's where you hang out and you don't get any privacy.

– ROBERT BRAULT

> *Oh, the comfort—the inexpressible comfort of feeling safe with a person—having neither to weigh thoughts nor measure words, but pouring them all right out, just as they are, chaff and grain together; certain that a faithful hand will take and sift them, keep what is worth keeping, and then with the breath of kindness blow the rest away.*
>
> – DINAH CRAIK

such a powerful tool. Your personal space plays a large role in how comfortable or uncomfortable you feel when dealing with others. It defines your comfort zone, and until you bring it to consciousness, it can keep you trapped, not allowing you to fully participate in and experience each and every present moment. When it is breached without your permission, it makes you feel uncomfortable and often even violated. The scientific community calls it Human Energy Field (HEF), which is the electromagnetic field our bodies radiate. It can be measured by scientific instruments, and its natural size varies from person to person. Once you become aware of and start using it as a tool, it can be expanded or retracted at will, and becomes like sensitive fingers, touching the world around you. You can then choose to include or exclude others in this space. Used consciously in conjunction with auditions, performances, networking, and schmoozing, it can help you to gain poise and confidence by actively and consciously inviting others into your personal space.

Several important medical doctors and psychologists have verified, through rigorous scientific testing, that what I have always referred to as Personal Space is something very real. It is an important part of how we relate to the world, and the world to us.

Gary Schwartz, Professor of Psychology at the University of Arizona, and Linda Russek, of the Heart Science Foundation, have discovered that 60 percent of our heart cells are made up of neural cells, which function similarly to the neural cells in our brain. So when you say that something is heartfelt or has broken your heart, it is the truth—our hearts do think.

Mae-Wan Ho, of the Institute of Science in Society, has proven that the heart produces an electromagnetic field 5,000 times stronger than that which is produced by the brain. It can be detected by scientific instruments up to 10 feet away, and is strongest from the body's surface to about

18 inches away. This measurable field continues indefinitely out into space, like radio waves.

Dr. Ho also says that, just in meeting another person—even before verbal dialogue ensues—one heart entrains with another, with a rapid exchange of information resulting in raised heart function, a rush of hormones, and a change in physiology. A different kind of dialogue begins.

We gather a great deal of information, which has no identifiable form or emotion, through our gut and heart. This information goes to the intellectual, intrinsic right brain, which starts to put it into a recognizable form. It then enters our thinking left brain, where it passes through three filtering systems, in this order:

Generalization: This filter starts the process of putting the pixels of what we are focusing on into a recognizable state. It identifies and categorizes similar incidents, situations, and experiences that have been established since childhood, even though these experiences might not seem logical if you were to stop and analyze them.

Deletion: This filter starts the alteration process, by leaving out certain details that don't seem to fit within a particular category or, in retelling a story, the parts we don't like.

Embellishment: This filter mixes the information with our existing belief systems, to create thoughts that we can express through language when we speak.

It seems that, instead of accepting incoming information as just that, we humans contaminate it with our own programming and belief systems. This often leaves us stuck, using our comfort zone as a kind of drug—we would rather stay stuck, because we are lazy, scared, or have no idea of who we are, and are afraid to find out.

So how do we use this information as a tool?

The first way to bring it to consciousness is to simply be aware that it exists. Raise both arms to shoulder height

> *The extent of your consciousness is limited only by your ability to love and to embrace with your love the space around you, and all it contains.*
>
> **– NAPOLEON BONAPARTE**

and stretch them out, slowly turning in a circle. Feel—mentally, physically, and spiritually—your personal space, the edges of which are defined by your outstretched fingertips. As you do this, consciously extend your personal space beyond this position, feeling the edges expand as you do; now contract that same space, making it smaller and bringing it closer to your body. Notice the differences in how you feel. When you are with friends, notice if you feel that your personal space expands to include them. When you are walking down the street, or perhaps with a group of folks you don't know very well, how far out does your personal space extend? Are others included in your space or not? Do you feel yourself being included in someone else's space, and if so how does that make you feel?

When someone you don't know comes up to you, notice if you feel yourself pulling your personal space in close to you, keeping them at arms length and not allowing them into that space. This is keeping the other person out. On purpose and consciously, try extending your space out beyond where they are standing. Invite them into your space. How does that feel? Probably much more comfortable. Did you notice a change in their response to you as well?

The uncomfortable, anxious feelings we experience when meeting new people, networking, or schmoozing come from us keeping our personal space tight against our bodies. Before you enter a room full of strangers, or as you stand ready for an audition, try consciously extending your personal space, filling up the entire room with it; you have just invited everyone in that room into your space. Now enter, and notice how much more comfortable you feel. Of course, this takes practice, and like anything else worth doing, you must be conscious of it all the time, until it becomes the habit.

As I said before, your personal space is a tool that, when extended, will help you feel more comfortable when auditioning, performing, networking, or schmoozing. Practice this many times before you try to use it out in the real world. You don't need anyone to help you with this exercise: Stand in a room of any size, and imagine a carpet that is as wide and deep as the entire room. Notice the color of the carpet. Make it a color that you love, or it may surprise you, and show up as a color you weren't expecting—that's okay, too. (It might even change color each time you use it.) Does this carpet have a design of some type? Does it have a deep, thick pile, or is it close cut and rough? Does it have a sculpted design, like many oriental rugs, or is it a tight, flat weave? Does it have fringe or tassels on the ends? With your eyes wide open, really see each detail of your carpet, hear the sound it makes as you walk barefoot over it, feel your carpet's texture and smell the essence of its fabric. Use all your senses to experience this—your very own "magic carpet" in your imagination.

Process: Once you have that in mind, remember that, for an audition or performance, you and your accompanist are both positioned on one of the ends of your magic carpet, which is rolled up and resting just at the tips of your shoes. (Or if you are networking or schmoozing at an event, enter the room and go through the same process, before you move on to greet others.) Now, still feeling, seeing, and hearing this carpet—as deep and as wide as the room—give it a small kick mentally with one foot, keeping your eyes on it's width as it methodically rolls out toward the back of the room. Don't rush it; really see, hear, and feel it unroll at it's own pace. Notice how wide it is. Again, don't be in a rush to make this happen. Time yourself, see just how long it really takes—it feels like it takes forever for your carpet to unfurl, but as you practice this, you'll understand the benefit of that. As the carpet finishes unfurling—when it hits the back of the room—allow your eyes to continue up the wall to a point about halfway up the wall; notice how powerful you feel, and that you are smiling all over on the inside. Once you have practiced this to the point that you feel confident with the process, try it on your friends. Ask if they noticed a difference in how you presented yourself—did they feel you exuded more confidence? Did you feel more confident? Ask if they felt invited into your personal space, and if they expected you to deliver an amazing performance, etc. With practice, you will see, hear, and feel the rug move, at a pace that is just right for this process to occur.

Isn't this kind of information amazing? It explains so many things, like when you meet someone for the first time and feel really close to them, or conversely, meet someone and immediately mistrust them. It also explains how we manage to stay sane when we encounter so many people every day, walking down the street in a large city, or using mass transit. At those times, we usually keep our personal space—our electromagnetic field—tight and close to our bodies, so that it doesn't get bounced around or misused. Up until now, we have unconsciously chosen to let our hearts entrain with others. With this new knowledge, we can consciously choose to start a silent and truthful dialogue with one person or with an entire audience. With practice, it is possible to learn the shape of your own heart field and use it as you do your mind, to touch the world around you, and to invite others to enter into your space and world.

SELF-ALIGNMENT

The final step in solidifying your Personal Brand is ensuring that both your inner (intrinsic) and outer (thinking brain) selves are aligned and in sync with it. To successfully complete this task, one needs only to notice, when living your Personal Brand—in conjunction with your full knowledge of your true belief system, and all your other inner systems, patterns, and traits—if they do or do not feel balanced within.

> *Perhaps we are looking at this from a wrong perspective, this search for the truth, the meaning of life, the reason of God. We all have this mindset that the answers are so complex and so vast that it is almost impossible to comprehend. I think, on the contrary, that the answers are so simple; so simple that it is staring us straight in the face, screaming its lungs out, and yet we fail to notice it. We're looking through a telescope, searching the stars for the answer, when the answer is actually a speck of dirt on the telescope's lens.*
>
> – JASON Q.

Being balanced within implies a physical feeling of openness, of overall symmetry and alignment within your body, which then allows your outer behavior to be in agreement with these inner feelings. It looks, sounds, and feels like you are smiling all over, from the inside out. You feel congruent, whole, and healthy. When you are congruent on the inside, it permits you to be consistent on the outside, which is a powerful way of showing others that you are ready for success and action. Because of the mind/body connection, you stand straight and tall, and naturally extend your personal space to invite others in.

On the other hand, being incongruent or out of balance causes your mind to wander, your thoughts to be chaotic, and too often, you feel out of control. You might feel uneasiness somewhere in your body, usually in your chest or abdomen, if your Personal Brand and your inner systems, patterns, and traits have not been successfully figured out. Often focus becomes an issue, because you're not quite sure what to focus on—your mind is constantly being distracted by jumping from one thought to another, lacking a source for understanding yourself—your foundation—to check against. Being out of sync, and not aligned within and without, can cause these reactions, and you might want to revisit this whole process to notice where the inconsistency might lie. Notice your posture and inability to extend your personal space when you are in this state.

It's harder to make choices if you don't know how you are wired on the inside. Having this knowledge gives you the opportunity to know where the difficulties might lie for you. Begin using your new tools and skills to help expand your thinking to create the outcome you want—to take action, rather than just react.

As you can perhaps now start to understand, the more that you know about the person inside the singer, the more flexible, curious, awake, conscious, and present you become.

When you start embodying, and living through, your Personal Brand, it becomes a compelling and persuasive way of communicating without having to say a word. You make the ultimate statement.

Creating and living your Personal Brand across all the roles you play in life—including the relationship you maintain with yourself—permits you to be curious, authentic, unique, real, empowered, flexible, and irresistible—not only will you feel good about yourself, but you will also draw others to you like a magnet, without having to work at it. Don't settle for the false façade that most people mistake for their Personal Brand. Take the time and energy to recognize, acknowledge, and then communicate your true self—your full Personal Brand—to the world. It will carry over into everything you do throughout your life, and you will then have only one behavior for all the many roles you play in life.

You are the only one who can truly make yourself happy, and define what success means to you. You learn that there is no one way, no ultimate path or exact time table for making your dream into reality, because there are no two people wired in exactly the same way. You become the active force in your own life.

Are you ready and willing to begin this lifelong journey? How will this impact you as an emerging artist? Are you ready to reveal who you are at your core level, and feel confident by being in control of your own life? Would you like to be able to leave any emotional baggage behind, and take action—rather than always just reacting—in situations that require your attention? Do you want to understand and manage your internal emotional state? Do you dare to take your power back, by becoming more of your unique, authentic self—your Personal Brand—allowing others to experience it without you having to say a word?

Answer these two questions honestly:

- How would you describe your life in eight words or less?
- Is your life proof of what you believe?

SUMMARY

This time, like all times, is a very good one, if we but know what to do with it.

– RALPH WALDO EMERSON

Representing and presenting your Personal Brand across the broad spectrum of roles that you play, within all of your relationships throughout your life, is an ongoing, all-encompassing experience. The benefits you experience from your ability to make decisions and choices, by constantly practicing and using your new tools and skills, is one safe and reliable way to come to trust in your *genuine* self. And with consistent practice, these tools and skills gradually become the default system, the habit.

I hope the strategies I have laid out in this chapter will continue to stimulate your sense of curiosity, throughout your entire lifetime, to pursue the quest for your most authentic self, allowing you to represent and present your unique Personal Brand with elegance and style. There is so much more information and material out there for you to discover, and to apply to your life. Getting better at being who you are is a lifelong journey, and one well worth taking, so get ready for a great adventure. You will definitely be living your life out loud, not just going through the motions or hiding behind rules and imposed lifestyles that others have tried to imprint onto you. If *you* don't try to make something out of your life, someone or something else will. *Avanti!*

Be who you are
and say what you feel,
because those who mind
don't matter and those
who matter don't mind.

– DR. SEUSS

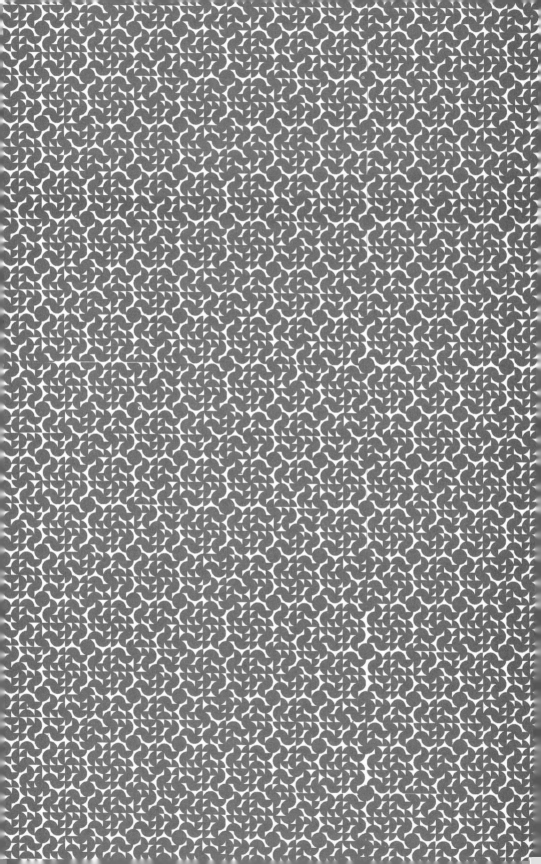

ACT III

business basics: user-friendly business skills and tools

HERE'S WHERE THE RUBBER hits the road. Even if you have the most amazing instrument, technique, and performing abilities, if you don't have an understanding of and habitual routine for doing business, getting your foot in that door as a professional singer will remain more of a dream than a reality.

Now is the time to start this process of deciding which business routines and systems will work just for you. As we've seen, each of us is wired differently, so you can now understand that no one plan works for everyone. It's up to you to take the information given and figure out how best to make it work for you. You will create your own individual plan, one that you can adapt and customize as you go. You will become a knowledgeable and inspired entrepreneur.

Most singers have been introduced only peripherally to the business aspects needed in building a career. For many of you, the realization that you need to be business savvy in order to have a career might make your mind go fuzzy, and you may have no idea where to start or what to really do.

If you continue to think the way you have always thought, you'll continue to get what you've always got. Is it enough?

– PAUL MEYER

> *In the modern world of business, it is useless to be a creative, original thinker, unless you can also sell what you create. Management cannot be expected to recognize a good idea unless it is presented to them by a good salesman.*
>
> **– DAVID M. OGILVY**

The first step in being able to use your business process without feeling at a loss, is to stop listening to the self-talk that says "I can't do it". That means you have to really wake up and expand your thinking to include the possibilities we are going to talk about in this section. Then you will be able to make the conscious choices necessary to help you see, hear, and feel that running your own successful business is possible. When you remain curious, flexible, and open-minded about this learning process, you will succeed. Remember, business is a process that can be learned—it is not emotional or personal.

Understanding how the business process can be individualized—continuously updated and adapted for you personally—will help you gain control over your fears and insecurities, and allow you to focus on the present moment and your next action, rather than being "off in your head," not knowing where to start or what to do. When you have these individualized tools and skills at your disposal—ready to make the necessary adjustments in how you do what you do as change occurs—you gain confidence in your ability to move forward toward your goals and dreams.

> *If you really put a small value upon yourself, rest assured that the world will not raise your price.*
>
> **– AUTHOR UNKNOWN**

So where do we start? Let's begin with this basic question: What business do you think you are in? The answer: *You are in the business of creating and maintaining relationships.* Yes, that is what any and every successful business is really about. Here is a sampling of those with whom you may already have or desire to create relationships: the audience, your family, friends, colleagues, those for whom you are auditioning, and yes, even a better relationship with yourself.

Creating excellent relationships means that you will make networking a priority. Whenever you meet new people, be present and prepared for the opportunity to build relationships and do business. Practicing these new skills and tools within all your current and future relationships, personal and professional, is part of the process, as is being present and conscious of the process as you continue to grow your network of connections. This allows you to recognize when opportunities show up, and decide how best to deal with them in that moment.

Before we delve further into the business basics that you will need to successfully run your career, I want to share with you a great organizational tool, one that might come in handy when it comes time to define your strategy and implement your tactics.

"Mind mapping" is essentially a method for taking notes and organizing ideas, diagraming them in a radial, non-linear manner, and encouraging a "brainstorming" approach to planning and organizing tasks. This approach to problem solving—defining goals, creating tactics for your plan of action, finding the source of personal issues, and in general, helping you to clear your head of extraneous details—allows you to focus on the solution, without getting stuck on the structure of it.

Though the concept of mind mapping has been embraced in various forms since the time of Aristotle, a British popular psychology author, Tony Buzan, repopularized its use in the 1960s.

Mind mapping may open up a pathway to organization for you that has not been available before. It's an effective way for some people to organize their plans and thoughts, while creating a record of that process, all at the same time. As always, keep in mind that we are all wired differently—mind mapping may not be your ideal method for organizing a plan of action—but if other brainstorming techniques have not been effective for you, give this a try.

Here is how the process works: First pick a project, topic, or idea to work with, for example, "need ideas to help me better organize my business." Write that central idea in

Mind maps can be constructed and adapted for a variety of tasks:

- Note taking
- Brainstorming (individually or in groups)
- Problem solving
- Studying and memorization
- Planning
- Researching and consolidating information from multiple sources
- Presenting information
- Gaining insight on complex subjects
- Jogging your creativity

There are also a variety of software applications available that facilitate this manner of brainstorming. If this way of working inspires you, and helps to set free your ability to understand and better organize your thoughts and ideas, it might be worth investigating how to integrate this kind of tool into your organization and planning.

the center of a piece of paper, to help keep you on point; as thoughts and ideas come to mind, of different ways to work with this project, write them down anywhere on the paper around the central idea, continuing this process until you feel satisfied.

Now take a good look at what your thoughts were. Start circling items that are similar or related, or that might work well in tandem, and draw a line from one to the other. Do this with the rest of the ideas you have come up with, until you feel you have completed the task.

On another piece of paper, write down in a list, either horizontally or vertically, those ideas that you drew together with connecting lines. Next, prioritize these items according to what needs to be accomplished first, and rewrite the list in that order. You may set off other unexpected creative ideas as you begin this part of the process, which is what you want.

Continue to write them down, finding the right place for these items in the list you have been making. This process is not about structure, but rather about freeing the mind to be liberated creatively. There is no right or wrong, good or bad about how to go about this process—use what works best for you.

Sometimes this mixing things up—finding new ways to look at a situation, project, or idea—helps the mind to change gears and start thinking in a more productive and spontaneous manner. It tells the "right brain" to wake up, and help you respond to a set of questions you haven't already thought out answers to.

Before you read the following questions, turn on the right hemisphere of your brain, and write down the first thing that comes to mind as you read the question, setting loose your stream of consciousness. You can always go back and ponder over the answers to these questions using your left (thinking) brain later. Let's begin!

QUESTIONS

- What do you imagine are the building blocks (relationships, trust, rapport, communication skills, research skills, resources, infrastructure, etc.) for developing your business?
- What helps link these building blocks together to form a business?
- Were there any unexpected, new and interesting concepts revealed?
- What is the difference between strategy and tactics?
- Which do you feel more comfortable with and what makes it that way?

Using the answers to these questions, start molding your own individual, unique, and authentic concept of how you want your business to work, just for you. Do this with your Personal Brand in mind from the earlier part of this book, so that every part of your business is congruent and consistent. You are the product, the company, and you run the business. That is in and of itself quite an extraordinary feat, and one that you are very capable of accomplishing once you put your own individualized plan of action in place.

Are you ready to step up, represent, and practice good business strategies and tactics? Let's go. Start this process by giving your management company a working name. This will help you stop thinking about trying to sell yourself as a singer—which is loaded with emotional implications—and instead give you a product to sell, which helps you to dissociate emotionally from the process, which is a necessary aspect of furthering your singing career.

Company Name: _____

SKILLS, TOOLS, AND OTHER PRACTICAL BUSINESS INFORMATION

Determine and Establish Goals

Goal, strategy/plan of attack, tactics/plan of action—these are all just ways to check in from time to time (usually daily) to see where you are now, if you are moving in the direction you want to be going, and are moving at a pace that works for you that will ultimately get you to your goal. You will be able to measure your success by looking at the results—the outcome of what you have just done—make adjustments if necessary, and continue to move ahead, while remaining flexible, and doing it all at your own pace. That's all there is to it.

Everyone has goals—success requires it. Most times, the things we want remain only wishes or dreams, because we haven't yet found a realistic and successful way of turning them into reality. Often we squander our precious time, energy, and money trying to imitate exactly what someone else did, rather than observing and incorporating different elements from several different sources, to help us figure out how to get what we really want, and go where we really want to go, on our own timetable. Following a path that doesn't make sense to you is a sure-fire way to lose your motivation, focus, and enthusiasm, causing you to feel frustrated, insecure, and afraid. How many of you have gone through the motions of what has been suggested by others—even if it makes no sense to you—and eventually just give up because you can't make it work for you? Blindly following someone else's actions or suggestions, especially if that approach feels incongruous to you and your way of thinking, can leave you feeling like a failure. You think something must be wrong with you, because you don't seem to be able to get it, while others are sailing along with this approach.

Because no one is internally hard-wired in exactly the same way, and we don't all have the same behavior, motivation, and work patterns or core beliefs, so it follows that no one strategy or plan will work for everyone. The good news is that you can weed through all the many different ideas that are out there, taking the bits and pieces that look, sound, and feel right to you, and then build your own strategy and tactics. When this happens you will become motivated and actually look forward to all the possibilities for your future. It's up to you to find what works best just for you so you can finally stop spinning your wheels and move forward.

For me personally, I have a general big goal with no specific timetable for completion in mind. Then I create what I think might be the bigger chunks needed for eventually completing my goal also with no specific timetable for completion in mind. Those are my strategies usually taking somewhere between a month to three months to complete through my tactics, the smaller details. I build a specific tactical plan for only one week at a time; that works best for me. At the end of that week, I can see if I put too much or too little on my plate and make adjustments accordingly and I can notice if I am still headed in the right direction.

Because I don't want or need a specific timetable to complete my strategies, I put less stress and pressure on myself while still feeling motivated and successful, as I can see what I have accomplished using these tactics over a particular week, and can then easily figure out what the next tactics need to be for the following week. I have tried other methods and ideas, but know that this works best for me. I also know from experience that if I put too much on my plate all the time I feel overwhelmed and guilty making it easier to just give up on the process altogether. There is no one way, method or path to accomplishing your goals and no one time table for getting there. Figure what works just for you, and adjust as you gain experience.

Answer these questions:

1. Do you already have a realistic and achievable goal in mind?

2. Do you have a plan in place to implement your strategy (bigger chunks) and tactics (the details)?

3. If so, do you know where you are right now within your tactical plan of executing your strategy? Write it down.

4. Where do you want to be strategically next week, next month, next year?

> Success doesn't happen by accident. You make it happen by focusing all of your attention only on what the next step is and how you choose to respond to the work that it requires. It's having a goal, putting a strategy in place to carry out that goal using simple step-by-step, daily tactics that work just for you. It will have whatever structure you devise if you feel that is necessary for you, and will happen on your timetable. It is always a work in progress; trial and error. This process doesn't need to be complicated. And the time frame can run from creating a goal for a week at a time to planning three years out.

> *You can create the energy to turn your dreams into reality by knowing what to say when you talk to yourself.*
>
> – SHAD HELMSTETTER

Possible Stumbling Blocks

In starting down this road, there are a few things that can get you stuck and keep you from moving ahead. Can you guess the number one reason we get stuck?

Fear of failure is the "granddaddy" of them all. If you ask any successful business person about failure, they will tell you to expect it along the way as a temporary condition of success and progress. It's not whether you should accept failure, but how you choose to deal with it that matters. Successful people treat failure as feedback. They don't take it personally, or allow any emotional impact to impede their quest of finding the lessons in whatever outcome occurs. They take the time to realistically understand and break down what happened, learn how and what did and didn't work, and move on with that knowledge in mind. That is why they often say, experience is the best teacher. And believe it or not, we learn more from our failures than we do from our successes. If we never failed, we would never learn anything.

There is a saying that, "Fear resides where knowledge does not exist," so the more you know about something, the less intimidated you will feel. And the more you can keep the emotion out of your rehashing of what just occurred, the quicker you'll be free to discover what went wrong, and how to adjust for the future.

Another reason you might find this process difficult is precisely because you *are* stuck in the place you are—not able to access the past or see the future. This is the result of your Inner Timelines, and the ability to understand these timelines—as well as discovering what forces motivate you in your life—are part of what I call your Inner Wiring Systems. This understanding of "how you are wired" will enable you to begin to identify your preferred patterns and systems, which are what create your own distinctive style. Once you recognize and contemplate the possibilities, you can begin using this information to further strengthen your Personal Brand. You will have more confidence in doing things your way.

DETERMINING WHAT MOTIVATES YOU

Again, this information is intended to help you figure out your own personal inner wiring, so that you can use it as a tool, to take you where you want to go in a manner that works best for you. There is no right or wrong, better or worse.

How am I going to live today, in order to create the tomorrow I'm committed to?

– ANTHONY ROBBINS

Are you motivated most often by the Stick:

> The glass is half empty; you are good at troubleshooting and solving problems, pinpointing possible obstacles during planning. You can also be motivated by being way too uncomfortable in a particular situation before you can take action, or wait until the last minute to complete a project, creating unnecessary stress; motivation is cyclical as a result. You can seem uninterested in others, because you are in your head and not listening. You usually know what you *don't* want, but don't often know what you *do* want.

or by the Carrot:

> The glass is half full; you always have your eye on the goal and feel energized as you move closer to your chosen outcome, feel all things are possible, know what is important to you. You can also bulldoze over others without noticing, because you are focused only on the outcome; you might forget to identify potential problems along the way, which may create larger problems in the future. You can forget to enjoy the journey and remain balanced, or create too-rigid rules for yourself, which becomes stressful.

Most of us use *both* styles for different situations, but we each have a preferred system. Most people want to either gain a benefit or avoid a problem.

MOTIVATIONAL TRIGGERS

> *Obstacles are those frightful things you see when you take your eyes off your goal.*
>
> — HENRY FORD

This next group of Inner Wiring Systems *trigger motivation*. Remember, no right or wrong, better or worse—it's just information to help you know how you do what you do:

- Are you motivated more by deciding, from your own internal values and standards, what choices, decisions and judgments to make? Or do you need outside direction, sources, references, feedback, etc. to help you make your mind up?

- Is making a choice easier when there are unlimited options, ideas, and possibilities? Or do you function better with procedures and processes, with a beginning, middle, and end to them?

- Are you motivated by evolution, revolution, or both? Or do you prefer stability? Knowing how often the bell for change rings will help to assist you in finding where your comfort zone is when it comes time to make important decisions.

These next patterns demonstrate how people *deal* with information, what type of tasks and environment they need to be most productive in a given context, and *how they get convinced* about something:

- What size chunk of information do you handle best: the big picture—the overview, the conceptual level—or specific details—the nitty-gritty, the linear sequence?

- Some individuals perceive and respond automatically to others' body language, voice tone, etc., and are interested in creating rapport, while others are more interested in the *content* of what people say, rather than creating rapport. Your sense of how well communication is going is based only on your own feelings.

- When there is a stressful work situation, how do you respond? Do you have an emotional response to the normal levels of stress at work? Do others say you are overreacting or are hypersensitive? Or do you perhaps first have an emotional response, and then have the ability to return to an unemotional state or not? Do you have no emotional response to stressful situations in a given context, which allows you to perform well in high-stress jobs or emergencies?

- What kind of environment allows you to be most productive: working independently, in proximity with others, or are you best when co-operating?

- When you organize your work, do you concentrate more on thoughts and feelings, or on ideas, systems, tools, and tasks?

- In order to be convinced about something, which "convincers" do you require to produce the confirming evidence for you to make a choice? Do you need to see, hear, read, or physically do something to produce the evidence you are looking for?

- Once you have the information, do you need to:

  - Go over the information several times, to convince yourself it will work or to learn something?

  - Do you need only a small amount of information to formulate your opinion, imagining what the rest will be?

  - Do you need to be re-convinced each time that you view the materials?

  - Do you need to gather information for a certain amount of time before you are convinced?

INNER TIMELINES

Unique among these systems, Inner Timelines are not hardwired, so understanding how to use each type within the appropriate situation can make many aspects of life more understandable and easier to deal with.

Time is the fire in which we burn.

– **DELMORE SCHWARTZ**

As human beings, we often talk about our experiences in terms of having already happened, happening right now, or potentially happening in the future. We describe these phenomena with such phrases as "a long time ago," "not having enough time," "future goals," or "stuck in the past." It allows us to experience the past, present and future. It helps create and keep perspective in our lives. It's about time which helps us organize and store our experiences as memories.

Why This Is Important

Inner Timelines are a crucial element in the ability to create and carry out goals through your strategy/plan of attack and tactics/plan of action. There is no right, wrong, better, or worse. Though we use both Inner Timelines—*Inside Time* and *Outside Time*, we usually have a strong preference for one or the other. And it is something we all use all the time—hundreds of times each day, but once you become conscious of its uses and power, it can become a great tool to help you consciously choose whether to be associated with or disassociated from your feelings or emotions in any situation.

There are two standard ways we associate with time. However, because we are each unique, these timelines can run in many different configurations aside from the two standard ways discussed here, Inside Time and Outside Time.

INSIDE TIME

> *Let's not forget that the little emotions are the great captains of our lives, and we obey them without realizing it.*
> – VINCENT VAN GOGH, 1889

Here is a description of what it's like to be Inside Time: It's like being in the back seat of a moving car, looking only out the side window at the scenery going by. It's a very clear picture of the immediate view, almost like snapshots rather than a movie. It is all you can see from the window—you can not see where you have been or where you are going. Again, remember that there is no right or wrong, better or worse to any of this—it's just a tool to be used in deciding how you want to relate to the situations you encounter and have to deal with.

- Physically, it usually passes front-to-back through your body. It's like standing on the yellow line running down the middle of a highway, looking at the line out in front of you. You can often see what is happening right now, but might not be able to see what's ahead, because there's a slight hill and you can't quite see over it. And you can't see the line behind you because it's "back there," and you don't have eyes in the back of your head.

- Those with this type of preference are more associated with the "now."

- Those experiencing events Inside Time feel strongly associated with their emotions in most situations.

- They can literally put the past behind them. This can be a wonderful tool to help keep you in the present moment. However, this can also make it difficult to access memories and utilize past resources and experiences. And because we tend to embellish the stories we tell ourselves about past experiences, they usually are filled with more emotion and feeling, clouding the truth of what really happened.

- It can become difficult to access the future because all you can see is the present moment. This makes it hard to create your Goal, build Strategies and Tactics and carry them out.

- Those whose primary predisposition is the Inside Timeline tend to live in a less ordered way and typically have trouble setting deadlines.

- They may also interpret appointments more flexibly, which can be misconstrued by others as being less dependable, which is not the truth.

- They do not lack the skills or energy to get the job done, they just don't connect what they are involved in right now with a deadline.

- They have a hard time dealing with date books and taking notes because they are not linear thinkers.

OUTSIDE TIME

> *The Future is something which everyone reaches at the rate of sixty minutes an hour, whatever he does, whoever he is.*
>
> – C.S. LEWIS

Alternately, being Outside Time is like standing at the edge of a road, watching a car approach from a long distance away, until it passes in front of you, then continues on until it again becomes a speck in the distance. You have a complete perspective, seeing not only the road directly in front of you, but also how far the road stretches out in either direction.

- Physically, your timeline runs left to right, about three feet out in front of your body. You are just outside the stream of time, watching it pass by in front of you.

- Those who prefer this timeline experience time in a more dissociated, less emotional manner. This includes their memories, the present moment, and their planned future, which may make them seem a bit uninvolved.

- They can see past, present, and future all at once. This makes it much easier to plan a sequence of tasks. It is easy to prioritize, create, and utilize strategies and tactics to reach a goal.

- They make and keep appointments precisely and expect others to do the same. It is easy for them to establish deadlines and take them seriously. Time-conscious Outside Timers are prevalent in the world of business, where time equals money.

There are any number of configurations of Inner Timelines beside the ones just described. They can run up above you, through you, down below you, or in a V-configuration. Your time line might be a circle—with you in the center, or perhaps standing on the line at some point in the circle. The line might go off at some sort of angle, with you either on the line or off of it. There are a plethora of possibilities.

Benefits of Understanding and Using Both Inner Timelines:

You will be able to maximize the results you are looking for by consciously choosing to be either emotionally in the moment, or standing just a little outside the stream of time, so that it is easier to deal with just the facts, putting them into logical order and organizing them in a step-by-step manner. It's being either associated or dissociated from your emotions in any situation.

Choosing the appropriate Inner Timeline will help you be able to access past resources, using what you learned—your past experience—as a tool for future endeavors. It allows you to create your own personalized process for reaching your goals, because you can see, hear, and experience the "whole enchilada" at a glance. You are able to figure out just how long a past project took to complete, the steps it took, which ones really worked and which ones didn't, learn from it, and directly apply it to a future project, making adjustments as you go.

There is another benefit to being able to use the appropriate Inner Timeline: one can stop playing those horrifying emotional games we so often experience with our family, friends, and colleagues. These usually involve what are known as our "hot buttons"—you know the ones I mean. It takes you away from who you are now, and puts you back into the same old emotional, frenzied game you have always played, which puts you on the defensive, feeling you need to protect yourself. Others know how to get a reaction out of you. By consciously choosing this new tool, you can sidestep these kinds of confrontations. Deliberately step off the emotionally charged "Inside Time" line. This allows you to notice, hear, and experience what is really going on, just the facts, so that you can choose to take some type of action if necessary or not. When you do this, the game is over, which can be very disconcerting for others until they realize that you can now have a real relationship, without the games, or perhaps they will move on. You get to stop constantly reacting, by making a conscious choice to use your new tools to initiate action.

Time is the most undefinable yet paradoxical of things; the past is gone, the future is not come, and the present becomes the past even while we attempt to define it, and, like the flash of lightning, at once exists and expires.

– CHARLES CALEB COLTON

Conversely, choosing intentionally to be in the present moment by stepping on the "Inside Time" line at appropriate times, i.e., auditions, performances, or intimate relationships, will be very rewarding because you are doing it on purpose. You are knowingly choosing to allow yourself to experience your emotions by using all your senses.

EXERCISE:

To find which Inner Timeline you prefer, follow these simple instructions. Read them through, then close your eyes, letting the mind and body come to rest, as you think about the task at hand.

- Think about a simple everyday behavior like brushing your teeth. It's something you have done in the past and will probably continue to do in the future. Think about having brushed your teeth this morning. Now think about brushing your teeth this evening. How about brushing your teeth right now? I'd like you to get a sense that you are taking on all these experiences at the same time, so that you can begin to notice what differences there are in *where* you spatially see, hear and feel this same event. Notice *where* each of these events is located as you move back and forth from past to present to future, then back again from future to present and past. Go back and forth several times until you can notice *where* you experience the past, then the present, and finally the future. What differences do you notice in *where* you have placed each of these experiences?

- Now I would like you to consider the opposite timeline, to experience how *it* might be used in certain circumstances to your benefit. After reading the instructions, close your eyes, and again let the mind and body come to rest, as you think about the task at hand.

- Remember the exercise we just did, where you discovered your preferred inner timeline? Go there now. As you get comfortable, try on the opposite Inner Timeline. You can do this by first stepping on the Inside Time line, noticing that you feel more in the present moment. Become aware of the emotional connection you have to some past memory or the outcome of a future event. Most times you can see only what is ahead of you as you stand on the line. Rest here for a minute, and explore the possibilities of how this timeline might work for you.

- Now experience the Outside Time line, by taking two big steps to the right, off the line; turn and notice the line running just out in front of you, being aware of how far it runs both to the left and right. Rest here a minute, and explore how this different timeline changes your insight and perspective of the same situation, and how that might impact your response.

- At your own comfort level, go back and forth between these two Inner Timelines several times noticing the differences and benefits of being associated or dissociated. This might feel a bit disconcerting and dizzying, but it's not harmful in any way. What would that other timeline allow you to do that you can't do with your present preferred inner Timeline? ***This next step is very important: Before you open your eyes always return to your preferred Inner Timeline.***

People usually have past, present and future events arranged along a continual line of some kind. This is a strong indication that the preferred Inner Timeline you just discovered for yourself is not arbitrary or just the result of my instructions, but is a significant way for you to sort through and respond to your experiences. The configuration of your Inner Time line may be different from how others experience and sort time. There is no right/wrong/better/worse. This new personal tool is there to help you decide "on purpose" where you consciously choose to be in your relationship to time depending on what your specific outcome needs are.

Having a conscious choice to be either associated with your emotions, by using the Inside Time line, or disassociated from your emotions, using the Outside Time line, gives you the flexibility to *consciously* choose which timeline will fit your current situation and your immediate needs. You now have another very useful new tool in your toolbox.

THE GOAL-SETTING PROCESS

First things first: Remember to consciously choose to use your newfound Inner Timeline tools to help you. Outside Time is the timeline to use for this process, the timeline where you are standing about three feet back from the line, as it runs left to right out in front of you. It permits you to see, hear, and experience past, present, and future arrayed out in front of you, all at the same time. You are able to be emotionally dissociated during this process, giving you the opportunity to initiate clear thinking. It encourages the visionary within to start working.

How does one actually begin this process of identifying a goal, and working towards it's successful accomplishment? How will you know you're ready to *begin* this process? What will make you that way? Like any journey, it requires forethought and preparation.

More than anything else, having the confidence to start your goal process requires ferreting out and identifying the appropriate information that makes sense to just you. Then it is easier to pick, choose, and try-on the systems that sound, look, and feel best for just you at this moment in time. Randomly write them down as you read through this section of the book. This will give you a starting point from which to develop your Business Plan. Take your time with this process as it will make all the difference between just going through the motions yet once again without a successful and satisfying outcome or being able to actually accomplish your goals as you continue to grow, change and make the necessary adjustments you need to move on into your future.

Getting Ready

DEFINITION OF GOAL, STRATEGY, AND TACTICS

Shoot for the moon. Even if you miss, you'll land among the stars.

— LES BROWN

A *goal* is the end objective of a project, the end purpose that drives you to achievement; it is the fulfillment of a dream.

Example: Become a managed singer. Make a living completely as a performer.

Strategy is defining the intention and objectives of your campaign to reach your goals. It involves the "big picture," the overview—the bigger chunks needed to help keep you "on point" as you move toward your main goal. Strategies give you the opportunity to measure and reevaluate the success and progress of what has been accomplished up to that point in time. It allows you to readjust, embellish or diminish, add or subtract, any ideas or processes that weren't as positive in their results as you might have imagined or were heading in the wrong direction, or even incorporate new ideas and decisions that seem relevant and part of the solution.

> *Example:* STRATEGY/BIG PICTURE: Refine and polish my product. Find appropriate entry-level programs and performance venues to gain experience.

Tactics are specific activities, the "detail work" of creating, selecting, and reaching particular and measurable smaller objectives. It is the detailed, short-term plan to get from A to B, B to C, etc., until you finally reach Z. It comes from a Greek word that means "science of arrangement." Tactics are the actual way in which the strategies are executed. It's the day-to-day, mundane, step-by-step work needed to get to your desired outcome. It's the daily "to do" list.

> *Example:* TACTICS/DETAILS: Set up times to work with coach. Get flat-rate envelopes and stamps to send in audition requests.

- get details of how to apply
- fill out and send in application form with fee

Regardless of the outcome, or your success in securing an audition:

- prepare pieces for audition
- practice visualizations for success
- make sure complete audition outfit is in order
- secure favorite accompanist, etc.

These tactics can be spread in any time configuration that works best for you. Perhaps, for some, they could all be accomplished easily in a week, while for others it's more realistically doable given a month's time. No one cares how you do it; just be sure to only put on your plate the amount of tactics that you know *you specifically* can accomplish in a particular time frame—whatever works best for *you*. And it may be that some weeks you find yourself capable of doing more, and other weeks less—that's okay.

PRACTICE TIME:

Build a Goal, Then Strategy and Tactics

Exercise: Before you can determine strategy or tactics, you have to have the goal. Here is one way in which you can decide if the goal you have chosen is the one that best fits the present moment. Then you can practice building a strategy (overview) and tactics (details) for achieving your goal successfully.

FINDING THE APPROPRIATE GOAL

- List just one very small possible objective. (Do an audition.)

- Mind map or list everything that could possibly prevent you from achieving this goal. (Money, not enough time to prepare, fear of failure, finding a really good accompanist, getting PR packet together, etc.)

- Next mind map or list all the benefits you would gain by achieving this goal. (Have the right people hear you, have a chance to network, possibly get a job, know you are working toward you goal, gaining confidence and experience, feeling like you are making something happen, etc.)

- List everything needed, including time, energy, money, and any sacrifices that you can anticipate having to make. (Pay for extra coachings, buy a new audition outfit, pay the entry fee, get PR packet together, ask for time off at work, no free time until then, etc.)

> *One half of knowing what you want is knowing what you must give up before you get it.*
>
> – SIDNEY HOWARD

- Finally, ask yourself this question: "Is this worth doing?" If you get a "yes," it's time to create your strategies and tactics to reach your goal. Be in the Outside Time mode—the disassociated, unemotional state—by stepping off your timeline and seeing the past, present, and future all laid out a few feet in front of you.

NOW IT'S TIME FOR YOU TO CREATE A STRATEGY

Figure out the large chunks or pieces needed to accomplish your goal. Mind map or write them down in any random order. Once you have finished with that process, prioritize your findings.

HOW ABOUT TACTICS

Starting with the first prioritized item compile a detailed list of what you believe it will take to accomplish this step: time, energy, things, stuff, and money. Go wild and crazy; think outside the box. It is fun. Make sure that you are satisfied with how the details look, sound, and feel to you before you move on. Doing this with each step may actually inspire and spark other ideas that you will want to incorporate into your tactics/plan of action.

FINALLY IT'S THE ACTIVATION PROCESS

To be successful with your goal, strategy and tactics you need to figure out how much you can comfortably put on your plate each day so you don't start feeling overwhelmed. Adjust as you go. It has to be right for just you, done on your own time table. Your particular inner systems and wiring are unique to just you, so why not find a method or process that fits your personal criteria to get you where you want to go? In doing so, you might realize that this process is not as difficult as you thought it might be. And it makes you feel successful, because you are!

What people want TO DO (or what we want them to do) determines Function; what people WANT TO KNOW (or what we want them to know) determines Content; what we want them to REMEMBER determines Brand.

– DAN ROAM, THE BACK OF THE NAPKIN: SOLVING PROBLEMS AND SELLING IDEAS WITH PICTURES

> *The road leading to a goal does not separate you from the destination; it is essentially a part of it.*
>
> – CHARLES DELINT

How did that work for you? What did you learn about this process that you might not have known before? Was it easier having this information *before* you started? Were there any "aha!" moments for you, and if so what were they? Did going through this small process give you a better view of what strategies and tactics might be needed to create a bona fide path for you to reach your final objective? What other information would make this process more user-friendly for you?

Following is an example of the whole process in action: Let's say that you need something from the grocery store. Your goal here is to get to the store, buy what you need, and return home with those items:

- Which store will you visit? Are you looking for a store that sells organic products? Perhaps it's all about price, or the store with the best selection of products, so that you can get all your shopping done in one stop.

- If you do need something additional from a different type of store, like a drugstore or liquor store, when will that task most conveniently fit into your trip to the grocery store?

- How are you going to get there? Will you walk, ride your bike, take a bus or cab, or drive your own car?

- When during the day are you going to do this shopping? Will you go after work, during your lunch break, in the morning on the weekend, or in the evening after dinner?

- What do you need to buy? Will you make a separate list or incorporate it into your other "to do" list for the day, or are there just a few items so you don't even need a physical list?

- Will you start in the produce department and end with the milk, ice cream and yogurt section or vice versa?

- As you are buying your items, do you check them off the list either mentally or physically to make sure you haven't forgotten anything? Do you find other items that you want to put on a new list for the next shopping trip or add to what you are going to buy today?

- Did you remember to bring your own reusable bags or do you want paper or plastic?
- How are you getting home with your groceries? The same way you came or is there an alternative and more convenient mode now that you have something to carry?
- Once you are home, what is your plan for putting your items away. Do some go into the fridge, freezer or pantry? Are there items that you plan to have for dinner and if so do they stay out because you plan to use them immediately?
- As you put your items away, do you double-check to see if you got everything that you needed?
- When do you start another list?

That's it! That is having a goal, creating a plan of action, and seeing it through. That wasn't too difficult, was it? We use this process hundreds of times every day, but rarely stop to notice that we are creating a goal and a plan to make it happen, so know that you are very capable of making this happen. And because, as I have said so many times before, there are no two people internally wired in exactly the same way, we don't have the same Inner Systems for dealing with life, our thought process and behaviors are all different, there is no one way of doing something that fits everyone, there is no one size fits all.

Before you start this process, take a look at how you are internally wired, what systems, patterns and traits drive your thoughts and behaviors. Figure out how you can use them as is or choose to perhaps acknowledge and adjust your thinking concerning them. Start by making a chart or list for yourself of your preferred inner systems, pattern and traits. This

Action expresses priorities.

– MOHANDAS GANDHI

will help you recognize the pitfalls when you hit a bump in the road and once you recognize you are stuck in a particular inner system, pattern or trait, you can then figure out and choose the best method of getting unstuck and moving on.

- Pay attention to how you function and what process you use when you go through anything that requires a procedure. Notice the which, what, how, when, where and why of the process you choose. And then see what happens when you transfer that same thought process and procedures to designing a career business project.

- Know that everyone has goals. However, most of the time they are just wishes and dreams because you haven't yet found a realistic, successful and "specific to you" way of making them into reality.

Habits are like comfortable beds: easy to get into but difficult to get out of.

– DENIS WAITLEY

Here are some proven ideas to sample as you start this interesting and unique process, in an effort to find what works uniquely best for you:

- ***Write down your goal.*** Goals once out of sight often become goals out of mind! Remember that while our mind is blessed with permanent memory we are quite often cursed with lousy recall. Written goals help clarify your thinking. It may take several tries before you come up with a winner so don't give in or up.

- If you want the best odds for realizing your goals, ***get specific and crystal clear about the details*** of what it is you want. (General goal: "Get in better shape." Specific goal: "Get in better shape by walking to work and back each day, eating smaller portions, cut out wheat products, and limit the bad fats in my diet."

- ***Decide what it is you want and why you want it***—not what you *don't* want—and state that in the positive. If knowing what you don't want is part of your usual thinking pattern, that might be the way to start this process, until you can clear the decks to find the hidden treasure of what it is you *do* want.

- *You must believe your goals are achievable.* This is not a wish, desire, or some pie-in-the-sky dream. Your goal has to be realistic, and in line with your abilities and talent. No one else can or should define your goals for you. Having completed the work in the earlier parts of this book will help you better understand who you are, what motivates you, and what type and frequency of changes you are comfortable with. Use this information to help develop goals you will be convinced you can achieve because you know how much you can put on your plate and accomplish realistically each day. To be successful, you must customize this process and carry it out on your own comfortable time table. You must also remain flexible because unforeseen "stuff" happens and you will undoubtedly have to make adjustments as you move forward on your path. And that's not a bad thing. Or you may try something that doesn't seem to work and that's when you need to feel free from anxiety so you can adjust whatever it is until it makes sense to you, or even change direction completely until you are once again moving in the direction you do want to go.

- *No process is or ever could be perfect, so don't wait* until you feel you have everything in place and feel safe before you dive in. It's a given that nothing stays the same so be prepared to adjust and make corrections as you go. It's not emotional, so step off your Inside Time line and keep doing it until you can actually see, hear, taste, smell, and feel only the real substance, the facts of what you are experiencing sans emotion.

- *Make a real commitment to achieving your goal.* This helps eliminate any wiggle room or excuses you might come up with along the way for not achieving your goal. If you do fall off the horse from time to time, and you will, don't beat yourself up because everyone does, even the "big boys" at the top

> *Whenever we take a chance and enter unfamiliar territory or put ourselves into the world in a new way, we experience fear. Very often this fear keeps us from moving ahead with our lives. The trick is to feel the fear and do it anyway.*
>
> — SUSAN JEFFEES, *FEEL THE FEAR AND DO IT ANYWAY*

of the business-world food chain. What is important is your ability to know when and how to make adjustments and then get back on and move forward.

- ***Be consistent.*** Be sure that what you want to accomplish is in sync with the gut feelings you sense inside concerning the goals you have written down. This will help you stay focused and motivated. In other words, don't try to follow someone else's plan and time table, if it doesn't feel right to you. You might want to use part of what is there, but not all of it. Try it out first to see if it is going to be something that keeps you moving toward you desired outcome and can be comfortably plugged into your own process and plan.

- ***Believe you are equipped and ready to acquire and receive what you are asking for.*** Use your Personal Brand as a touchstone, to help you remember who you are and what you are committed to, as you become the example of that to the world. This will keep you in tune with what is bona fide and valuable to you.

- Risk is involved, so ***be prepared to step out of your comfort zone*** once in a while. The fear that you feel when breaking this barrier is usually some rule or belief that you may have put in place when you were a child, and it's time to perhaps change your habitual routine to embrace a more realistic attitude. Being afraid is OK only if you allow yourself to consciously feel that particular emotion, then allow it to float away or step out of it, so you can recognize only the truth of the situation and take appropriate action or not.

- ***Remember that what we call mistakes and failures are only feedback.*** That is how you grow and learn what works just for you. It keeps you moving toward your goals and living life on purpose. It strengthens your Personal Brand. Stretching your comfort zone takes trust in yourself and courage, and it starts with the first step, so try it and notice how you feel before, during, and after. Then do it again. (*Disclaimer:* This does *not* mean purposely engaging in any hazardous or harmful activities or actions as a means of stretching your comfort zone.)

- **Experience is a great teacher.** The road to success is paved with those who have experienced temporary failure. This is how you learn. You notice what went wrong and figure out after the fact how to correct it or notice what lessons you learned from it that might be applied to similar situations or problems that come up in the future. Or perhaps you have stepped out of your comfort zone and actually achieved something that you though impossible. That is also how we learn. After the fact, stop and notice what steps you took and the sequence of how it all worked so you can do it again with some other idea, situation or problem.

Creating and using these tools will help keep you focused and motivated to do the work. Success is a choice—you must decide what you want, why you want it, and how you plan to achieve it. No one else can, will, or should do that for you.

Try this: Rehearse your success in your imagination several times each day. Write down, in as much detail as you can envision, how the process of reaching your goals will look, sound, and feel, as you move step by step toward your successful goal—your intended outcome. Write it out as a movie or TV script, with dialogue not only for yourself, but also for each additional character you will come into contact with along the way who will help you reach your goal.

Next, spend time each day watching yourself—up there on the screen, playing your role in this movie—several times throughout the course of the day, without allowing yourself to leave your seat—your place in the audience. Enjoy watching yourself in this disassociated manner. Notice how having achieved your goals will look, sound, taste, smell, and feel. When doing this exercise, be sure to view the story as a spectator—only watching yourself and your

Success isn't a result of spontaneous combustion. You must set yourself on fire.

– ARNOLD H. GLASOW

fellow cast members up on the screen, and being very specific about the details of the story.

Rehearsing the outcome in this way will help bring your goals to mind more often and help keep you on track and motivated to achieve them. Seeing yourself up on the movie or TV screen being successful not only fills you with confidence, but because you haven't yet physically completed the actual process of reaching your goal (gone through this experience of becoming that person on the screen telling their story) it saturates your whole being with a real desire that motivates you to make that story into a reality.

These suggestions for settling on a goal are transferable—they not only work in your singing career, but for anything else you would like to accomplish in your lifetime as well. Now it is time to understand how to build your strategies and tactics for each goal.

Create a Structure to Hang Your Goals, Strategies, and Tactics On

Don't say you don't have enough time. You have exactly the same number of hours per day that were given to Helen Keller, Pasteur, Michaelangelo, Mother Teresea, Leonardo da Vinci, Thomas Jefferson, and Albert Einstein.

— H. JACKSON BROWN, JR.

There are a plethora of ways to create a structure on which to hang your main goal, strategies, and tactics. Or it may be that you don't need a big, scary structure to hang your "stuff" on. You do, however, need to figure out what suits you best. The best way to do that is to try several different types of available structures. Or better yet, check out several differing options and then build your own. Or just build your own method of dealing with the goal process without a concrete model anywhere on the horizon.

It could be as simple as this: once your goal has been established, you simply check in weekly/monthly to see if you are headed in the right direction in a timely manner and if not make the necessary modifications before moving on, always keeping your eye on the eventual long term outcome/goal you want. This gives you the flexibility to re-evaluate and fine tune your strategies (overview) and tactics (details) without falling off the horse completely almost day by day until you feel satisfied with the plan of action you have created and put in place.

Or maybe you may need to see the "whole enchilada" at once, to help keep you on point, motivated and focused. Everyone is different, so figure out what works best for you. There is no perfect, right or wrong way to make this happen, but it is easier, and helps keep you focused and motivated, if you go through the process suggested, seeing what does and doesn't work for you. I personally think that this "structure" thing is one of the biggest road blocks that often keeps people from even trying to reach their goals. In reality all that matters is figuring out how to best reach your long term goal at your own pace. The degree of progress you experience will depend on how much you are willing to actively participate. Research several different types of organizational structures—family tree, list, pyramid/inverted pyramid, funnel, building blocks—to find one, or a combination, that work best for you, or as a starting point to create your own.

As you make the first draft of your longer-term goal, strategies/plan of attack/overview, and tactics/plan of action/details, you will start finding new ideas, resources and information that can be added into your plan along the way. You know, the idea that one thought leads to another, or you hear what someone else is doing that sounds like it might work for you, or you read how another successful singer or business person achieved their success, that sort of thing. It is a process and a journey, not just a means to an end so be prepared for altering and making adjustments as you work toward your goals. When you build a process that works just for you and put it in place, you will notice that your mind is consistently drawn to it as you move through each day. It helps keep you on point, focused and moving forward. And it is always flexible and adjustable, never written in stone.

One cannot manage too many affairs: like pumpkins in the water, one pops up while you try to hold down the other.

— CHINESE PROVERB

> *Life is either a daring adventure or nothing. To keep our faces toward change and behave like free spirits in the presence of fate is strength undefeatable.*
>
> — HELEN KELLER

> Pursuing your dreams and goals might cause some people in your life to be envious, or fearful that they are "losing" the former you. This can cause them to be critical of your new aspirations and plans. They become "dream stealers." Develop the tenacity to stand up for what you want out of life, by representing and presenting your Personal Brand at all times. Realistic goals that may have seemed far away and out of reach, eventually move closer and become attainable, not because your goals shrink, but because you have the tools, skills, and courage to grow and expand to match them.

OVERLAPPING GOALS

The journey is really the best part of reaching any goal, which on its own can oftentimes seem anticlimactic, so put a new goal into place just before you finish the current one. And you can run different goals for different parts of your life concurrently, so that you always remain inspired.

Be honest with yourself and step up to the plate by taking responsibility for your actions, even if it sometimes feels uncomfortable and risky. Remember to expect "failure" along the way—treat it as feedback and a lesson learned before moving on. Know what goals you want to achieve, and how you want to live your life in order to make that happen. Get out of your emotions, wake up, and stay alert, so that you can begin to see previously overlooked opportunities that will bring you closer to achieving your goals. Always find the best method for just you to achieve what you want. If you want to succeed, you have to step up to the plate and take a swing at the ball, until you hit it. Trying doesn't count. As Yoda said, "Do or do not—there is no try."

ACTIVELY RUNNING YOUR BUSINESS

Now that you have a goal and a plan of action crafted just for you by you, it's time to understand and build a powerful company to help expedite and strengthen your Personal Brand into a salable asset using all your new information, skills and tools. Here are the jobs that need filling: Office Manager, Business Manager, PR Manager, Financial Officer, and Client.

OFFICE MANAGER

Setting up an efficient and organized office is, in the beginning, a lot of extra work. The reward comes as you start to do business in an organized and professional work space specifically meant to reach your companies goals. You have everything that you need in place for running your successful business. You represent your company's Brand in a consistent manner, and are committed to making a specific time each week to keep the business running smoothly by responsibly taking care of the mundane and necessary tasks at hand. Developing your business routine introduces self-confidence and order into an oftentimes already overtaxed and chaotic day.

JOB DESCRIPTION:

- Organizes and manages paperwork
- Takes care of mail
- Makes sure there are supplies on hand
- Reorders supplies as needed
- Answers phones
- Makes calls
- Keeps web site updated
- Tracks appointments and updates calendar
- Maintains and updates mailing lists
- Keeps office running efficiently
- Represents Company Brand

STRATEGIES FOR OFFICE MANAGER:

1. Schedule a regular time each week to work at your business. This is as important—possibly more so—as all the time you spend making yourself performance-ready.

2. Unless it is an emergency, always make calls Tuesday through Thursday. Monday and Friday in the business world are usually spent catching up or getting things off one's plate. In other words, they are too busy to take on anything new and you will not have their attention.

Another stumbling block when pursuing your dream is that the amount of work required to run a business while still having a part- or full-time job, performing as often as you can, taking lessons and going to coachings seems overwhelming and undoable. By breaking it down into specific job components, the work load get's divided up into clear-cut segments. The advantage is that you can then create an exclusive identifiable personality for each of these jobs within your business, like playing a character in an opera, and then you, as that character can do that job which keeps it autonomous, independent, and disassociated emotionally from you, the product, the client, the singer that your company is working for. It's another opportunity to be creative and practical when running your business.

3. Back up all of your computer business information at the end of each week.

4. Make hard paper copies of all your important information and documents. This way if you have a computer meltdown or power failure, you will not be stranded.

5. Replenish materials and supplies before they run out.

THE TACTICS:

- Know proper phone etiquette. "To whom am I speaking?" is proper grammar, and a nice way to find out someone's name. Jot the name down for future use. Use their name during the conversation which also helps you remember it and starts creating a relationship.

- If you are not speaking to the right person, ask with whom you should be speaking. Get a name, write it down, and ask if they are available.

- If you have to leave a recorded message, speak like you are on stage—clearly, precisely, and slow enough for the person receiving the message to be able to understand. Already have a concise message in mind before making the call.

- Leave your name, number and the best times to reach you. It should be a short concise message so they know who and what to expect when they call back. Represent your company's Brand.

- It is impressive and a great courtesy to ask if this is a good time to speak. If not, ask when it would be convenient for you to call back and then do it.

- When returning a call remind the other person that you were asked to call back at this time. It is professional, not personal or emotional.

To speak and to speak well are two things. A fool may talk, but a wise man speaks.

— BEN JONSON

Filing System

If you already have both a computer and paper filing system that works for you, congratulations! If not, here is one way of accomplishing this task.

You will have both computer-generated and hard copy files of all business transactions that get backed up each week. Inside Time Liners, don't panic—this is one of those times when you will want to step off your line, face it square on, and observe the process that needs to be done. There is no room for emotional attachment or personal feelings here—this is business, and you are working as the office manager.

In the business world, everyone is paid in two coins: cash and experience. Take the experience first; the cash will come later.

– HAROLD GENEEN

1. Create a separate file for each contact (company, competition, apprentice program, summer program, etc.) that you are applying for.

   - Keep hard copies, even if you are applying online. (One never knows when there will be a power failure, computer glitch, or possibility that your materials won't be received.)
   - Put all correspondence, forms, filled out applications, proof of payment etc. in the appropriate prepared file. If it becomes necessary to correspond or speak with someone about any issue, you will have all of your information right at your fingertips. You will have dates, canceled checks, etc. available to corroborate the facts of what paperwork, phone conversations, etc, have been done on your end, along with any extra information they might have given you.

2. On each file tab write the name of the contact. (Arizona Opera, TOP Summer Program, etc.)

   - Inside the front cover keep all the names of those with whom you have spoken, the date, and note whether they are auditory, visual, or kinesthetic so you can further your relationship with them by speaking to them in their preferred inner language (auditory, visual, or kinesthetic).

- If you have sent in your application or have applied online and haven't heard within two weeks, e-mail or call to make sure they received your materials. Of course, if they put in their ads, "do not call," then don't.

- Once you get an audition date, write it in red on the cover of the appropriate folder along with the time, place, and date. Secure your favorite accompanist right away, and write their name, e-mail address, and phone number on the cover as well. Enter all of this information into your calendar, including on your phone or computer.

3. Your manager will also be handling these files, so make sure that they are all complete and up-to-date.

4. Make a separate file for copies of each résumé item and one for all of the originals.

5. Put several PR Packets together except for your client's letter of introduction and perhaps a DVD or CD so they are ready at a moment's notice. (It's always good to have your client—you the singer—take one with them along with their audition aria sheet, to the audition and ask those for whom they are auditioning if they need it.) Rebuild and replace your client's PR Packets as you use them.

6. Often you are asked to send your client's PR packet materials via e-mail. There are many reliable web sites that allow you to keep your client's electronic information (résumé/bio/photo, etc.) online, to use as needed for e-mail applications, and that can also be easily updated when necessary.

7. When your client's PR packet needs to be sent by domestic mail, I've found that the most economical method of sending these materials is to use flat-rate envelopes. The cost of stamps is the same, regardless of the destination in the U.S. Get a dozen envelopes and the proper postage for each, so that you are ready to do business at a moment's notice.

Web Site

With today's online tools and programs, there is no excuse for your client not to have a professional web site.

- Make and keep the web site professional looking, with all pertinent information on how to contact your company. That means all of your client's contact information goes on all PR materials—sound clips, DVD clips, reviews, photos, up-coming events, etc. And always remember to represent your company's Brand.

- Keep your client's web site updated. Make sure that the most recent audio and video clips are available on the site, as well as on any other online sites where that material is available. Make sure the site is well-organized and easy to navigate, so that visitors can easily find the information they are looking for.

Time Management System

Give yourself 10–15 minutes each day, morning and evening, to sit quietly and internally center yourself, even if it means getting up earlier. You might want to start by reading something inspirational, then set some type of alarm for the time you have allotted this practice, close your eyes and quiet your thinking mind. When the alarm sounds, once you are back to the real world, you can then, with a more focused and clear mind, plan your day or in the evening, prepare for the next day. I have used the same book for years for my morning and evening inspirational reading. The book is *Discover Inner Peace* by Mike George. There are many short and powerful messages, sort of food for thought throughout the day.

- If it helps your day be less frantic, get up earlier to get some of the necessary business tasks off your plate.

- Always get the hardest thing done on your "to do" list, first. It really makes a huge difference in how the rest of your day goes.

Looking at the proliferation of personal web pages on the Net, it looks like very soon everyone on Earth will have 15 megabytes of fame.

— M.G. SRIRAM

Time is what we want most, but…what we use worst.

— WILLAIM PENN

- Follow the schedule you have set for yourself, but also know that unforeseen events and changes do happen, so remain flexible.

- Check your "to do" list every day, especially in the beginning to see if you have put too much or too little on your plate. Adjust as you figure it out.

- Handle mail only once. Open your mail and put the dates that the bills are due on the back of each envelope and in a pile, throw junk mail away, put any audition information in the appropriate files, look through catalogues and mark any pages with items you want to purchase and throw the rest away. No muss no fuss.

- Make a block of time for making or returning business phone calls or business e-mail.

- Turn your phone off while you are doing business, learning text or practicing. That leaves no excuse for distractions or interruptions. Folks can leave messages.

- Listen to your messages all at once. Jot down any information you need to follow up on, then erase all unnecessary items.

- Leave frustrations and stress behind. On your way home from work, whether you are driving, taking the subway or bus, or walking, find a place that will work for you to "drop off" an imaginary bag of emotional, work-related stuff for the day. Put all your worries, frustrations, anger, etc. in it, tie it up tightly, and drop it in the same place each day. You will be surprised that it will be there in the morning, for you to pick up if you want and take back to work with you.

- Don't take yourself and life too seriously. Laugh a lot, or at least compel yourself to mindfully turn the corners of your mouth up into a smile, even if it is an effort, many times each day. Notice how that makes you feel, lighter, happier and less emotional because you have changed your inner energy.

MANAGER

Having a professional agent/manager probably won't happen until you have a serious, consistently growing professional career already in place. Most present day managers/agents are looking for someone who has had lots of performance experience, has already signed future contracts, and is salable in today's market. That means you have to create a strong character to play this role, one that you can then step into and portray when it's time to do business as the manager.

The superior man understands what is right; the inferior man understands what will sell.

– CONFUCIUS

JOB DESCRIPTION

- Keeps the business running efficiently
- Works with you, the Singer, when putting together and updating a PR packet
- Establishes and maintains important business relationships. Is always networking and is a great communicator knowing how to use the inner language system (found in Act II) when dealing with others
- Puts Companies strategies and tactics into action to sell you, the product
- Reviews auditions and performances with you, the singer
- Negotiates contracts
- Helps singer with the proper etiquette for differing venues if necessary
- Meets with other staff members when necessary
- Aids PR Manager in finding appropriate venues/contacts to send the singers's materials/PR packet to, and follows-up

Here are some questions to answer, to find out who you might want on your roster if you were the manager. Who would be the ideal person you would want to represent your Brand and Company? Build a profile:

- What would they look like?
- How would they behave?
- How would they dress?
- What positive performance attributes do they possess?
- Do they emit a unique, authentic, and consistent energy and image that represents who they are, whether performing, just being, or in conversation?
- Is their Brand a "fit" with the reputation and standing of your Management Company?
- Does your client have a plan of action? What is it?
- What are their strengths? Weaknesses?
- What kind of rapport do you have with them?
- If you were an Artistic Director or Conductor, would you want to rehire this person and why?

Now it's time to turn the tables:

- When you audition, how do you think the people you are auditioning for perceive you?
- Do you have a Personal Brand that represents and presents the unique and authentic you well?
- How do you want to be seen and known in the opera industry?
- If you were the manager, would you want to have you as a client? Why or why not?
- What are your strengths? Weaknesses?
- Have you modeled yourself after a specific person or persons and how has that helped you?
- What specific aspects of the people you have modeled yourself after inspire you?

- How do you feel about the difference between the answers you gave as Manager and Client?

Your answers will help you better understand both roles, that of the performer and of the manager, and might perhaps give you a new perspective of the person you want to model when stepping into that Manager role.

CONSTRUCTING YOUR PR PACKET

Your PR packet will not only represent you as the singer, but also the Company and your Personal Brand, both on paper or in the virtual world. The colors, font, and style are all personal choices, but remember that simple is always better. You want those who are looking at your materials not to be distracted by the art work; this is business.

Normally your PR packet will get only about a 20-30 second cursory look, so make a very clean, professional looking and easily understood format. Make sure your name and how to reach you is on each and every item in your Packet whether virtual or hard copy. You want to make sure no matter what happens to your PR packet, they know how to get in touch with you. If you are not sure what look you want or like for your materials, go online and check out what others are doing. Most singers today design and generate their own supplies on their computers, which is a much more budget-friendly proposition. If you choose to do this, don't forget to print your materials on good-quality paper, and always check and recheck spelling.

When building your PR packet, here are a few ideas to keep in mind:

- This is often, your initial and sometimes your only opportunity to present yourself to potential clients/customers.
- Make it worthy of your best. It is quite often an expensive undertaking, so be sure to use the best materials you can afford.

It doesn't matter how many times you fail. It doesn't matter how many times you almost get it right. No one is going to know or care about your failures, and neither should you. All you have to do is learn from them and those around you because... all that matters in business is that you get it right once. Then everyone can tell you how lucky you are.

— MARK CUBAN

- Represent the Company and your Personal Brand.
- You want this packet to be consistent with who they encounter in an audition.
- This packet is your visual calling card. Do not include a CD or DVD if it is not required.

GUIDING PRINCIPLES

1. As I said before, it can be a pricey item, so do your homework to find the best you can afford.

2. Offer your PR packet only to those at the right entry level for you right now. Again, only include a CD or DVD if it is required. Making this part of your presentation without having it requested will only irritate and annoy those that will be looking through your packet and could even keep them from considering you altogether. It tells them you can't follow instructions and are not professional.

3. Make sure all spelling of titles, names and addresses are correct before you send your packet. Let a second pair of eyes proof read all of your information before copies are made for your files and packet.

4. Have your name, address (optional), e-mail address, web site, and phone number on all of your materials. Check the spelling before printing.

5. Keep all colors, fonts, designs, and paper consistent throughout your materials, even if it is in a virtual presentation. You will also need stationery and thank-you notes, both with corresponding envelopes. If you are offering a hard copy of your materials, it is more professional to present them in a folder. Don't forget to include a business card.

6. Let your Office Manager know when it is time to reorder and recopy materials before you run out. Also, give them a heads-up when you have additions to any of your client's—you, the

singer's—materials, so the necessary changes can be made to your PR packet.

Staying on top of your business will help make it easier to manage, and you to be more professional. What should your packet contain?

- Cover letter
- Business card
- Publicity photo
- Resume
- Short bio
- Reviews
- Letters of recommendation
- CD or DVD (only if required)

Cover Letter

This letter is printed on your professional letterhead stationery which has all your pertinent contact information already printed on it. This can undoubtedly be the most important part of your PR packet, especially if you have an introduction from someone of influence in this industry. It should be brief, to the point, and one page only.

First Paragraph The first paragraph of your cover letter needs to tell those to whom you are writing what it is that you want, and if appropriate, who it was that suggested you contact them. If there is someone of influence you know whose name you have been given permission to use to introduce yourself or who personally recommends you, put that name in the first sentence of your letter. Know that those receiving this information will follow-up with your personal contact to ask for more specifics about you. Remember, business is about creating and maintain-

Won't you come into the garden? I would like my roses to see you.

– RICHARD B. SHERIDAN

ing relationships, and referrals from those of influence are worth gold.

> *Example:* Janice Mayer suggested that I contact you. She recently heard me in a production of *Cosi fan tutte* in Portland, Oregon, and thought my talent might be of special interest to your company. In speaking with Ms. Mayer, she asked if I had the role of Figaro in *Barber of Seville* in my repertoire. She said that you will be mounting a production of that opera next season and are currently looking for a Figaro, and feels that I would a great addition to the cast you have already assembled.

Know that this has to be legitimate, because they will pick up the phone and call Ms. Mayer. When someone of influence is interested in your talent, don't be afraid to ask if you might use them as a reference, or if they know of any upcoming opportunities where you might use their name as a reference, or if you have an upcoming audition for something, could you possibly use their name in your letter of introduction. The worst that can happen is that they will say "no." Then say, "Thanks, I understand your position," and move on—this is business, not personal.

Second Paragraph Highlight your skills and give them your background as related to *this job only*. This is not a résumé. I repeat—this is *not* a résumé. Tell what you are best at and why they should use you. If others of influence had nice things to say about you or your work, you can add that here. Sell your Personal Brand. Let them know how you can be a benefit to them and make them money.

> *Example:* The role of Figaro fits me perfectly. Even though my voice may be a bit bigger and darker than most who sing this role, my ability to sing the coloratura passages comes with great ease. Nathan Smith, who staged the most recent production I was in, was utterly amazed at

my vocal agility and loved working with me and I with him. When we brought a promotional sampling of this opera to the schools and community events, getting to spend time with the kids and audience members was such a treat and I know it helped get many of them to want to experience opera and bring their parents along.

Third Paragraph and Closing Let them know again your enthusiasm for this job, and state your method of follow-up. If you say you will call by a certain date if you haven't heard from them, then place that date on your calendar and do so. It shows that you are professional.

> *Example:* I hope that you will consider hearing me. I love getting to know this wonderful character of Figaro better, each time that I have the opportunity of performing the role.
>
> Thank you for your time and attention. If I have not heard from you by September 23, I will take the liberty of calling you.
>
> Warmest regards,

Make a hard copy of the letter and create a file for this company if you don't already have one. This makes follow-up easier because you know exactly what you wrote and when, etc. If you have follow-up telephone calls or e-mails with this company, keep a note of whom you spoke to, the date and time of the call or a copy of the e-mail exchange. Try to note if they are auditory, visual, or kinesthetic, so that you can reply to any further correspondence or phone calls in their preferred inner language. You are in the business of creating and maintaining relationships (see Act II of this book). This is good business and shows that you are professional, and those hiring are always looking for someone who not only sings and performs well, but who is ma-

If you don't get everything you want, think of the things you don't get that you don't want.

– OSCAR WILDE

ture enough to take care of themselves. It is never personal or emotional.

Publicity Photo

This is an immediate and lasting visual impression of who you are. It communicates what you want others to know about you—friendly, warm, strong, happy, fun, professional. It lets others see who you are as the person, not just the singer. It shows the artist as the person the audience would like to get to know personally and see perform again. It is your visual calling card.

You might eventually need two photos, one as described above—the real person inside the singer, and the other, which can be done at a later time, a more glamorous or dramatic shot, one that will tell others what type of roles you play, and which may be used more for publicity. Both types of photos need to be done by a professional. Depending on the current trend, it could be done as either a black-and-white or color photo. This is another financial investment that is worth your best effort. You are building a portfolio of how you want others to see you as you fully represent your Personal Brand.

Many singers express disappointment and frustration over their new headshots because they simply took someone else's word regarding a photographer. They didn't yet understand how important it is, to do the necessary homework towards finding the right photographer before making their investment of time, energy, and money:

- They didn't check the photographer out online to see if they liked any of their work.

- They didn't make an appointment to go visit the photographer and the studio in which the photo shoot would take place, to find out if they had rapport with the photographer and were comfortable in the space.

> *A person who has good thoughts cannot ever be ugly. You can have a wonky nose and a crooked mouth and a double chin and stick-out teeth, but if you have good thoughts they will shine out of your face like sunbeams and you will always look lovely.*
>
> — ROALD DAHL

- They had no agenda, they asked no questions; they didn't really know how much it would cost, or how many photos the photographer would take for them to choose from, so the outcome was less than stellar, and they wound up feeling cheated, angry, and like the victim.

Remember that mistakes and failure are part of what happens in the process of building a business and a career. It's always about how you choose to deal with the lessons that you learn from the experience that's important. It's how we learn everything.

How do you find a good photographer and what should you expect?

Warning: Because you already know that not everyone is internally wired, thinks, or behaves alike, it is very important to spend the time finding the photographer with whom you will have the greatest rapport, so that you can get the photo that best represents who you are on the inside. Seeking out a good photographer today is usually quite easy.

It is always useful to ask your singer friends which photographers they have used and what kind of experiences they had. Did they have a good time at the shoot and were they pleased with the end results? This could be a photographer you might want to check out for yourself.

Music industry publications and online are also both great resources for this kind of information.

Choose a couple of possible photographers and meet them in person to find if you have good rapport. Just because someone recommended them doesn't mean that you will get the same good results. Without rapport and mutual respect between you the artist, the photographer and the space in which you will be photographed, you will not get the photo you were hoping for. Don't settle for something less than what works for you. Take the time to look through their portfolios either in person or online to see if this is the

Those first few steps into the professional world of opera require courage. Being a little scared to take those really important first few steps outside of your comfort zone can feel overwhelming. However, knowing that you are willing to try new things that might fail, is part of how we all learn. It's an opportunity to gain some important feedback. If you want to be successful at this business, you have to do your homework then have the guts to follow through even though you may fall off the horse a few times. Gaining experience by being successful "one small step at a time" into new territory adds to your confidence, and gets and keeps you motivated.

kind of photo you are looking for. Do they all look like models posing or do they each show their individual personalities and jump off the page at you? Do the photos represent how you want to be known and remembered visually? Bear in mind, you are paying for this.

If the photographer and/or space doesn't feel comfortable and is not what you are looking for, thank them for their time and move on to the next photographer on your list.

By doing your homework, both you and the photographer will know what to expect from each other, which will allow you to work in tandem toward that ultimate great outcome. The process may seem like a lot of additional work, but in the end there are fewer misunderstandings, less frustration, and more positive productivity. Like the other elements of a career, it's about creating and maintaining relationships. It's business.

FACTS – QUESTIONS – GENERAL INFORMATION

Photographers can charge anywhere between $250 to $1500 and up for a shoot. There can be hidden costs, so ask exactly what is included in the price you are paying.

- Do they have a make-up artist they like and use regularly? What is the additional expense? If not, could they recommend someone? Otherwise, do the homework and find someone on your own.

- How many finished 8 × 10 prints are included in the price, or can you download the images and make prints at a photo reproduction firm or from your own computer?

- How long should you plan to be there?

- Is retouching and digital editing included? Can you be there while it is being done?

- What is the procedure if you don't like any of the photos? Do you get your money back?

- Does the photographer listen to your suggestions?
- Is the photographer using a digital camera? How many photos will be taken? The more shots that are taken, the better the opportunity for you to relax and try different poses, outfits and attitudes.
- How soon will you be able to view your photos?

You can ask the photographer to mark which photos he or she feels represent you best. E-mail your photos to teachers, coaches, friends, and family, and have them give you the numbers of the ones they prefer.

You ultimately make the final decision, keeping in mind that this is about having others see the real you, your Personal Brand. It's not a magazine image of a model's face, which is usually more concerned with the composition of the photo itself. What you want is your personality and energy coming off the photo in a powerful way, and it should mainly come through the energy and interest in your eyes. Be objective when you look at your photos: Is this someone you would want to hire? When you are being photographed, remember this: try to create a memory that allows your eyes to come to life, something that makes you light up and puts a smile on your face from the inside. You want this to represent your Personal Brand to a tee. This photo will generally be good for three to five years.

Photo Duplication

There are many companies that specialize in reproducing headshots for actors and singers at an economical price. Most photographers will usually recommend a firm whose work they know to be good. You will also no doubt have an electronic version of your photo, to send out or for printing your own copies as you need them. It is better to have a vertical (portrait orientation) photo, because of how it looks and fits into your PR packet. Your name should be printed on the front of your photo, in the area at the bottom of the photograph, using the same font that is on your other materials.

Print stickers with your name, e-mail address, and phone number, and place them on the back of your photo in the upper left-hand corner. If your materials are in a virtual format, make sure your contact information is incorporated. That way, if for some reason your photo becomes separated from your other materials, you can still be contacted.

Résumé

This document is a synopsis of your performance experience. It is important that you make it clear, organized, and easily understood, regardless of what format you are using, virtual or a hard copy. Many times your résumé gets only a cursory 20–30 second glance—in reality, the letter of introduction is often the most important part of any PR packet, especially when an influential person in the industry has given you permission to use their name in introducing yourself.

Above all, make sure all the spellings are correct. Check and recheck. You will find a sample résumé in the appendix. A single page is best. Begin each category with the most recent performance or event date. You might not need or use all of the categories mentioned below, but they are possibilities, and will probably change as you gain experience and can leave off some of the less-professional information.

- *Roles Performed:* name of opera, character, company performed with, stage director/conductor and date performed
- *Performance Ready Roles:* These are roles that have been coached, perhaps performed in concert venue or with a group of other singers, or done with a lesser opera company.
- *Roles in Preparation:* This gives those hiring an opportunity

> *We should be taught not to wait for inspiration to start a thing. Action always generates inspiration. Inspiration seldom generates action.*
>
> – FRANK TIBOLT

to see what you are currently working toward and where you are going vocally.

- *Oratorio:* same format as roles performed
- *Musical Theatre:* same format as roles performed
- *Concerts:* name of work performed, conductor, where and when performed

As you continue to expand your professional performance experience, these next categories will eventually be dropped from your résumé:

- *Summer/Apprentice/Training Programs:* name of program, where and when attended
- *Awards:* titles and dates
- *Education:* Unless you are applying for a degree program, this is usually unnecessary to include on your résumé.

Short Bio

This is a publicity blurb that will be used in programs, newspapers, and for other publicity. *It is not a résumé!* It is a concise overview of the current highlights of your career. It should also, like your photo, give the reader an idea of who you are personally. It needs to compel the reader to want to know more about you, and want to support you by becoming a fan. Check all spelling. Start with a powerful, theatrical assertion:

> From her beginnings as a young performer growing up in a small rural town in New Mexico, to winning audiences' rave reviews, Ms. Smith has generated a loyal following with her persuasive acting and delicious voice.

Now back it up with facts:

> At her most recent recital, Ms. Smith's innovative program and beautiful singing was not only enthusiasti-

What lies behind us and what lies before us are tiny matters compared to what lies within us.

— HENRY S. HASKINS

cally appreciated by the audience, but she received a glowing review from the *San Jose Sun.* Jack Place said, "a beautiful program, a beautiful voice, and a beautiful young woman."

Last, let everyone know what's coming up in the future.

Having recently won the Pit Award, Ms. Smith will next perform at Town Hall in New York. While there she will coach with Maestro Tullio, in preparation for her debut as Inez in *Il Trovatore* at Albert Hall in March of this year. If you would like to learn more about Ms. Smith, please go to www.anitasmith.net.

CD

This is your auditory calling card. This is another expensive investment, so get the best you can afford. This item may or may not be needed with each PR packet.

> *If you don't know where you are going, you will probably end up somewhere else.*
>
> **– LAWRENCE J. PETER**

- Most times five opera arias are required: two in Italian, and one each in German, French, and English. Only if it is appropriate for your fach, include one Mozart aria. Depending on your fach, you might also want to include Russian, Spanish, or Czech arias.

- If you are sending your materials off to several different types of venues, it would be wise to record a master CD with a few diverse art songs, crossover pieces, sacred pieces, an orchestral concert piece, and a musical theater piece. You can assemble it as money and time permits. You can then select the appropriate pieces to be duplicated onto a CD for each venue as needed.

- Secure your favorite accompanist in plenty of time.

- Leave enough time before your recording date to work intensely with your accompanist so you truly become a team.

ARIA READY GOLDEN RULES

- Rule of thumb: a 15-minute recording requires 2–3 hours of recording time. Book your time accordingly.

- If recording five or more songs or arias, break your recording session into two days. You will be surprised at how much energy is required to do a recording. It is different from working with a coach, or with an accompanist in a rehearsal or performance.

- Test sound levels, and take the time to listen to the playback of each piece. This assures you are getting what you want and spending your money wisely.

- Book your favorite accompanist way ahead of time.

- If you have a great recording of yourself made in the past year, you might include that on your CD as well. Listen to the recording before you add it to your CD—it might be remembered in a better light than it actually is, and you want to present your current best technique, sound, and artistry.

HOW TO FIND A RECORDING STUDIO

This process is very similar to finding a photographer. Always do your own homework. Ask your colleagues, teachers, and coaches for recommendations, but check them out for yourself before you book a date or spend any money. Find out what their experience with the studio and engineer was, and look for reviews online or in trade publications.

When solving problems, dig at the roots instead of just hacking at the leaves.

– ANTHONY J. D'ANGELO

- Make sure that you have good rapport with the engineer and feel vocally comfortable with the physical studio space, by making an appointment to check them both out. Sing a few notes while in the space, and notice how it sounds and feels to you. Are there any ambient noises that might be picked up by the recording? Are there any distractions? Do they have pets or smoke, and are you allergic?

- Digital recordings allow for easier editing. You will usually receive a master CD from which to make copies and add selections to your web site. Listen to the final edited CD master in its entirety before paying for the recording, in case there are any mistakes or blips. This gives you a bit of leverage in fixing any problems.

- Ask the engineer how much experience he or she has had with recording opera singers. You need to be sure they know how to allow for the extremes of an opera singer's dynamic range.

- Are there hidden cost items? If so, what are they and how much will they cost?

DUPLICATIONS

Most of the time you will burn your own copies from the master CD as you need them. If this needs to be done professionally, always begin by asking your recording engineer for references.

When done professionally, make sure the engineer has a correctly spelled list of the selections, in the order in which you would like them to be copied. Regardless of who is burning your CD, the first selection on the CD must be the piece that you feel you sing best, just like when singing an audition.

- Listen to the entire CD before you pay for it, to give yourself some leverage if there are problems.

- If done professionally, how are mistakes and errors handled?

- How long will the process take?

LABEL

Make your label consistent with your other materials in color and font. Make it clean, clear and in the same order of what is on the CD. Check and double check all spellings.

There is nothing more unprofessional than misspelling the name of the opera, aria, or composer.

Make sure your name, phone number and e-mail address are on each CD. You may also want to put your photo on it to help remind them of your Personal Brand.

Reviews

This is a wonderful and professional way to let others know how you are doing, and a wonderful tool to keep in touch with those on your A and B lists. Send them a copy of your review, along with a short note, by post or via e-mail.

Here is one system for making hard copies of reviews for your physical (versus electronic) PR packet:

- Cut the entire review out of the newspaper or magazine. Cut out the name of the newspaper or magazine along with the date it was published.

- Paste all of this onto a plain piece of paper in a neat and readable way. Highlight the portion of the review that pertains to you. (If the review was not favorable to your colleagues, leave these portions out if possible.) Only make copies from this mock-up. Put the copies in the appropriate file, and the original in a file marked "original reviews for copy."

- If there are reviews online, cut and paste them into a document that can be printed out. Make sure that you have the name and date of the publication included, and be sure to highlight your portion of the review.

- Make several hard copies for the files to be used in putting your PR packet together. This way, you are also never left unprepared should your computer be down for any reason.

Letters of Recommendation

There are two types of letters of recommendation. One is the kind required for a specific application, and the other will be from influential people who want to facilitate supporting your career by helping to make introductions and connections.

APPLICATION LETTERS OF RECOMMENDATIONS

As soon as you get the application and know these letters will be required, already have several people in mind that might write a letter for you. It is a professional courtesy to give those you would like to write this letter plenty of time to do so. It's annoying to have someone ask you at the last minute, because it does take some careful thought, focused time, and energy on the part of the person who is writing the letter, so give them plenty of time.

Use your Outside Time line, disassociated from your emotional state. This is not a personal or emotional situation. It is a professional and business matter.

Make a list of everyone of influence that you have worked with within the last year and contact them to see if they would be interested in helping you. Know that not everyone will be available or willing to write this letter for you. And remind yourself that this process is not personal, but business.

Most times the application will give specific instructions as to what information is needed by the writer. If not, these are items to suggest:

- How long have you worked with this singer?
- How innately musical are they?
- What kind of stage presence do they possess?
- What is their command of languages?
- What do you feel their career potential is?
- How reliable are they?
- What kind of performance instincts do they possess?

- What kind of colleague are they?
- How fast do they learn?
- Any additional items they may want to add which they feel would be important or significant

It is a great courtesy to e-mail a partially written letter to those willing to do this favor for you. Create a template for a regular business letter with the name, address, etc. of the person or company you are returning it to, a greeting ("Dear Mr. Smith," or "To Whom It May Concern:"), and a closing ("Warmest regards," etc.). They will then only have to fill in their recommendation information, print the letter on their letterhead, and sign it. You can also supply a pre-addressed, stamped envelope, so all they have to do is stick it in a mailbox, or you can pick it up from them at their convenience. Remind them again if their signature is required on the back of the envelope.

Taking the time to write a letter of recommendation or fill out a musical reference is a great courtesy for others to do for you. Show your appreciation by sending them a handwritten thank-you note, being sure to check the spelling.

SUPPORTIVE LETTERS OF REFERENCE

Who are the people you've worked with most recently that feel strongly about your career potential and talent? Make a list of these individuals, and begin the process of asking them if they would write a general letter of reference for you to put into your PR packet.

Character is what emerges from all the little things you were too busy to do yesterday, but did anyway.

– MIGNON MCLAUGHLIN

- When writing this letter, they need to include something about how they know you, your character, work ethic, talent, and potential.
- Ask to have ten copies printed on their letterhead stationery, with their original signature on each copy. Pick the copies up

> *Even if you're on the right track, you'll get run over if you just sit there.*
>
> — WILL ROGERS

at their convenience, or include a self-addressed, stamped large envelope (you don't want their letters to be folded), and have them drop it in the mail to you.

- When you receive the letters, file them into the appropriately labeled folder.

I can't stress enough how important it is, to let those that are willing to help you launch your career know how much you appreciate their help and support. Write a short, hand-written note saying thank you, and keep them apprised of your career as it unfolds. Check for correct spelling.

Presentation folders

When a physical (rather than electronic) PR packet is required, show others that you care about how you represent yourself and your company by the way you introduce your materials. Present your materials in a pocket folder that co-ordinates with the other stationery products in your packet. This keeps all of your information together in one convenient packet.

- You might glue your business card or create a sticker with your logo, name, and contact information to put on the front of your packet. It should look interesting but simple, clean and professional—remember, this is business.

- Make up several PR packets in advance and keep them in an appropriate file. This makes doing business so much easier, because when and if you need a packet at a moment's notice, you won't have to spend time finding all the components, then hurriedly putting them all together in some haphazard, unprofessional way.

- Domestic flat-rate envelopes and stamps are the best way to send your materials. You can keep a dozen or so on hand and resupply them as needed.

- Make sure every item in your PR packet has your name, phone number, e-mail address, and web site URL on it. If your materials get separated for some reason, they'll still be able to contact you if they are interested.

You can also put a file tab on the side of your PR packet with your name, voice category, and phone number, making it easier to find your materials once they have been filed.

Arrange the materials in your packet thus:

- Opened left side of packet: Letter of introduction

- Opened right side of packet: Starting from the last item, letters of recommendation, reviews, résumé, short bio, and your photo on top. Add a CD or DVD if appropriate.

- Place your business card in the slots cut for this purpose on the inside of the folder.

AUDITION AND PERFORMANCE FOLLOW-UP

A very important part of being a manager is following-up with the client/singer after both auditions and performances. This is a way for both you the singer, and you the manager, to understand from both points of view how you did, and where there is room for adjustments or improvement. You will find that as the singer, you will be more emotionally attached to or associated with your observations, and as the manager, you will be less emotionally attached, or disassociated (stepping off your Timeline) with your observations, allowing your overall interpretation of the same event to be more objective. Using this combined overview will assist you in having available a more realistic, constructive, and accurate picture of the event you are reviewing.

Produce an audition information sheet where both the singer and the manager can record their impressions of the overview and outcome of the audition or performance. There are also various software applications available which

Piglet sidled up to Pooh from behind. "Pooh!" he whispered. "Yes, Piglet?" "Nothing," said Piglet, taking Pooh's paw. "I just wanted to be sure of you."

— A.A. MILNE

> *How can a society that exists on instant mashed potatoes, packaged cake mixes, frozen dinners, and instant cameras teach patience to its young?*
>
> **– PAUL SWEENEY**

can be useful for keeping track of this kind of information. The audition information should include the name of the company, competition, or program for which the singer auditioned; the names of whom you sang for, along with their positions, if possible; what the singer wore; what, if anything, was discussed with those who listened, etc. This will serve as a template to get you started with this important part of your job as manager. Using this tool on a regular basis will help you to identify any problem areas that might need some work.

As manager, if follow-up is necessary, keep it short and to the point. This will probably be done by e-mail. If a phone call is required, it is important to make a short list of questions or comments, and have it available to refer to as you speak. Remember to actually listen to the other person during the conversation. Don't try to second-guess or impress the other person; simply take the time to really listen to what they are saying, and respond appropriately and honestly. Have any appropriate files available, so that you can add any important comments to the information you already have amassed. Also, write down the date and time of the call, and to whom you spoke. It will all pay off in the long run. Try to ascertain whether the person with whom you are speaking is visual, auditory, or kinesthetic; make a note of it and use it, to the benefit of you both.

In today's virtual world, sending your materials in electronic form via e-mail seems to be the norm. There are companies out there that, for a small fee, will keep your materials at the ready for this kind of use. Once you have an account, it is easy to access and make any necessary updates. There are also specialized software products you can purchase that can help keep you organized and better prepared for a singing career. One that I particularly like is a program called "Velvet Singer," put out by Bill Bennett, and available at www.velvetsinger.com. It is also important that you continually send those interested in your career to your web site. That means you have to continually keep it updated with the most recent audio and visual clips of performances and events, and post all current other information.

The constant process of change within the world of social networking technologies are moving at such an extraordinarily fast pace that much of what happens in the virtual world transforms daily. In writing this book I realize that it is impossible to keep up with the amazing shifts occurring within these virtual tools, so it will be up to you to figure out how to adjust the information to work within the parameters of this new technology.

However, all business is still about creating and maintaining relationships, including the one with yourself. Remember that business is not personal or emotional. When you use these skills and tools which involve being both associated and disassociated with your emotions, you are able to look at an event from both view points, and keep a record of the combined results. You will learn to become more objective and reflective when dealing with the outcome; you will treat it as essential information and feedback improving your opportunities to succeed.

Dealing with people is probably the biggest problem you face, especially if you are in business. Yes, and that is also true if you are a housewife, architect or engineer.

— DALE CARNEGIE

CONTRACTS

There are four main types of contracts we will examine here: training/apprentice program contracts, non-union contracts, AGMA union contracts, and self-created contracts.

Training/Apprentice Program Contracts

There are no two training/apprentice programs alike. They can range in duration from a few weeks to a full year or more. They can be with big companies or smaller ones. They can be training- or performance-oriented, or a combination of both. In some cases, you will mainly be performing in an outreach program for the schools and local communities, and might

> *There are so many men who can figure costs, and so few who can measure values.*
>
> – AUTHOR UNKNOWN

make up the chorus for the main stage performances. In others, you will have the opportunity to take classes and perform small roles, perhaps even understudy a leading role with the main stage performances. Or there might be a combination of all of these. Some pay a stipend, while others pay a regular salary. Some offer AGMA union contracts, and others don't. There are many questions you need to ask before accepting a training/apprentice program contract; here are a few to get you thinking. Talk this over with your voice teacher, coaches, and manager.

- What kind of salary/stipend will you receive? How often do you get paid? What are the hidden costs? (Very important.)
- Does your contract include housing and transportation?
- Will you have to share your apartment/room/bathroom with someone else?
- Will there be someone there to pick you up at the airport?
- How do you get from where you live to work each day and does the company pay for it, or do you pay for it?
- What exactly will you be learning and from whom will you be learning it? What skills and tools will you add to your knowledge as a performer?
- What will be expected of you as a performer?
- Will you be expected to cover main stage roles? Will you receive an additional fee for this?
- Will you receive adequate rehearsal time, and musical and staging preparation to prepare a cover role?
- If you should have to step in as a cover for the lead in a performance, is there an extra fee for that?
- Will you be expected to sing in the main stage chorus?

- Can you be released from your contract to accept outside employment, if you have free time?
- Can you be released to compete in a vocal competition?
- What are the repercussions of getting out of a program if you really feel strongly that it is wrong for you?
- Is there someone you can talk to who will listen to your concerns, without fear of being terminated?
- If you love the program, can you re-up? Or can you move up to a contract as soloist?
- What happens after the program is over? Does this company have first right of refusal on your services for a given period of time, even after you've fulfilled your obligation to the contract you signed?
- What kind of references can you get for your résumé packet?

Non-Union Contracts

When you sign one of these contracts you need to know exactly what you are getting into. You really need to have everything spelled out in detail. Most non-union contracts are based on AGMA rules. However, read the fine print and ask questions. If you have a manager, make sure you go over the contract with him/her. Some of the questions you need answered whether you have a manager or are acting as your own manager are:

- How much are you going to be paid and when will you be paid: one lump sum, after each performance, per diem and performance pay by the week or month, etc.?
- If you are you paid per performance, do you receive a per diem fee to cover your expenses during the rehearsal period? When will you receive this money?

- Are you paid one blanket fee for the time you are there, no matter how many performances, rehearsals, and publicity work you do? When do you receive this money? Again, on a weekly basis, etc.?

- Are travel arrangements taken care of or do you have to pay out of your pocket? What about ground transportation once you are there?

- What are the housing arrangements? Do they meet your needs? Is there air-conditioning, heating, roommates, pets, private bath, quiet, piano, etc.?

- Exactly what role(s) will you be singing?

- How long are the rehearsal periods each day?

- How many performances are there and how are they spaced out over the performance period?

- Do you have a day in between performances or are they back to back? Often times this is the norm with smaller companies and you have to be prepared to sing a whole role this often, so know it going in and understand the best way to make this right for you.

- Are you being used for publicity performances for which you won't be reimbursed, or is this part of the package?

- Are you expected to sing at schools in an abridged version as part of the company's outreach program? If so are you paid or is this part of the package?

- Will you receive an audio/video tape of your performances as part of your fee?

AGMA Union Contracts

AGMA—the American Guild of Musical Artists—is the union representing opera soloists and choristers in the United States. You can see a copy of the basic AGMA national agreement and learn what the rules are on their web site, www.agma.com. This AGMA contract is a standard document. It includes the date of the contract, role performed, rehearsal and performance dates, and fees and per diem information.

Let your manager, if you have one, negotiate your contract—it is better for everyone. If you don't have a manager, step into the model you have created for your imaginary manager and do the work using these guidelines:

- Make sure you read through and understand everything on your contract before you sign it. Make any necessary adjustments. Don't *ever* let your manager sign a contract without your approval.

- AGMA has determined what constitutes a leading role, a supporting role, a feature role, etc. They have a corresponding fee scale for each of these categories.

- Everything is clearly stated in this standard contract, and all the working conditions clearly outlined. There is little room for confusion.

- Every company has a different letter of amendment, so their working rules might change. However, most times it is possible to negotiate better terms or fees; it is your right. The more in demand you become as a performer, the more money you can potentially earn, so keep that in mind when and if you choose to ask for more money. In other words, keep it business, not personal. Don't negotiate yourself out of this or any future jobs by developing a reputation of being difficult to deal with because you got emotional when it was not appropriate.

- There are two lines of a union contract which you can initial that make it possible for you to work in a union house—even if you aren't a member of the union—in a right-to-work state. Cross out and initial the line that recognizes your artist obligation to the union, as well as the deduction authorization line. You will continue to have all the rights and benefits of

If you have a job without any aggravations, you don't have a job.

– **MALCOLM S. FORBES**

> *Learning is a treasure that will follow its owner everywhere.*
>
> **– CHINESE PROVERB**

a union contract, while avoiding having AGMA union dues deducted from your paycheck.

OTHER INFORMATION ABOUT CONTRACTS:

- I have found that it is to your advantage to have the company pay directly for things like housing, transportation, including ground transportation, (taxi/car to from airport to hotel) and per diem because you are then obligated to only pay state/federal taxes and commissions to your manager on the amount you receive in the check you collect at the end of your engagement. Know that sometimes you may be paid weekly, monthly, per performance or one lump sum payment.

- Again, you want to make sure that you read every word of any contract you sign, and if you have questions, or need some clarification or revisions, contact the company or your manager, if you have one, and speak to them about it.

- Once you have signed a contract, the company will need other information such as your body measurements, head measurements for wigs and hats, and your shoe size. They usually send you a form to be filled out that you return to them. Be honest about your real measurements. You don't want to get there and have your costumes, wigs, shoes and accessories not fit. That is very unprofessional.

- They will ask for your publicity materials and several photos. Once there, they may ask you to do some publicity work to help promote their production. This kind of work is a great way for you to show your professionalism, and is an opportunity to do some networking on your own behalf. If you are popular with the public and can help put "butts in seats" at the theater, you have created an additional reason for them to re-hire you. You may be asked to promote on TV, radio, or for other media. You might also be asked to sing at clubs, community functions, or schools. Here is another opportunity to endear yourself to the public and create a fan base.

- Ask which edition and what publisher of the score they will be using. Rehearsals are always easier if you are literally on the same page as the conductor and stage director.

- Ask if they are planning any cuts or dialogue/text changes in the music and if so, would they please send them to you.

Creating Your Own Contract

When you get a job that requires a contract, or you want to create a contract between yourself and another party, go to www.agma.com and look at one of their professional contracts, to help you understand what it covers. You can use it as a template to write your own contract for any upcoming event. Your own contract doesn't need to be long, technical, or involved like a union contract, but it should cover all parties' essential needs.

If a man love the labour of any trade apart from any question of success or fame, the gods have called him.

– ROBERT LOUIS STEVENSON

- Read through the suggestions given for all the other types of contracts to make sure you have carefully thought through the points you want to make.

- Once you build your own contract, file a copy for future use when and if it becomes necessary to write another one.

- It may take some negotiation in order to create a win-win situation, so stay on your Outside Time line, where you can keep your emotions in check and out of the picture. Always remember, this is business, not personal. Working through this kind of experience helps you better understand the importance of being accountable and personally involved in all aspects of your own career.

Knowing you have done the work required to secure a contract that works for everyone involved in a production, is a self-esteem booster. Each step you take gives you more pertinent information and insight, as you make your way forward into the professional world of singing. It gives you the experience needed to feel more self-assured when dealing with the unknowns in your future.

MARKETING/PR DIRECTOR

> "It is not because things are difficult that we do not dare: it is because we do not dare that they are difficult."
>
> – SENECA

Continually adding fans and prospective patrons to your clients mailing lists is a big part of building a career. It requires great networking and schmoozing skills and tools that help keep your client's name out in front of the public whether done in person or via the virtual world. It also requires researching to find the right entry level venues for you the client. This is the work of the Marketing/PR Director.

JOB DESCRIPTION

- Sell the well-branded product, the singer. Find appropriate venues to help promote your client.
- Keep client's name in circulation by networking, creating and maintain relationships.
- Make sure PR materials are current
- Support & represent the company brand.

PRODUCT SALES: SOURCES FOR FINDING APPROPRIATE COMPETITIONS, JOBS, AND APPRENTICE PROGRAMS

What is important about this and how will it be useful to you? Sending your materials to just anyone or everyone shows others that you have not done your homework—you are not acting professionally. You will create the wrong (and lasting) first impression, by sending your materials to companies, orchestras, festivals, summer programs, apprentice programs, competitions, etc., that are not at your current entry level. Those that receive the materials do not easily forget this kind of faux pas, making it harder to get your foot in that professional door, so why waste your precious resources, time, energy, and money making a wrong move and a bad impression?

More often than not, PR packets are sent in electronic form via e-mail. Make sure all of your materials are updated with your client's most current information.

If you aren't sure what level your client, the singer, is working from at the moment (local/community performing organizations, professional chamber ensembles, B-, C-, or D-level theaters and orchestras, etc.), ask their teacher and coaches for a recommendation. There are also several resources available where you can research to determine your client's appropriate entry level situation:

- *Musical America:* National/international singer's bible. Published annually, specifically for the music industry. Contains information on managers, telling you a little about each and who is on their roster. You can also learn about which opera companies, orchestras, festivals, apprentice programs, summer programs, or competitions would be right for you. All are rated by size, budget, number of performances per season, etc. New editions are available for purchase, or can be accessed at a library or on their web site, www.musicalamerica.com.

- *Opera America:* The national service organization for opera in the U.S. Provides a variety of publications, online resources, workshops, and networking opportunities, a great non-profit organization that caters to the opera profession. You receive many benefits by becoming a member, including a group health insurance option, newsletters, monthly workshops, etc. Their web site is www.operaamerica.org.

- *Classical Singer* magazine: Lists auditions of many kinds, including some church jobs, and advertises many classes, workshops, etc. They can also help you create your own web site, and offer an online program where you can keep all your pertinent audition information, which can often be used for online applications. Web site: www.classicalsinger.com.

- *Backstage:* Aimed at performers in straight theater, musical

The ultimate pertinent information you are looking for when scoping out managers, companies, programs, etc. is information that gives you insight into who each of the players are within an agency or company. Do an internet search to find out more about each team member as a person, so that you can tailor your introduction (or letter of introduction), making it more personal and real. Notice by the words they use when writing about themselves, if they are visual, auditory, or kinesthetic, and use that inner language system when speaking with them or in any correspondence. This helps create instant rapport. When you have specific information about the individuals for whom you'll be singing, it often helps to alleviate the fear and anxiety; because you feel you already know them somewhat, they are no longer strangers, but fellow human beings.

When looking for a manager or agent, find out the type of venues where most of their singers perform. Are they A-, B-, C-, or D-level venues? Then figure what your entry level is, and further explore the agents/managers that are working with singers at your entry level. Next, explore those in your voice category on their roster. If there are only one to five singers that sing the same repertoire that you do, then perhaps this agent would be a good one to put on your short list for further exploration. Find out how often and where their singers work. If there are a dozen singers in your voice category, find out how often and where they all work as well. Some managers/agents love good voices and will take you on as a client, but if they already have too many similar voices on their roster, only a very few get the jobs. Do your homework. And yes, this is tedious work, but will pay off in the long run. Stick with it.

theater, and crossover. There are occasionally opera auditions listed as well. Web site: www.backstage.com.

- Local/Community Performing Organizations: Ferret out as many as you can in your own community or within a 50 - 100 mile radius. Ask what they are planning for their next season and if you find that there is something appropriate for your client, tell them you would like to arrange an audition. This is a great way for your client to get their feet wet, try a new role without the pressure of reviews, and/or get more experience at performing.

Teachers, coaches, and peers often have their own network and resources for getting information as well. Don't be afraid to ask them for suggestions. Here are a few of the many online resources available to you for finding information on upcoming auditions and performance opportunities, once you have identified your client's entry level:

- Yvonne's List (You can sign up through Facebook)
- www.bravuravox.com
- www.yaptracker.com
- www.operabase.com

As the Marketing/PR Manager, research becomes a big part of your job. When you find just the right niche for your clients entering the professional world of opera the PR Manager is then responsible for making sure the proper PR materials are available and sent to that venue. Each referral that you gain is worth gold, and gets added to either your "A List" or "B List" of contacts.

Keeping Track of Contacts and Mailing Lists

As the PR Manager, you are responsible for going out into the professional world of opera to gain access to the fans, patrons of the arts and those of influence in our industry and that is mainly done through networking and schmoozing. This is how the backbone of interest in your client is perpetuated as this essential information is collected and added to your company's Contact/Mailing List.

I have found that having two lists works well. You can call them whatever works for your company, but for our purposes here I will call them the "A List" and "B List." Both lists are important. The A List will require frequent tending to because these are the folks that do the hiring, or are of influence in this process in some way. Each time your client wins a competition, enters an apprentice program, performs, etc. you send out a concise, short notice via the virtual world that keeps those on the A List informed of your client's progress and growth as a rising performer. This also helps keep your clients name in front of those hiring. The B List helps create an audience for your client's performances and is usually their fan base, which includes family, friends, colleagues, etc.

The "A List" will contain the names, e-mail addresses, physical addresses, phone numbers, and any important information of anyone who might move your client forward on their career path and are either in the opera industry or associated with the professional performance world in some way. They can also be those who have given financial support or given you contacts of worth. This is a never-ending, ongoing process and might be the difference in getting your client a job or not.

The "B List" will contain names, e-mail addresses and phone numbers of your clients friends, fans and family. This list will undoubtedly be the longer of the two in the beginning phase of your client's career.

Networking and Schmoozing

What's the difference between networking and schmoozing? Even though both networking and schmoozing are, sim-

> When sending out e-mail to your A or B Lists, always put your own e-mail address in the "To" line, and the other recipients' e-mail addresses in the "Bcc" line. The email looks more like it was sent to each person individually, rather than arriving displaying a long list of recipients. It is also a courtesy to ensure the privacy of the other individuals on your lists.

> Often it is not only what you know or how great a talent you have, but who you know and how comfortable you are with this networking process. Critical, if not crucial, to career building, is connecting with those who have already built reputations and connections. I have noticed that often singers fall into one of three categories: They are either naturally comfortable, and enjoy people and the networking/schmoozing process; they create a façade, become over-zealous and a bit too forceful, using an unnatural "overdrive" mode that tends to push people away; or else they just don't do it at all, because they feel too awkward, vulnerable, and afraid that just being themselves is not enough.

ply put, ways to exchange information, ideas, and resources, there is a slight difference between them. Here is how I see this difference:

Networking not only involves great communication, the exchange of information, ideas and resources, but also you go with an agenda and are looking for a specific outcome when meeting with others. It is about what you want to accomplish by making these business connections. Another difference is that doing business can be done in either the virtual world via e-mail or over the phone or it can be done in person as long as you go with a particular agenda that needs a specific outcome. It means doing business; it's not personal or emotional.

Schmoozing on the other hand, has more of a social connotation. It is the art of engaging in clear, meaningful conversation in more of a social setting, and can be done for pure enjoyment as well as cultivating business relationships. However, often we engage in schmoozing without having a business agenda or particular outcome in mind. It is worthwhile to train yourself to be very present when engaging in any kind of social or business intercourse. It's learning to listen without letting your mind wander. When you schmooze, you create an occasion to put your new people skills to use to help others feel comfortable and engaged in conversation and communication. You can network while you are schmoozing, and schmooze while networking, but they are in my book, two slightly different skill sets.

Both networking and schmoozing, like everything else, require skills that need to be practiced often, in order to make the process feel natural and comfortable. When performers are without a character to play, they are often shy and tongue-tied. To engage in this process of networking and schmoozing with panache, you might want to revisit the "Inside Out" section in Act II of this book, and work through it once again in a mindful manner, to reacquaint yourself with many of the personal skills and tools. And of course, if you live and represent your Personal Brand, you will always be exactly who you are, no matter the circumstances.

Just like getting really good at performing, experience is the best teacher. So get out there and on purpose practice and perfect your personal skills with your friends and family. And do it before you try some of these skills/tools with someone you don't know well. Your best chances for success are to connect physically, mentally, and spiritually to all the aspects of networking/schmoozing and to gain as much experience as you can before applying it to your business. This is how you will gain confidence and feel comfortable with this process. The more positive experiences you have, the more poise you gain. And know that just like everyone else using this tool, there may be temporary failure along the way, so don't take it personally or get into your emotions, simply use it as feedback, learn something from it, then try the new improved version the next chance you get.

So, how do you successfully conquer your fears, and actually learn to enjoy networking and schmoozing? How do you break the ice, be yourself, socialize with grace and ease, and still look professional? Or pick up the phone and make a "cold call" with confidence? It can be a daunting experience or an opportunity to enjoy the conversation and company of others. First, let's get comfortable with networking:

- Always go with an agenda. It could be to meet and create rapport with a certain person that you know will be there or to make a particular suggestion to a specific person. You are looking for a specific outcome so go prepared.

- Create situations that enable you to be around those in your profession. Network in such a manner that people enjoy having you around, which will keep your name more on their minds if they, or someone they know, is looking to recommend or hire a singer in your fach and entry level.

And remember, no matter where you go, there you are.

– CONFUCIUS

Remember, if you're headed in the wrong direction, God allows U-turns!

– ALLISON GAPPA BOTTKE

Make sure to familiarize yourself with the local social customs of greeting, if you are in a foreign country, which can often be very different than your own. Find out ahead of time how to handle meeting people for the first time. Being aware of and following local social and professional customs, when either networking or schmoozing, shows respect, and is professional.

- Listen closely to find out their preferred inner language system and then speak their inner language to create rapport.

- It is a professional courtesy to use Mr. or Ms., or whatever title one uses with a specific profession, like Dr. or Reverend, etc., when speaking with someone you've just been introduced to. Allow them to give you permission to call them by their first name, otherwise address them as I've suggested. This is good business and shows respect.

- Get to know your contacts' interests outside of their job title. Do an internet search to find what they are interested in besides business. Getting to know others before meeting them in person helps you feel less like strangers when you do finally meet. It also gives you an opportunity, if appropriate, to bring up subjects you might have in common. As you gain rapport during an event, you can easily talk about subjects besides business, getting them to also share their opinions and views of unrelated work subjects. Be informed yourself. Find common ground as you build your relationships by talking to them about what they are reading, what movies they like, their hobbies, or what their favorite restaurant or kind of food is. Remember that this is still business and still networking; act professionally, show respect, and use your skills. Know them for who they are, not just what position they hold.

- Become a great listener! Take the time to really listen to what those who are giving you information are saying. Don't try to create an answer or be thinking of a point to make while you are listening to them. People love to talk about themselves so ask a few pertinent questions, then really listen to their story. By listening for real, you will find points in their conversation that will prompt you to ask further questions and make real conversation. You will be favorably remembered.

- Speaking of asking questions, may I suggest that you alleviate the "why" question from your repetoire, and start your questions instead with "what" or "how." Asking a "why" question often feels combative, and the person being asked might feel the need to defend themselves. Try it out for yourself and notice the difference in the kind of response you get.

- Have a creative, informative, and always updated web site to which you can direct those that are interested in knowing more about you. (This is an important tool for both networking and schmoozing.)

More business decisions occur over lunch and dinner than at any other time, yet no MBA courses are given on the subject.

– PETER DRUCKER

If there is real rapport, or you feel this is someone you would like to add to your professional A or B List, ask if it would be okay for you to do so—"Would you mind if I kept you updated concerning my upcoming performances?" It's always best to ask for permission, and a professional courtesy. If they say "no," don't take it personally or allow yourself to get into your emotions. This is business. Simply let it go, so that you can stay present and involved in the conversation. That kind of attitude lets them know something really important about your business ethics.

Because the music world is so small, always follow up on all advice and any leads you are given, and do so in a timely manner. They might not pan out, but make the calls or send the material. An unlikely contact may turn into a great opportunity. Remember, the person who gave you the contact may actually follow up, to find out if you did or didn't make contact with the leads they gave you.

Always make the right impression by doing what you say you will do. It's good business. Represent your Personal Brand—make your word your bond.

- If you say you will send information, send a CD or DVD, or contact someone, do it!
- Let others know how much you appreciate their willingness to share information, leads, or advice with you, by sending them a handwritten thank-you note, and do so within a window of

> *Lots of people want to ride with you in the limo, but what you want is someone who will take the bus with you when the limo breaks down.*
>
> **– OPRAH WINFREY**

one or two days from when you received the information. Make sure to check all spelling.

- Keep and update the database of your contacts regularly. If you had a conversation with a particular person who talked quite a bit and with passion on a particular subject, see if you can find any interesting information about that subject and send it to them periodically. It shows that you were listening, and makes an unexpected good impression.

- If you had particularly good rapport with someone, it wouldn't hurt to send them a short and concise handwritten thank-you note, to let them know how much you enjoyed their company and conversation. They will much more likely think of you when they are networking themselves, passing your information along to others. That is what you want. Represent your Personal Brand.

- If you hear about a job that is not right for you but would be for one of your colleagues or friends, pass the information along to them. They might reciprocate.

- Always give more than you get. Don't forget—networking is a two-way street. If you are asked for advice or information, give it generously.

Keeping in touch by creating a habit of networking will pay off. And yes, it is a lot of work, but that is your current job—creating and maintaining relationships. That's good business. Keeping those who have interest in keeping abreast of what you are currently doing professionally will help to keep your name circulating in the opera world. And that just might get you a job.

The Art of Schmoozing

Without the proper information, skills, and tools, it can be daunting to be at a social event where you don't know the majority of the guests. Here are some suggestions and basic rules for "working the room" in a social setting. Please keep in mind that, if you are in a foreign country, you need to find out ahead of time what local social customs are appropriate for each occasion. This shows others that you are respectful of them.

- If you know ahead of time who some of the people might be attending an event, do an internet search on them, to find out more about them besides their job title. This gives you an opportunity to get to know them a little before you actually meet them. It also gives you occasion to talk about your possible similar interests.

- At any social function, give yourself time to enter the room, roll out your "magic carpet," inviting everyone into your personal space, observe what is going on, and get settled. Do not assume that you are the only one who is feeling ill at ease. Take the time it takes to feel comfortable. Represent your Brand. Smile if you catch someone's eye or vice versa. Look and feel friendly. Expect to be accepted and liked. Move with confidence and grace. Remember that this is more about making the other person comfortable.

- Moving clockwise or counterclockwise around the room, notice if there are any familiar faces. Is there anyone you have seen or been introduced to before? Reintroduce yourself, and if you can, let them know where you have made their acquaintance. Or ask them where it was that you met them?

- For the most part, the majority of the people at this social event don't know who you are, and frankly don't care—unless you can show them why they should by engaging them in conversation, and then really listening to their response.

- If you can't remember someone's name, say so, then ask for it and use it as often as possible to help you remember. You can also try finding something about them to help you remember, like their clothing, a color, or a physical feature or attribute.

Once you have someone engaged in conversation, the best advice I can give you is simply to give them all of your attention when listening. Really hear what they are saying. It is then much easier to respond in a natural, unforced manner, and with genuine interest.

Informal conversation is probably the oldest mechanism by which opinions on products and brands are developed, expressed, and spread.

– JOHAN ARNDT

If you want or need to move on to another group, and need to break rapport—move away from the person to whom you've been talking—here is a great skill to know. When you have their full attention (and *only* when they have stopped speaking), put your hand on their arm, which breaks rapport; remove it quickly once you have their attention, and say, "It has been great meeting you (or seeing you again), let's stay in touch, etc.," and move away. It's an effective way to break rapport, and works like a charm. It's important not to physically touch them until they've finished talking—if you make contact with someone *while* they're talking, they'll think you're actually *more* interested in what they're saying, rather than understanding that you need to move on. Try this technique out several times with friends prior to attempting it during an important event.

- Talk about the weather, the performance you have just seen, the food and drink, etc. This will help break the ice. Ask "what" and "how" questions—people love to talk about themselves. Then listen to their response. Avoid discussing religion, politics, or money in these situations.

- If the party or reception is after one of your performances, be gracious in accepting compliments from others. Don't tell them how you could have done this or that better, etc. It takes the magic away from how they perceive you.

- Never approach a twosome talking. This is usually a personal conversation. Try either someone who appears to be alone or a group of three or more.

- Don't sit down unless you really need to. For most people, this is a signal that you don't want to be bothered. Stay up and moving—even if your feet hurt!

- Always have plenty of business cards at the ready. This is a great business tool. If you exchange cards, write on the back of theirs where you met them, what they do, and if you are supposed to get in touch with them. Then follow through.

- Again, listening is the most important part of any conversation in which you will be engaged. It shows interest and respect for the other person.

- You always want to been seen and treated as a professional. Make sure you look the part.

- Once you have made a complete circle in one direction, go back around the room in the opposite direction, catching any newcomers and to say your good-byes.

- If it is a hosted event, always find your host/hostess before leaving and thank them for a lovely evening/afternoon, etc. Make sure to send a handwritten thank-you note (check spelling) no more than two days later, saying what a great time you had.

- If you are invited to a dinner party, tactfully try to find out who the other guests will be in advance, and do a little research, using the internet or other sources, on what they do for a living, and what their interests, hobbies, likes and dislikes might be.

- Being well-read in several subjects yourself is a great help in feeling comfortable and confident. There are so many web resources to give you a variety of information, in the form of current news stories, gossip, science, food and restaurants, and sports events, so that you can be up to speed on what is going on in the world enough to join almost any conversation. And not knowing everything allows others the opportunity to fill you in and make them look and feel special.

- Always remember to thank your host and hostess before you leave and again and always send a handwritten thank-you note no more than two days later. Check for correct spelling.

Make sure you know how to handle the place settings if you are invited to a formal sit-down dinner. You don't need to be caught off-guard. It means spending a few minutes online checking out the proper etiquette for such an event. If you are not sure how to deal with an item or food, wait and watch those around you. Then follow suit.

If you are still feeling a bit unprepared or nervous, go back and work through Act II. It will help you to "polish up" your Personal Brand, and remind you of those qualities and goals that help to define it.

Schmoozing can be a lot of work or a lot of fun—it's up to you. Giving people an opportunity to get comfortable with you, and becoming a consummate listener, will help you to put your best foot forward. When you engage in conversation with someone, give them your full attention by being very present. This will ensure that you will be favorably remembered as someone with whom they felt at ease and in rapport, that you listened to them and were genuine. It's that simple. As you can see, networking and schmoozing are an important part of building a solid professional singing career. Creating and maintaining relationships is a big part of your job, and you now have the skills and tools necessary to accomplish this task. Experience will only make it better.

Waiting for the fish to bite or waiting for wind to fly a kite. Or waiting around for Friday night or waiting perhaps for their Uncle Jake or a pot to boil or a better break or a string of pearls or a pair of pants or a wig with curls or another chance. Everyone is just waiting.

— DR. SEUSS

> *The number one problem in today's generation and economy is the lack of financial literacy.*
>
> — ALAN GREENSPAN

FINANCIAL OFFICER

Knowing how much you spend each month on your business gives you an opportunity to eventually create an accurate budget within whose parameters your company must work. Keeping track of your client's weekly expenses is an invaluable tool when it comes to tax time and is especially beneficial if your company is ever audited because you have all of your client's financial information already prepared and easily accessible.

JOB DESCRIPTION

- Craft a Budget
- Keep track of expenses - receipts – pay bills
- Preparation for tax time

Crafting a Budget

Money is an important element in setting up any business and yours is no exception. Learning how to manage your money is an essential component of feeling empowered, and helps keep you in control of your business and life. It helps generate that healthy balance I have talked so much about.

Crafting a budget is a relatively simple process. Knowing what monies you have to work with each month, both personally and professionally, keeps you on track. And it is a tool to help you make wiser decisions about how you want to spend your hard earned money. This is a very personal matter, so make sure your budget reflects your needs and goals. The better you understand your whole financial situation, the more precise your budget will become, which in turn will grow your self confidence.

No one else is going to see this, so be brutally honest about where and how you spend money. Devising a budget that is written down and living within that budget will give you a sense of control over your life and where you are going. Remember, this is only a guide, which will undoubtedly change as your life situation, work, goals, and needs change. Nothing here is written in stone. However, there is no worse feeling than not knowing where you are financially, so take the time now to put this process in place if this is not already a practice you follow.

Here is one way in which that can be done. There are two things you need to pay attention to, income and expense. It is really that simple.

Start by creating three lists: Income, Fixed Expenditures, and Varied Expenditures. Make these lists as accurate as you can. There is no right or wrong to any of this. It is simply a guide to help you better understand your current money situation.

- *List #1-Income:* List all the monies you make regularly each month. If you have a full time job, it is the monies you receive every month. If you, like many young artists, have a temp job or do freelance or short-term work, check your past six months of paycheck receipts from these jobs and find the average amount that you made. There will be months where you made more and other months where you made less, but there should be a median point between these two. If you have a regular church job, include that and any other monies you make on a regular basis from singing, etc. That is what you will put down as your monthly income.

- *List #2-Fixed Expenses:* List all of your monthly bills that are usually pretty similar in amount each month, every quarter or year. These might include things like rent, gas/electric, water, phone, student loan, cable TV, credit card debt, car payment, car insurance, taxes, and etc.

- *List #3-Varied Expenses:* List any expenses that occur every month, but are not fixed in amount. Average them out: grocery expenditure, gas for your car, entertainment, eating out, cleaning bills, repair bills, voice lessons, coachings etc.

Once you have totaled each list, add list 2 and 3 together. Now simply subtract this total from the total of list 1 and you will know how much either over or under your budget you are. This will give you a very clear picture of what you need to do next. If your expenses are under or about even with how much you make a month, congratulations! If your expenses are over the amount you make a month, there are some changes you might want to address:

- Look carefully at everything you spend that is truly not necessary (coffee at Starbucks, lunch out, manicure, etc. These are usually *wants*, not needs. If you pull these items out of your list, how will it affect your bottom line? Will it make a big enough difference in having a balanced budget, or do you need to make more changes?

- How much credit card debt do you have? What is the interest rate of paying off that debt on a monthly basis? Is it worth it? Credit cards should ideally be used only for emergency situations and paid off in one to three months. Call your credit card purveyor and ask for a reduced interest rate. If your credit card bills are way out of hand find a reputable counselor that deals with helping those that are deep in debt. If you are feeling guilty or shameful about where you are financially, step off your Inside Time line and leave your emotions "over there," on that line, so that you can deal with the "facts" of this situation. Remember this is business. If you really feel lost, check out some of Suze Orman's books, or visit her web site and blog.

- Whether your friends are fellow performers already semi-established with their careers or those making a living doing something else, when you see them going out on a regular basis or having more discretionary monies to spend, it is often hard to discipline yourself. They might have all the current fashions, get their nails done weekly, have all the newest electronic gadgets, order food to go, have tickets to the ball games, etc. However, they do not have the added expenses of preparing for a career in singing. The question for you is, where do you want to put your priorities? Is it worth the momentary gratification of doing or having a thing right this minute or would you feel better about yourself if you stayed within your budget? They can afford to spend their money on different things right now. Your time will come.

- Maybe you need to get a second job. A church job might make all the difference in helping to balance your budget. From that you might start getting other free-lance singing jobs at weddings or funerals. Depending on the religion, you must be prepared to give up your Saturdays, and/or Sundays every week, and be prepared to attend an evening rehearsal every week. But it could give you the extra money you need for that extra lesson or coaching you want to take, or the music you need to buy

- Consolidate your debts if you can. You will then have only one payment a month to make with only one interest rate instead of several smaller ones each with their own interest rate and high pay back amounts. If you choose to do this, make sure you get a loan with a fixed and low interest rate.

- Check with your school loan financier to see if you can arrange to pay only the interest on your loan. This is called "requesting forbearance during economic hardship". Tell them you are not in a position to start paying off the debt yet. Each call will be good for about 6 months and you will only be paying the interest on your loan. This can usually be done for several years, until you get on your feet.

Knowing what you have to spend each week or month financially will make you feel empowered, confident, balanced, and professional, allowing you to enjoy and focus on the other aspects of your life. If you see on paper how you spend your hard-earned money, that will hopefully stick in your mind the next time you want to throw caution to the

The individual who wants to reach the top in business must appreciate the might and force of habit. He must be quick to break those habits that can break him—and hasten to adopt those practices that will become the habits that help him achieve the success he desires.

– J. PAUL GETTY

wind and spend money unwisely. Working toward a career is about being responsible for the choices you make—lots of self-sacrifice and even more self-discipline. Advertising today often makes it seem as if we are entitled to have all the "stuff" that is available. "They" want us to buy everything, and are happier when we put it on a credit card for which we won't even have to make a payment for 6 months. Is what you are considering a *need*, or a want? Or is having an extra voice lesson or coaching, or getting your résumé packet together, more important? How about saving extra money for a rainy-day emergency?

A BUDGET CHALLENGE

You can still have fun while sticking to a budget. Enjoy the challenge of finding either free or inexpensive ways to do it:

- Rent a movie instead of paying money to go to one at a theater. Have a move night at your place where everyone chips in with the cost of the rental, and have everyone bring their favorite movie snack.
- Go to free concerts.
- Get out in nature and bring a picnic.
- Have a potluck dinner party.
- Make your own birthday and event cards. Instead of buying a gift, give a coupon for a back or foot rub, cleaning someone's house, helping someone with their computer, or taking their dog for a walk.
- Check out the possibilities of getting a grant or scholarship to help pay for your lessons and coachings.
- Find a sponsor to pay for your lessons and coachings.
- Hold a benefit for a program or workshop you want to attend. Be creative.

It really doesn't take long to craft a budget. Once you know what that is—income minus expenses—you'll be more aware of how you want to spend your hard-earned money, and at the same time feel more in balance with the rest of your life.

Taxes

DISCLAIMER: *The information given here is designed only to provide you with some general ideas for tax preparation and record keeping. This is not a substitute for legal advice or the advice of a Certified Public Accountant. For specific tax questions, always consult your legal advisor or CPA.*

You, as a performer and entrepreneur, are responsible for knowing how much you owe in taxes on your income. Aside from the federal income tax, many states also have income taxes (in New York City, there is also a city personal income tax). The purpose of this guide is to give you a sense of the basic information needed to make tax time less of a burden. By recording your income and keeping organized records of all your related expenses, you will have all that pertinent information available when needed.

> *The income tax has made more liars out of the American people than golf has. Even when you make a tax form out on the level, you don't know when it's through if you are a crook or a martyr.*
>
> **– WILL ROGERS**

Keeping very accurate financial records with organized backup materials will help you keep from overpaying taxes, and simplify the amount of time spent preparing your tax forms. If you are ever audited, this will make the process easier, because you will already have the backup documents available, organized and ready for inspection.

Oftentimes, performers/musicians receive a paycheck where an employer has already withheld taxes and other deductions. As an entrepeneur, you are responsible for calculating and paying the taxes on any other income you make during the year for which an employer has not withheld taxes. This means you have to keep track of all of the monies received for services rendered, and all of your expenses pertaining to your performance career. You have control of both what you make and what you spend.

> *Did you ever notice that when you put the words "The" and "IRS" together, it spells "THEIRS?"*
>
> – AUTHOR UNKNOWN

You will most likely have two sets of forms to fill out, one form for your federal return and one for your state return. Because state income tax varies from state to state, we will deal only with federal income tax here. If you plan to do your taxes yourself, there are a few IRS forms you need to become acquainted with:

- *Form 1040, U.S. Individual Income Tax Return:* You may include itemized deductions (which you will list on Schedule A), and any gain or loss from your business (on Schedule C).

- *Form 1099-MISC, Miscellaneous Income:* If you were hired as an independent contractor, your employer should send you this form as a record of your income. Even if they don't, you still have to report all your income from contract work (on Schedule C).

- *Form W2, Wage and Tax Statement:* You should expect a W2 form from your employer if you receive a paycheck on a weekly, bi-weekly, or monthly basis.

If you made $600 or more, after expenses, as a self-employed musician by year's end, then you are required to file a tax return. Tax laws change on a regular basis. It is smart to find a CPA whose business caters to musicians and performers. They will be current on all laws, will help you get organized and see that you don't pay more than you are required to by law. They will tell you what forms will work best for your situation.

The good news is that as a self-employed musician you can claim deductions for business expenses on your tax return. This means that you must keep accurate records, and have the appropriate backup materials to substantiate these deductions. Deductions must be for your business only, not for personal use. In the music industry, this can often be difficult to define. Your CPA will be able to help clarify what are and aren't considered acceptable business deductions, as well as inform you of the most current tax laws, and what kind of documentation is required to substantiate your deductions for the IRS.

If you show a business loss, you must demonstrate that you are in business for the purpose of making a profit—you just haven't done it yet. The IRS will allow you to declare a net loss on your income tax return, for any two tax years during a five-year period of being in business. In other words, you must show a profit three out of five years, or the losses will be disallowed and you may owe additional taxes.

If you don't have the necessary support documents for your proposed tax deductions, or declare a net loss more than the allowed two out of five tax years, the IRS may categorize your musical activities a "hobby," and disallow your deductions. So take the time on a weekly basis to keep great records. If you don't already have a way to keep track of your weekly expenses, I have provided a sheet for this in the appendix—you may want to add or subtract items from it to make it applicable for your own personal situation.

- Requirements for deducting car costs are strictly enforced by the IRS. You must keep a log of business mileage and be accurate Or find out from your CPA what is legally allowed.

- Grants and fellowships are no longer partially excludable. List this money on the "Other Income" line of your Form 1040.

- If you choose to use a tax accountant, the taxes they prepare will only be as good as the information you give them. Make it clear and accurate.

- Your tax records, both federal and state, must be kept for a minimum of three – maximum of seven years after filing.

- All of your records and backup support material should be stored together and marked with the appropriate tax year for easy identification.

Of course the truth is that the congresspersons are too busy raising campaign money to read the laws they pass. The laws are written by staff tax nerds who can put pretty much any wording they want in there. I bet that if you actually read the entire vastness of the U.S. Tax Code, you'd find at least one sex scene ("'Yes, yes, YES!' moaned Vanessa as Lance, his taut body moist with moisture, again and again depreciated her adjusted gross rate of annualized fiscal debenture").

— **DAVE BARRY**

- You must retain all receipts for personal property pertaining to your career, such as musical instruments, recording equipment, etc., for as long as you hold this property and for three years thereafter.

> Man is not like other animals in the ways that are really significant: animals have instincts, we have taxes.
>
> — ERVING GOFFMAN

As a performer, you could be self-employed *and* an employee of an established business. (You could, for example, have a regular church job, do other performances, *and* hold down a regular nine-to-five job.) This requires great record keeping. You may want to consult a CPA or tax accountant who understands the complexity of tax accounting for this profession, or who works regularly or exclusively with performing artists, to help you initially set up your record keeping, and perhaps have them prepare your taxes.

Ask teachers, coaches, or colleagues for recommendations of a reputable CPA or tax accountant accustomed to working specifically with performing artists. Here are some questions you might want to ask a CPA before you consider employing them:

- Ask in advance how much they charge per hour. Are there additional costs for using additional forms?

- Ask for an estimate of their fee in your situation. (How long they think your appointment and their work filling out the forms will take.)

- Ask what specific documentation they will need from you. Wasting their time wastes your money. Be organized and prepared.

Here are some simple tips for keeping the kind of records that you will need for tax purposes. If you have access to a computer, there are several simple, relatively inexpensive software programs, like Quicken or TurboTax, that can help organize your records for you.

- Always ask for a receipt. Keep all receipts that pertain to anything you do as a performer.

- Make sure the receipt states what the money was spent for (coachings, lessons, practice space, business cards, office supplies, electronic devices, etc.). If it doesn't, take the time to write the date, item, and why you bought it on the back of the receipt. If there's no receipt, create one on the spot. Ask for a piece of paper and have the clerk sign it and fill in the appropriate information (date, item, and how it will be used).

- When paying by credit card, the receipt usually has all the information you will need on it. If it's not itemized, have the clerk fill in the information, then you need only to note on the receipt how you intend to use the item and you're done.

- If your receipt is for entertaining, write on the back the date, who your guests were, why you were entertaining and the topic of conversation.

- If paying with a check, keep the canceled check. If you pay with cash, get a receipt with the date, the recipient's signature, and the purpose of the expenditure. If paying with a credit card, you'll not only get a receipt, but will also have a record on your monthly bills.

It is much easier to complete your tax forms if you have already separated your deductions into categories. The following are some suggested categories. If you have questions or are in doubt, always check with a qualified accountant.

PROFESSIONAL SERVICES

Voice teacher, pianist/coach, language/drama coach, dance teacher, fencing teacher, Alexander technique teacher, accompanist, agent/manager fees, etc. If you pay with a check, keep the canceled check. If you pay with cash, get a receipt with the date, the recipient's signature, and the purpose of the expenditure.

Ask your accountant to recommend a journal or workbook available to performers for recording tax information. I have also provided a simple weekly worksheet in the appendix, to help keep track of your professional expenses. Make it your own by adjusting what you need to keep track of. After it's filled out, staple all of your backup receipts for the week to this worksheet and file it away. At the conclusion of the year, you will have very little to do to prepare for tax season.

RESUMÉ PACKET

Business cards, stationery and envelopes, paper, folder and envelope for presentation, photo costs, CDs, DVDs, on-line services and any other costs incurred when putting together your packet.

EQUIPMENT

Digital recorder and microphone, iPod/CD player, piano, keyboard, computer or laptop, cell phone, Blackberry, etc. The costs involved with purchasing and maintaining equipment used for your business can be used as a deduction. You can also take a deduction for the depreciation of certain equipment over time. If the equipment is not strictly used for business, only a percentage of these amounts can be deducted.

CAR EXPENSES

Requirements for deducting car costs are strictly enforced by the IRS. You must keep a log of business mileage and be accurate. If you use your car often for business, put a small notebook and pencil in your car. Log the miles whenever you travel for your business.

- Write down your starting and ending miles from your regular odometer. Subtract one from the other and put the mileage in your notebook with the date and why the trip was made. Make a habit of it.

- There is also a standard deduction per mile allowed by the IRS. Ask your accountant for the current information.

- Tally the mileage at the end of the year.

- Keep parking fee receipts, toll receipts, and the standard deduction for all of the miles driven for your business use (a flat rate per business mile or the miles you have logged) of driving your car for business. That includes about everything that you do for your car, from repairs to replacing parts, insurance premiums, license plates, and depreciation. But you *must* have receipts for all of these things, and are required to keep an accurate mileage log. Oftentimes the flat-rate deduction will amount to a larger tax deduction, though you still must keep a mileage log.

DUES, MUSIC, BOOKS, AND PUBLICATIONS

Union dues, subscriptions to singing industry publications, online sites, books used for aiding and educating you for your business, any music scores you buy, etc.

PERFORMANCE AND AUDITION EXPENSES

The cost of clothing/shoes and accessories used exclusively for auditions or performances. The cost of laundering or dry-cleaning your performance clothing. Repairs or alterations to performance clothing/shoes. Cosmetics, hairpieces or wigs, beauty parlor expenses used for performance only.

TRAVEL EXPENSES

The expenses that you incur while traveling for business are deductible. Plane, taxi, train, bus, subway, or any ground transportation while on business can be deducted. Hotel or lodging expenses, laundry, tips, telephone expenses, etc. are also deductible.

Only 80% percent of meals while on business are deductible, so create a separate category for this. If you are entertaining a client, save all of your receipts and be sure that you write on the back the cost of the meal, name of the person, and what business was discussed.

RECITAL EXPENSES

The rental of a hall, rehearsal space, publicity material, mailings, flyers, accompanist fees, any expenses that are incurred while preparing or performing a recital. Performance clothing, shoes, etc.

Setting up this process does take some time, but once it is in place and you faithfully take care of your business on a weekly basis, it becomes the habit and easy—everything is at your fingertips when you need it. If you *don't* do this work and make it a habit, waiting too long to file your receipts and record the necessary information, you probably won't remember what some of the items were for, or the dates they were purchased. Then it becomes a *real* chore, and lots of work.

UTILITIES

All long distance phone calls and a percentage of your local calls used for business purposes are deductible. Also faxes and a percentage of your expenses for online access are deductible. You must have copies of the bills with your business calls clearly marked as backup material.

BUSINESS SUPPLIES

DVDs, CDs, batteries, paper, pens, pencils, folders, files, envelopes, copies of music, documents, etc. Business supplies with a life of less than a year are not depreciated.

POSTAGE

Any postage not included in any other category that is used for your business.

MISCELLANEOUS

Anything for your business that does not already have a category goes here.

You'll find a blank form with these categories in the appendix for your use. Customize it to fit your specific needs and make several copies. (Keep the original to make additional copies in the future.) Make enough copies so that you have one for each week of the year, one for yourself to tally each category at the end of the year, and one for your accountant.

Put the blank forms in a file folder that will also hold all of your receipts for the past week. At the end of each week, with your checkbook, blank form and the receipts, fill in the amounts you spent in each category for that week. (Don't forget to check your monthly credit card bills for business items you spent money on as well.) Total each category. Staple the corresponding receipts onto the back of the corresponding week's report and file it in a new file folder called "Business Tax Information (with the appropriate year)."

When it's time for taxes, all you have to do is add up each category for its year-end grand total. These totals can then be put onto the extra form you made for doing your own taxes, or it can be given to your CPA/tax accountant. The categorized business expenses are now ready to be used on your tax form. Make sure you keep one for your records as well.

Once you have completed your taxes for the year, put all the forms with their stapled receipts in a manila envelope and mark the envelope with the appropriate year. Then keep them all in an appropriately and clearly marked box that holds only tax information. This also guarantees that if you are audited, you have all the pertinent information in one place, organized, and available. You must keep these yearly records for up to seven years.

Organization, having the correct information and implementing this process are the keys to making tax time easier. It's up to you as to how hard or easy you make this yearly task.

Fundraising

As a singer you will quickly find out how expensive it is to prepare for a career. Until you get your foot on the lower rung of that proverbial professional ladder, you need to be very resourceful and self-reliant when it comes to generating the monies needed to develop your product and make a career. You are an entrepreneur representing and presenting your Personal Brand, your product, and as such must believe that you have something unique and authentic to offer. As you gain a solid vocal foundation and start polishing your product, it is imperative that you are able to find ways to generate monies for moving your career forward through summer programs, competitions, and auditions. You must also continue honing your skills as a singer by working with more advanced coaches and perhaps even

It's good to have money and the things that money can buy, but it's good, too, to check up once in a while and make sure that you haven't lost the things that money can't buy.

– GEORGE HORACE LORIMER

an influential voice teacher who can make important introductions for you. This takes creativity, vision, and tenacity.

Or maybe you are ready to find a patron, sponsor, or an organization to help build your business from the ground up. An aspiring artist and young professional are always looking for ways to help finance their careers. You must learn to think like a business person who is promoting their product. Remember that this is business; it is not personal or emotional. Here are some of the more conventional ideas for raising funds:

- Schedule a concert six months out, so that you have time for organizing the details.

- Get a local organization interested in becoming a sponsor for a specific project where you might perform in return for their financial help.

- Find a patron who would be willing to help support you until you have hit the big time. In return, offer to be the entertainment at dinner parties, holidays, etc.

- Apply for a grant.

Forget that there is even a box that you can think outside of. With all the many wonderful sources for networking in the virtual and electronic world, find interesting and productive ideas that you think will work for helping you build a campaign worthy of your talent and vision.

As you move further up the rungs on the professional ladder, here are some suggestions on how to find, create and maintain a relationship with a sponsor or patron. This is someone or an organization with lots of discretionary money who wants to assist you in building your business and seeing it become successful. This requires a specific process. You first need to check through your mailing lists to see if you already know someone who fits the above description. When you have a couple of prospects in mind, contact them to see if they show any interest in getting together to allow you to present your well thought out proposal for helping you build your career and business. Then you have to put a business proposal together that you will ultimately present to them. Here is how that works.

Begin by making two lists. The first list will contain the items you would like to have financed, the individual expenses of each, and the time frame for your project. It could be something like 6 months worth of voice lessons, coachings, etc., or it could be for a specific project, like a summer program, a competition, or the expenses for an audition tour of Europe, or perhaps you want to present yourself in a concert where you will invite managers, conductors, etc.

The second list will be a list of everyone and every organization you know that might be of assistance in funding your project. For example, investigate any organizations you belong to: church, work, community groups in your area like opera guilds, Rotary Clubs, Kiwanis, garden clubs, etc. Talk to your immediate and extended family members, your doctor, dentist, lawyer, the owner of the local car dealership where your family bought their car, your voice teacher and coaches. Do an extensive internet search for specific people or organizations that might be interested in a project such as yours.

After you have finished the research for your two lists, it is time to put together a well thought-out and succinctly structured business plan. Your package should contain:

- A letter of introduction, written on your professional stationery, stating who you are, who suggested you contact them, what you feel you can accomplish with their help, and the benefits they will receive from helping you. These, for the most part, will be their involvement and close association with you as performer, i.e., going backstage after performances, free tickets to your events, perhaps having you entertain at their parties, and the joy of watching someone go from an aspiring professional to a professional singer. If they don't know you as a performer, you can offer to send them a CD or DVD, direct them to your website, or perhaps arrange to sing for them live. This will give you another opportunity to be in touch with them personally.

> *We are so accustomed to disguise ourselves to others that in the end we become disguised to ourselves.*
>
> — FRANÇOIS DUC DE LA ROCHEFOUCAULD

This letter must be able to capture their imagination and passion, so you will need to dig deep to find an honest, novel, and real way to express that. Keep this letter of introduction to one page, if possible. In your closing salutation, thank them for their time and attention, and let them know that if you haven't heard from them within two weeks, you will take the liberty of contacting them. Mark your calendar, and then follow through.

- If possible, include a letter or two of recommendation from someone who either knows the person you are addressing and/or is influential in our industry.

- On a separate sheet of your stationery, write an interesting one-page story containing information about your particular voice category, stories of the current or past singers in this fach that have influenced you and the roles and operas they sing, and how you intend to carry on this tradition.

- Compile a detailed list of expenses with defined categories. (*Example:* Summer Program: CATEGORY 1: Cost of program. CATEGORY 2: Flight, hotel, food, ground transportation to and from airport. CATEGORY 3: Performance clothing and shoes. CATEGORY 4: Purchase of scores or music for program. CATEGORY 5: Costs of preparing music or roles before you go—voice lessons, musical and lyric diction coachings.) These categories are important, because by breaking your requests down into smaller segments, you are more likely to have someone interested in perhaps helping you with at least one part. Once you have a commitment from one sponsor who will help you with a specific portion of your business, it will be easier to encourage others to become part of your support team. When putting your plan together, don't forget about asking for things like frequent flyer miles, or perhaps being able to stay in someone's home, etc. Be very creative when approaching your prospective sponsors.

- Include a current publicity photo, bio, résumé, and CD/DVD.

Getting experience in presenting yourself to sponsors, patrons, and organizations is the next step. You will want to practice your presentation first, by trying it out on a friend or two before presenting it to a prospective parton or sponsor.

Once you feel you are ready, do a mailing of your business plan package to the list of prospective sponsors you have compiled. If you haven't heard from your prospective patrons within the time frame you gave them to answer, follow up with a call to see if they are interested in making an appointment to go over your plan in person.

- When you present your package to a potential sponsor or patron in person, be sure to bring one for yourself. This way you will literally be able to be on the same page as you go over your plan together.

- If they feel they can't help, always ask if they know anyone else who might be interested in a project like yours and to keep you in mind if they think of some way they could help. If they give you a referral, ask if you may use their name in introducing yourself to the person they have suggested contacting.

- No matter the outcome of a meeting with a potential sponsor or patron, always write a handwritten thank-you note, to let them know how much you appreciated their time and attention; make sure everything is spelled correctly.

- Ask if you may stay in touch by keeping them updated with important events as they occur throughout your career. If the answer is yes, add them to your mailing list. As they see your progress, they may want to help at a later date.

- If the prospective sponsor is the president of an Opera Guild or some other group or business organization, your business plan might be something they will want to present to their entire group for consideration of their sponsorship. Or you might suggest that you would love to perform for their organization free of charge to help promote yourself.

Present the materials for your business plan package in an attractive presentation folder. Check and re-check for correct spelling. Make up several presentation folders in advance, so that you will be ready to make a presentation when you find an interested party, and need only to add a letter of introduction and a couple of your business cards.

Knowing that you have done this work, and have an impressive business plan packet together and ready, will help keep you motivated to find the sponsors, patrons, or organizations to help support your career. Remember to have several presentation packets prepared, so that you are ready when the time comes to present yourself or an unexpected opportunity arises. The work will have already been done, which helps you feel prepared and professional.

Grants

If you want to apply for a grant for a specific project, there are a number of great resources available to you.

Research for leads in finding appropriate funding sources. Do a search online to find the best fit for your project. If you are in New York City, the Foundation Center is a great place to start. You can also find them online at fconline. fdncenter.org. If you go in person, plan to spend an entire day—it is a learning adventure for sure. There are very qualified people there to help guide you through this process, to narrow down finding the information you need. There is no such thing as a stupid question, only an unanswered one, so ask away.

> *If you're not playing a big enough game, you'll screw up the game you're playing just to give yourself something to do.*
> — PETER MCWILLIAMS

- You need to have a specific project in mind before getting involved in this. Writing a grant proposal is basically a compelling argument as to why the funders should specifically fund your project. Why are you qualified to do this project? What is your track record so far? What evidence of probable success can you offer? What do you plan to accomplish through the project? What will the results be? How will you evaluate your success? Will there be any results for the community? What's in it for them?

- Contact funders for current guidelines and applications. The best way to contact them is to call or go online and see if you are a good match.

- Read the materials very carefully to make sure there is a good match between your goals and the funders' interests. Don't try to make what you want fit the funders profile, as it will be a big waste of your time, energy, and money. Continue looking for the right match. You will find it.

- Following the guidelines, begin to write your proposal. Write from your heart, with passion. Keep your writing easy to read and interesting. Tell them your story. Make them interested in your project and you. Use an active voice when writing. Let others read your work to see if it grabs them. See what they would change to make it better. Then decide what to use or not.

- Slim your proposal down by editing. Then proofread it yourself again and ask others to do so as well, just to double-check your information. Ask for whatever help and advice you need to get the job done. That may mean calling the funders themselves.

- Check spelling and math for errors. There can't be any—they are very picky about this.

- Make your proposal clean and well-organized, using bullets and headings to emphasize your main points and paragraphs.

- Don't ever give more than is asked for—it will not help. Follow their instructions to the letter. If they want or need more information or materials, they will ask for it.

- When you receive the grant for your project, always keep in touch with your sponsors. Send them a thank you note. Invite them to your project, if applicable. Send them tickets to the event, programs, reviews, etc. Keep them in the loop and interested. Put them on your "A" mailing list.

- Acknowledge them on your posters, programs, press releases, advertisements, etc. Because of your professional handling of this project, they may want to sponsor you again for another project in the future.

Because preparing for a career in singing is an expensive venture, it is important to look for sponsors, patrons or institutes that give grants to help support you while working toward your career. The best way to achieve this is to put together a well thought out business plan that is properly put together and well presented to those who might be interested in giving their support to you whether it is a sponsor, patron, or applying for a grant. There is money out there, but it is up to you to find it and keep it. A great motto for taking the plunge in the financial support arena is: "Leave no stone unturned." Always be networking and looking for interesting ways to help move you forward on your journey.

THE CLIENT—YOU, THE SINGER

Your company will not be able to sell and promote you, it's product, if you don't have the goods! This is not a profession for the faint of heart or those with any romantic notions, or a fantasy of what the lifestyle of an opera singer is like. It requires sacrifice in many areas of your life, plus having a beautiful natural instrument, great vocal technique, intrinsic performance instincts, musicality, passion for the music and story, and a burning desire to pursue a professional singing career. You also have to love networking, have some business savvy, and cultivate the skills and tools to consistently represent yourself—your Personal Brand— with panache.

An Indian guru appeared, clad in a loincloth. As he began to adjust my spine, like a chiropractor, I protested. "Stop, you're giving me a lot of pain." "No," he responded, "I'm giving you change. It's your resistance that's giving you the pain."

– AUTHOR UNKNOWN

JOB DESCRIPTION

- Realistic perspective of your talent
- Capacity to preserver and grow as an artist
- Ability to remain curious and flexible
- Love and propensity of and for business
- Passion and fortitude over the long haul
- Represent and present your Personal Brand at all times

This is the time and place to once again check in and do a recap of all the new tools and skills you have acquired, and review all your inner systems, patterns, and traits, so that you can put them into play when necessary, as well as to help remind you, if you get stuck or caught in your emotions, that you do have choices. So stay awake and present, and recognize the opportunity to be able to help yourself in these moments.

Life is like playing a violin solo in public and learning the instrument as one goes along.

– SAMUEL BUTLER

It's time for you as the client/singer to step up your game, and forge your own steady path at your own pace to the finish line—your goal.

And if, along the way, you discover that it's time to consider a different goal or path, bravo! More than anything else, life is about being content and happy with what you do, who you are and how you make all that happen in a sane, conscious, and mindful manner.

Once you have your ducks in a row, it's time to put all of your preparation to the test, and that happens in the form of auditioning and performing. We are going to start this section by talking first about the auditioning process, then job selection, rehearsals, and performance protocol, and finally the follow-up process that shows everyone that you are a professional in each of these areas. Knowledge is always power! The more you understand, the better prepared you are; the better prepared you are, the more you are finally ready to see and partake of the many opportunities that may have been there all along. Avanti!!

THE AUDITION PROCESS

> You'll always miss 100% of the shots you don't take.
>
> — WAYNE GRETZKY

Do you think in terms of strategies and tactics, and having an agenda, when thinking about auditioning and performing? Performers might feel they have done their job because they have completed the work it took to arrange and be granted an audition, and all that is left to do is focus on singing well. *Au contraire, mes amies!* The best auditions and performances happen when you go with an agenda. You are there to do business and to do your job in presenting the product. There are strategies and tactics that need to be implemented during this process of presenting yourself in an audition. The rest of the job entails creating and maintaining relationships which requires follow-up when you have finished your job of performing in an audition. That is good business all the way around. Preparation, action, and follow-up.

The Event

> When in doubt, make a fool of yourself. There is a microscopically thin line between being brilliantly creative and acting like the most gigantic idiot on earth. So what the hell, leap.
>
> — CYNTHIA HEIMEL

Auditioning is a process which is interesting, subjective, and provocative. Some might look at it as a necessary evil; I offer an alternative viewpoint. At this juncture, most of your formal training is complete. Don't get me wrong when I say that—yes, you still need to explore and expand the more exacting aspects of vocal technique, interpretation, languages, etc, but if you are auditioning, you must have the basics down by now. Experience is now going to be the best teacher to help solidify and hone your craft. Getting comfortable with the means of getting a job is just another part of this process. It is not unlike any other profession; you get better by doing. Getting work *is* your "job," and auditioning is just a word we use when describing the process by which that is done. It's now your *job*, nothing more, nothing less. The more you start using these words—"I'm now going to go do my job"—and believing it is your truth, the more quickly you will begin leaving all the emotional baggage out of the mix, which instantly changes the feeling and tone of this process of auditioning. If you don't believe me, try this: Speak these sentences one at a time, pausing between to notice what emotions are triggered, if any, with each sentence. Now think about how applying this to your habitual auditioning routine will help change your attitude about this necessary process.

1. The audition is tomorrow. I need to get all my materials together so I can be ready.

PAUSE – Notice how you are feeling. What emotions do you notice and how do they make you feel?

2. I have another job coming up at the end of this week that I need to prepare for.

PAUSE – Notice how you are feeling. What emotions, if any, do you notice?

I rest my case. It is now up to you, which words you want to benefit from using when seeing, listening to, and reflecting on this idea of auditioning. If you haven't had much experience doing this "job" yet, here are several simple professional tactics that will help make the event go smoother.

Go back to whatever section of this book resonated with you concerning the issue of comfort zones, to reacquaint yourself with the skills and tools available for breaking loose and getting unstuck from the stranglehold that your comfort zone creates. And don't forget to use your practiced Magic Carpet, for networking and schmoozing as well as auditions, inviting those listening into your personal space.

Tactics

Dress for success. Make sure you have all the pieces of your outfit clean, pressed, and ready to go. Let others see that you respect and take pride in yourself as you become even more of the young professional looking for a job. In other words, represent and present your Personal Brand.

Women: You want those experiencing your presence to be aware of what you can do vocally and dramatically, how you can take them through your story on a journey, so don't distract those listening with a flashy outfit that takes away from your performance.

There is no actual law that says that a person of inner beauty cannot also maintain an appearance.

– ROBERT BRAULT

> *If men can run the world, why can't they stop wearing neckties? How intelligent is it to start the day by tying a little noose around your neck?*
>
> **– LINDA ELLERBEE**

- My experience as an adjudicator tells me that simple is always better. That means an ensemble that fits well, makes you feel great, and shows you to your best advantage; a suit, tailored dress, skirt and sweater, etc., preferably with sleeves.

- Use scarves and/or jewelry to help give some bling and color if you feel it is part of your Brand. If you choose dangling earrings, make them tasteful. Make sure they don't get in the way of your performance, make noise, or distract those listening by too much movement.

- Can you sit comfortably in your clothing. Occasionally you are asked to sit and talk with those for whom you are singing. If you have a skirt that is too short or has a slit that can't be controlled while sitting, find another outfit.

- Wear heels, even if it gives you only a small lift. If you're not comfortable walking in 4-inch heels, don't wear them. Wear heels that are comfortable when you walk, stand and sing.

- Wear makeup. If you don't know how to apply it, go to any makeup or department store and have someone help you. Then practice putting it on..

- Keep your hair up and away from you face. Your face is the most expressive tool you have when you present yourself.

- Behave as if you already had the job. Represent your Brand.

> *Clothes make the man. Naked people have little or no influence on society.*
>
> **– MARK TWAIN**

Men: Simple is always better. You are interested in capturing others' attention by your ability to take those listening, watching, and experiencing your story on a journey.

- If you want to make a statement, wear a suit. Dark suits are best. If you need help with your wardrobe, go to a men's clothing store or department store and ask one of the sales people. They are usually very knowledgeable not only about what looks good on your body type, but on making sure the fit is perfect. They can also help you pick out a shirt with the proper collar type and color, and ties or accessories.

- Wear a shirt and tie that complement your suit, coloring, and each other. If you feel a tie is not appropriate, then wear a dress shirt, open at the collar, with or without a suit jacket—whatever is appropriate.

- Make sure your shoes are polished and match the color of your belt. Be sure your socks coordinate with your shoes and the color of your suit.

- Be sure your hair and facial hair are clean, trimmed, and neat.

- Dress as if you already had the job. Dress for success.

Allow enough time to be early to your event. This gives you time to get a drink of water, go to the bathroom, get focused and centered, etc. before you present yourself. If you are not sure of the physical location of the event, go online for both that information and a place to park if you are driving. If you are in a different city or country, determine ahead of time what options are available for getting to and from this event, and just how long it will take.

If you are sick, or have to cancel for some other reason, try to let those for whom you are singing know as far ahead of time as possible, so that they don't waste their time, energy, and money with an unused time slot. Make your conversation or e-mail short and to the point. They don't need to know the circumstances, only that you are ill or there is a real emergency—they don't need or want the details. This is part of living your Personal Brand and becoming professional. It shows others that you are thinking of more than yourself. And by offering this professional courtesy, you may be given an opportunity to audition at a later date. First impressions are important, so stay healthy. And whatever you do, don't start setting yourself up for failure by getting stuck in your comfort zone and making "getting sick" a

Always be a first-rate version of yourself, instead of a second-rate version of somebody else.

– JUDY GARLAND

convenient excuse for not doing your job. That will kill your career chances. Stepping outside of your comfort zone is always risky and scary.

- Make sure the accompanist you trust and want to share this experience with is available and book him/her ahead of time for that date. Do not forget to reconfirm the date and time a few days before the event.

- Double-check your book of arias meant for the accompanist. Make sure the pages are clean, have all the notes on each page, and are clearly marked with your particular cuts, added cadenzas, starting and ending places, breath marks, etc. *Do not* put your music in plastic sleeves. It not only makes it hard for the accompanist to turn pages, but also creates a glare which often makes it difficult to read the music. Paste the pages back-to-back, or print two-sided on a page, and place into a three-ring binder, odd-numbered pages on the right, with the names of the arias placed on tabs on the appropriate pages.

- If they are supplying the accompanist, find out who it is and see if you could arrange a time to work together a day or two before the event. (That goes for when you are out of town as well.)

- If you are using the accompanist furnished by the company and there has been no time to work together before this meeting, take the time when you give them the music to point out any cuts, special endings, rubatos, or rallentandos you will be taking. Don't take long to explain—they are professionals.

- It's wise to bring a PR packet along. You can offer it as you enter the meeting along with a list of your audition arias on a separate sheet of paper. They may or may not want the packet, but will probably take the aria list. It shows that you have prepared as a professional for this event.

- *Do not* take a bottle of water in with you—it is very unprofessional. Get a drink of water before you go into the meeting, and if it is truly necessary and you simply can't make it through just a few arias without a sip of water, excuse yourself for a moment and go out and get a drink of water.

One of the most interesting ways to feel more comfortable with those you're auditioning for is to find out all you can about them as people—not just what they do for a living, but who they are outside of the business they are in. What's their background, what outside interests do they have, where did they grow up, etc.? It also helps to research the background of the program, company, or competition you want to work for or become part of as well. Research of this kind allows those whom you're meeting with to seem less like strangers and more familiar, and they won't seem so intimidating. When you know someone's personal story, you realize that they are people, just like you, doing their job, just as you are.

If just doing your job still seems too intimidating, you might want to try creating a model of a person or persons who you deeply admire, and really step into that model or conglomerate of models of excellence, to see how it fits. Make sure that the model you choose supports and represents your core values and Personal Brand. Acting "as if" may be the answer to overcoming anxiety and nerves. It may be a persona you want to use when doing this particular job in the future. Make sure you try it out several times on friends and family before going public with it. And make sure it supports your Personal Brand. This is called modeling excellence.

Stay focused in the moment. Don't let your thinking mind, "The Brat," take over with its incessant, damaging inner babble. Instead, try this as you wait to be called into the audition: focus on letting the back of your tongue relax, and focusing your gaze on a particular object. Slowly, allow your gaze to move outward to the peripheral aspects of that object. Stay in this place for as long as you can. You can notice how it clears your mind and keeps you in the pres-

> Many performers use this technique of modeling excellence in their work. The pop star, Beyoncé, uses this strategy, saying that she is rather shy and needs to put on her "performing brand" when it's time for her to hit the stage.

ent moment. Always practice these kinds of exercises before using them for a real event. It's a fascinating process to participate in.

Once you are ready to do your "job" at this audition, take your place, then roll out your Magic Carpet, inviting all into your space, give your name and what you will start with, and begin.

ALWAYS start with the aria that makes you feel most comfortable, gives you the most confidence, and shows off what you can do to your best advantage. This is the aria you could sing well if someone woke you up at 3 in the morning and said sing. They might or might not ask for a second piece. They may even stop you somewhere in the aria and say thank you. This is neither bad or good. It means they have heard what they need to hear. Remember those that listen or adjudicate hear singers all the time and know what they are looking for and don't always need to hear you sing through the entire piece. If they are looking to fill a particular role, they might ask for a particular aria, or they may have heard all they need to hear. If however, you have prearranged to sing for a specific role, they will definitely want to hear specific sections of that opera, so be very prepared even if it is on book.

Never agree to sing something you have not prepared or don't feel is ready, even if they beg you to do so. Suggest instead that you would like the time to prepare it and would be happy to arrange another time to sing it for them. Remember that this is business, and as a professional, you want to present the product—your Personal Brand, you the singer—at its best. You don't want to appear less than the professional you are.

Almost every man wastes part of his life in attempts to display qualities which he does not possess, and to gain applause which he cannot keep.

– SAMUEL JOHNSON

After the Audition and Follow-up

No matter how much better you think you could have done your job, do not talk about it or show your emotions until you are out of the space physically and alone. Continue to represent and present your Personal Brand throughout this process. That means do not share it with the accompanist, or anyone else waiting to audition. If you feel the need to vent emotionally, try the following; When you get home, set the timer for anywhere between 10 to 15 minutes, and then let it rip! Allow yourself and your "Brat" to call yourself whatever names need to be expressed without editing. Yell and scream, get down and dirty by rolling around in the bottom of your mucky, humiliating self-loathing. And you have to go through this process at its full-blown level until the timer goes off, even if it starts feeling silly or unproductive before then. As soon as the timer goes off, you are done! No more thoughts of what was or second-guessing any notions those listening might have had. Instead, employ your time and energy learning from this particular experience, what you did well and where there is room for improvement and how you might want to go about making that happen. It's always about learning, adjusting and getting ready for the next job opportunity.

This is a great time to bring all your new tools and skills, inner systems, patterns, and traits to the table, to help you sort out what is real and how you might better adjust some of your thinking to give you the most productive results.

If the accompanist is someone you didn't know well or at all, and you find that you have great musical rapport, make sure to get their information and add it to your list of accompanists. Having a list a accompanists in the places where you do most of your auditions is very handy, because during the busy audition season, the few you know may already be booked. If you really liked working with this accompanist, you may want to schedule a couple of working sessions to get better acquainted musically and personally. Maintain a current list of available accompanists and share it with your fellow singers.

When you get home, both you and your manager need to fill out your audition page. Write down on the back of the page what things went well and what things need improvement from both perspectives. Also, record all your expenses on your weekly expense sheet (accompanist, cab, etc.). You can find both of these forms in the appendix.

Lastly, send a handwritten note to the person for whom you sang, thanking them for the opportunity. Let them know that you look forward to the prospect of working with them in the future. Check and double-check the spelling. I know from firsthand experience that it can make the difference in getting jobs, into apprentice programs, etc. You will be remembered for all the right reasons. It helps to put your name and Brand on the musical radar map.

Having the knowledge of what to expect when preparing for and performing (doing your "job") at an audition, will help take some of the anxiety and mystery out of the experience. Knowing that you have done everything possible as both singer/artist and your own business manager to make this a great experience will help you perform with confidence. The next job opportunity will become easier and more fun as you learn from the past, make the necessary adjustments from the lessons learned and simply repeat this process over and over successfully into the future.

Second-Guessing the Reasons Why

> *What you think of me is none of my business.*
>
> **— TERRY COLE-WHITTAKER**

Again, second guessing why you were stopped in the middle of the first piece you were singing, why you weren't asked for a second piece or any other second guessing questions you might have is a waste your time and energy. Having been on both sides of that coin as singer and adjudicator, I know from my own experience, that there are a plethora of reasons that have, most times, nothing to do with you or your singing. If you ever wondered what some of the reasons might be, here are a few ideas to consider:

- *First impressions* Your overall impression on others when you enter the space to sing is of paramount importance. Those hiring or adjudicating know the minute you show up if you are going to be good at what you do. So have your act together, represent your Personal Brand, and back that up with a great performance by doing your job. Show others that you are happy to be there and have this opportunity by being genuine and authentic. And above all, have fun!

- *Voice type* Perhaps your voice is to big, small, light, or dark to match with the rest of the cast that is already in place. Perhaps they hear your potential and will keep you in mind for a future production.

- *Repertoire* Auditioners get confused if you offer pieces that are from several differing voice fachs. They might feel you haven't settled down vocally quite yet, and no matter how well you sing they will probably pass you over.

- *Physical appearance* There may be an existing costume that those hiring need the person they are hiring to fit into. Or perhaps the rest of the cast is especially short or tall, and hiring you would make the overall piece feel out of balance, especially if the stage is a small one. (If you happen to be especially tall or very large, have your own generic costumes made and let them know by indicating this on your résumé.

- *Other factors* The part might already have been cast and these auditions are only a formality or an opportunity for those listening to discover new talent. Holding auditions is a way for companies to advertise themselves and prove their worth. They might not need any new singers at this time. They do however, need to keep their name before the public and at the same time know what new talent is out there so they can continue to build a pool of possible singers for their future productions.

Beauty, to me, is about being comfortable in your own skin. That, or a kick-ass red lipstick.

– GWYNETH PALTROW

These are just a few of the many, many reasons why you might not have been chosen this time around.

So stop wasting your time and energy trying to second guess the reasons they didn't select you. Instead take

A word of advice: The time spent before and during an audition or performance requires you to be purpose-driven. The many tactics that are needed to prepare you for a particular event, no matter what it is, require your time, energy, sometimes money, and focus each day. When this period of concentrated purpose has ended, there can be a feeling of let down or depression. That is normal. Give yourself a day to recover physically, mentally, and spiritually, then get back to your normal daily routine and on to your next project.

action, don't just react to what you think the answer might be. Use the suggestion of going over your audition from you, the singer's, point of view, then change seats and let your manager tell you what they thought went well and where there could be some improvement. Remember, don't have any preconceived idea of what they might say. It really works, but you have to try it to believe it. That way you can learn as much as you can from each new experience, and apply those lessons to any future situations, as you continue to get better at your craft in every way. This allows you to become more of *who you are* as you grow, representing and presenting your Personal Brand.

Your belief system in tandem with all your other inner systems, patterns and traits, create your reality and there is no other law. Continue getting comfortable with those parts of you, and use these new tools and skills to help you be more of your Personal Brand in all that you do especially when it's time to do your "job".

Unscheduled Audition

If you hear about an audition that you in your heart of hearts and those that support you, believe is right for you but have not been able to arrange an opportunity to sing for them, find out when and where the audition will take place. Go there prepared to sing. Before the event starts, or during a break go into the event space with your PR packet to ask those listening if there happens to be a no-show or unexpected cancelation, would they allow you to fill that audition time slot. Or perhaps they would listen to you just before or after the lunch break or at the end of the day. Be pleasantly assertive representing your Personal Brand in a professional manner. It is usually possible to snag someone else's accompanist to play for you and of course you have to pay them whatever fee is agreed upon. It is a wild card, but worth a try if you really believe that this particular opportunity to sing for these particular people would get you the job.

Make sure you have the correct title and mailing address for those you were able to sing for so you can send that very important handwritten thank-you note making sure all the spelling is correct. Even if you don't get to sing for them, send them a note saying that you hope they will include you in their audition schedule the next time they are in town. And check and recheck your spelling. Put them on your "A" mailing list so your name stays in their mind with your upcoming performance events and reviews.

It is important once you get your name out there to keep it circulating. That is done by continuing to sing well, presenting your Personal Brand at all times, getting jobs and networking. Keep those on your "A" List updated on your successes and apprised of any upcoming events. And just like everything in life, you get better at going through this process we call auditioning, and what I call doing your "job," by gaining more and more experience. You will continue to learn something new about yourself and your expanding comfort zone by getting comfortable with and continually utilizing your new-found inner systems, pattern and traits and then applying this knowledge to help expand your Personal Brand and singing career.

Every time you don't follow your inner guidance, you feel a loss of energy, loss of power, a sense of spiritual deadness.

– SHAKTI GAWAIN

Job Selection

I feel it's important to say something about this subject because sometimes it's hard to know, especially at the start of your career, which jobs may benefit you and which may not. Many of my own students ask me how to best sort, select, and choose the best jobs for them right now. And that is the key point: You might feel overwhelmed or in doubt about whether it is the right thing to be doing at that particular time. Sometimes you simply have too much on your plate, but feel you cannot turn down a job opportunity, es-

It's important to learn how to allow your attention to rest where the working surfaces meet and when it is time to change from one task to another, to be able to stop what you are currently doing, leave all thoughts and emotions involved in that project there as you walk out of that imaginary room and close the door. This allows you to leave everything associated with what you were just doing behind that closed door. You will step into the empty, peaceful imaginary hallway for a moment, not permitting any old or new thoughts in, giving yourself time to center and breath. When you feel ready, you can open whatever new door you choose to that will occupy the next task, event, problem, etc., and be there without having drug the baggage from the last project to distract you from what needs to be done now.

pecially if it pays. Here are a few ideas to consider when offered a job:

- Understand and be certain of what roles you should be currently singing. Stick with the roles within your present voice category until you have had several years of professional experience getting those particular roles under your belt. Once you get comfortable with performing within your fach it may be that you are offered a role a bit beyond what you are singing at the time. Always check in with your teacher, mentor, coaches when approached with this type of offer. It might be just the right role/piece to help you grow vocally and dramatically. My advice is to do only one such new role every couple of years and get that securely under your belt by performing it with several different companies while you are continuing to stay within your normal fach. This gives you time to grow into that role and experience it in varying circumstances. As you gradually add other new roles from this new fach, you may find that you have made a controlled, smart and positve change into this new fach. Your voice will have had the opportunity to grow holistically in the right direction without being pushed or rushed.

- Know how much work you can handle comfortably before accepting anything new. Your intention should always be to give all of your attention to each job you have. For example: would you feel comfortable performing a major or minor role in one opera while learning another role or piece of music or singing an important audition, and having a full or part time job all at the same time? Be honest about how that works for you? There is no right or wrong. Is that overwhelming or can you easily change gears as you move from one task to another?

- No matter where or what size role you are performing, you want to treat each opportunity with professionalism. You never know who might eventually become a person of influence and importance within your cast and crew whether it is a community program, semi-professional, or professional situation. It could be the conductor, a stage director or colleague who changes positions within the framework of your performance industry going from in front of the footlights to behind the scene or even into the management end of some company or into a management agency. You always want to leave a great impression that you are a complete artist, can behave in a professional manner and are a genuine human being. You can do that best by being true to and representing your Personal Band.

This is another great arena in which to employ your well-practiced inner language, rapport, and listening skills. And if you feel yourself listening to the messenger instead of the message, step off your emotional Inside Time line, leaving the emotion "over there," so that you can clearly understand what is really being said. This is business. And don't be tempted to accept the wrong job just because it pays you something; another opportunity will present itself. There are three main reasons for accepting an engagement:

1. To make money

2. To be heard by and to work with influential people who might get you a paying job in the future

3. To benefit from the experience of performing a particular role for the first couple of times in a safe, comfortable situation

Do not think you have to accept everything that comes your way. Experience is useless if it doesn't create a positive outcome for you. It just becomes a time and energy stealer that could be put to better use doing another task within your business plan. Remain smart, awake, and use your management team to help you look at where you are right now and where you eventually want to go and the best path to take to get there. Always checking in with your management team gives you a more well rounded and often dif-

Quit now, you'll never make it. If you disregard this advice, you'll be halfway there.

– DAVID ZUCKER

ferent and interesting perspective from which to view your progress. You have the tools in place to help you make important decision, so use them.

Rehearsals

With the time and budget constraints of today's world, the amount of rehearsal time prior to performance is short and concentrated.

Knowing all you can about the composer, librettist, time line of the story, customs of that time and place, your character and establishing ideas about the relationships between characters will give you a huge edge on being comfortable with the rehearsal process. This means filling out a detailed character chart for your character and also for every other character in the piece and researching as much as you can about every aspect of the time line in which this piece takes place plus what inspired the composer and librettist to write this piece.

You also might want to work with a drama coach who specialized in this particular type of role or contact someone who has had a lot of experience singing this particulate role to see if they might be interested in working with you on it. This kind of work helps confirm you as the professional.

Often if the entire cast are novices, the work you will have done to prepare yourself for this job—your understanding, expectations, and actions as the character—will actually elicit the kinds of reactions and responses from the other singers' characters that you expected, and will help establish the tone of the story being told. This works especially well if the stage director doesn't have a strong concept of the character, or there isn't much time to develop the character in rehearsals.

However, always remain flexible and curious if the stage director does have a different and specific idea of who your character is and how the interaction is to take place.

> *"Come to the edge," he said. They said, "We are afraid." "Come to the edge," he said. They came. He pushed them... and they flew.*
>
> – GUILLAUME APOLLINAIRE

When this occurs, be open and invest in their ideas with confidence. This is a great way to start creating within yourself, the process of constructing your ultimate rendition of this character. It's how it is formed, by incorporating bits and pieces of others' ideas of the character. And if there is no time for discussions or expectations for your character from the stage director, you will at least have a base from which to work.

Always arrive with your music and words memorized; work your music with a drama coach, a lyric diction coach, and a music coach before you get there. Secure your success by being prepared. This is your work insurance. By doing this kind of work, you are more likely to be rehired and your name given in recommendation to other companies.

Entering the higher level of professional performance for the first time can seem overwhelming, even though you have had experience rehearsing for previous productions. The feeling is somewhat similar to the difference between being a senior in high school and a freshman in college. Every time you move up the ladder in the professional world, it seems like there is always something new to discover and learn. You might feel a bit intimidated by the ease and professionalism of those with whom you are working. Remember, the only difference is that they have had more experience, the opportunity to work with their skills and tools more often and all done within professional circumstances. They also might have had the opportunity of performing with several of your current colleagues, including the stage director and/or conductor, so that also creates a different dynamic within the rehearsals. Take advantage of learning from the consummate professionals in your cast by watching, listening and absorbing what they do and how they do it. In some cases it may be what not to emulate.

The choice is yours as to how you want to be perceived by the company you are working with, so be smart and pre-

Many of life's failures are people who did not realize how close they were to success when they gave up.

– THOMAS EDISON

Remember, everyone is a good example; some people are good examples of what to do, and some people are good examples of what not to do.

Here is a great opportunity to stay out of your emotions, and use your communication, rapport, and listening tools and skills. Knowing how you learn best, which inner systems, patterns and traits of the motivational systems you use will allow you to understand when you are falling off the horse and under their habitual spell. Once felt and recognized, you can then choose to change your mind about how you want to handle the situation in a more productive and professional way.

pare yourself before you even get there. Keep your personal tools and skills at the ready, so that you will feel confident in handling whatever is thrown your way, as you continue to represent your Personal Brand. Here are some points to consider regarding rehearsals:

- Dress comfortably but professionally—don't go in cut-offs and a t-shirt. Wear something that is appropriate, causal, and comfortable to work in. As a woman, you might request a rehearsal skirt to practice in. Be true to your Personal Brand, the professional image you want to create and maintain, no matter what anyone else is wearing.

- I can't stress this enough: Go having your music and words memorized and in your voice. There will not be time to have someone teach you your music or words. It is rude, unprofessional, and insulting to your colleagues and management, which includes the conductor and stage director, when you are not prepared. When another colleague comes not knowing their part, you will quickly realize how you view them as unprofessional, as well as your annoyance that their lack of preparedness is holding everyone else back. This singer will probably not be asked back.

- Introduce yourself to the other cast members and to the conductor and stage director. It is not uncommon to feel a little uncertain and like an outsider when rehearsals first begin. It is possible that the other cast members have worked together at different times in their careers. Once you are involved in the process of rehearsal and performance, this feeling should go away.

- Never get involved in the politics of the company. Be friendly with the staff, but keep it professional even when you fraternize or socialize with them. Getting too close can create a very uncomfortable situation for you and could hurt your chances of being hired back.

- You may be asked to represent the opera company at an event, or do interviews for the local TV station or newspaper. Make sure to get copies of any publicity materials you appear in. Be gracious about it—in the long run, it is publicity for you. It also makes you a good candidate for a return performance with the company. To put "butts in seats," the public and audiences need to love you, and this is another opportunity for them to get to know you.

- Ask if there will be an audio and/or DVD made of the performance. Make sure you get copies of both if available. Excerpts can then be used on the CD/DVD you send out with your résumé packet, and also used on your own web site, as well as other appropriate internet sites to help promote yourself.

- There will be musical rehearsals with the other cast members and the conductor, so even through your part is memorized, bring your score. This way you can mark any pertinent and specific directions the conductor may have for you. At the end of the day, study the specific items in your score so you can be better prepared for tomorrows rehearsals.

- For working purposes, at the start of rehearsals the set will most likely be lines marked off with tape on the floor in a rehearsal room. You probably will not see the actual set until at least dress rehearsal. If you feel the need, and there is time, arrange with the stage manager to spend a few minutes on the set when it becomes available, so that you are comfortable.

- Often the first staging rehearsal is a talk-through, where the stage director gives only the logistics of where to move and when. Bring your score and a pencil to mark your movements. This is often done as you're singing, so you will need to have your score and pencil with you throughout the process.

When returning to the place you are staying after a day of staging rehearsals, spend time going over your notes on the staging that you put in place that day, practicing it in your imagination, and once that is secure, putting it into the context of the whole opera scene by scene as the staging progresses over the rehearsal period. This will help you feel secure and allow you to get off book as soon as possible. Your imagination is a great place to practice, so use it.

If you do not yet have a method of marking your stage directions down, there are some shortcut markings that are helpful for notating the directions in your score. Make a small diagram in your score on the appropriate page for each set change. Use these diagrams and stage direction markings to study and prepare for the next day's rehearsals.

- "**X**" means to cross
- "**→**" means to move to another place on stage in the direction of the arrow
- "**L**" refers to stage left, and is to your left as you are looking at the audience
- "**R**" means stage right, and is to your right as you are looking at the audience
- "**U**" means upstage, toward the back of the set.
- "**D**" means downstage, toward the audience.

These markings will be used together in a sequence to tell you where you need to move. You can also use the initials of each character to remind you to whom you will be crossing or moving toward. (XDSL to D = cross down stage left to Dorabella.) This will allow you to make notations quickly, and more importantly, be able to understand them later when it's time to study the day's work.

Be attentive during rehearsals. Do your work with concentration and have an open mind. Don't goof off! Play is for after rehearsals or during the breaks, even if others don't adhere to this practice. Stay focused and professional.

- Never leave the rehearsal without asking permission. (There is usually a stage manager at these rehearsals taking notes, etc and they will be the one that will need to know.)

- Remember that most rehearsal periods aren't very long anymore, so make the most of them. Don't wait until the performance to act and react as the character. Practice what you want and need to do as the character. Don't be inhibited. It will be your reputation and Personal Brand on the line when you perform. Do the work.

- If something within the staging doesn't work for you, speak up. It has to be comfortable for you. Simply say you are having a problem accomplishing their goal and could they perhaps show you another approach to make it work. If you have a major concern about your direction make an appointment to discuss it with your stage director privately. And whatever you do don't be on the defensive. Try to ask questions that use "how" and "what," rather than "why." "Why" questions often make others feel they need to defend themselves and their position, and creates an unhealthy atmosphere and relationship.

- If you can, use your props during rehearsals. If the actual prop is not available, use a "rehearsal prop."

- If you have a tricky costume, headpiece, shoes, etc., ask to rehearse in them. I have found that wearing the shoes I will be performing in and a rehearsal skirt helps me establish the feel of my character and how to move as the character. (most women buy and bring their own performance shoes which are usually bought in a dance store.)

- During costume fittings, be flexible, but if something does not work say so and see if you can have some adjustments made so you are comfortable. The same applies to shoes, wigs, jewelry capes, and hats.

Worry is a darkroom where fears are developed and enlarged.

— TERESA EAGEL

The costumes you will be wearing, unless they have been made specifically for you, will have been worn many times by others. I have made it a practice to bring my own new under-arm sweat guards, to have stitched into my costume for my performances. (They also come with straps so that they can be taken on and off as needed, and hand-washed in between performances.) It is a courtesy to others, as well as to yourself.

- There may be a costume parade for the stage director, designers and others. This is to see how things flow and look on the singer, how they work with the set as well as how the costumes look with lighting.

- When you move to the set on the stage, practice on it as much as is possible. There may be different levels or stairs to work with. Get comfortable.

- Often during the rehearsal periods, the lighting may continue to be adjusted. Don't let that throw you.

- Stay out of the way backstage. The stage manager will call you when it is time for your entrances. Always be courteous to everyone backstage which will be easy to do if you continue to represent your Personal Brand.

- There might be what is called a *sitzprobe* rehearsal (from the German, literally, a "seated rehearsal"), where the entire cast assembles on stage in front of the fire curtain or in a rehearsal room with the orchestra and conductor to sing through the complete opera prior to the dress rehearsal. This usually does not include the chorus. Bring your score just in case there are last-minute suggestions or adjustments.

- If you are lucky, you will be given a dressing room. If it can be locked, bring what you want and need to be comfortable. Leave your valuables at home. The dressers will take very good care of you if you represent your Personal Brand, by being genuine, friendly, and courteous, and not acting like a diva.

As you can see, you are finally able to put to good use all the many personal, business, and performance skills and tools that you have acquired, in almost every aspect of your performance process. Knowledge is power, and it is very satisfying to realize that you are continuing to grow and change while you continue achieving professional status. All your hard work is paying off. Experience is the best teacher, and this is just the beginning.

Performance

This is the moment you have been working toward. This is the time to trust all the many things you have learned, how prepared you are and allow yourself to enjoy each moment of the performance. Permit yourself to let go of the student and become the artist, the performer, the professional. Let the passion you feel for the music, story, and character you are portraying touch the audience. It is your time to take the audience on a journey. Scoop them up in your arms and gently return them after the performance. Enjoy yourself.

An important reminder: Don't try anything new that might upset you physically or mentally before a performance. (Foods, prescribed or over the counter medication, first time chiropractic or acupuncture appointment, massage, etc.) Stick to your tried and true routine.

When it comes time for performance, we often take ourselves off track by imposing impossible expectations on ourselves. The best advice I can give you is to know you are as prepared and ready as you can be at this stage of and point in your career, and are going to give your OPTIMAL performance. You are there to do a job. You might notice that just having read that word, or saying it out loud, instantly relieves that feeling of stress you have placed on yourself with your expectations, and makes you feel like you can accomplish it. Thinking of giving an optimal performance leaves all kinds of room for knowing that you might fall off the horse here and there, and that's okay—you can recover and get right back on. It also leaves open the opportunity to have one of those performances in which the stars and planets are perfectly aligned, and you perform way beyond your wildest expectations. But, as a rule, optimal is where you want to be focused—that is respecting your humanness, and getting the "job" done. You are not a Greek hero or any other performer, current or from yesteryear; you are, however, unique and authentic, just because you are you, and that is enough. Here are some suggestions for the day of performance:

> *Chase down your passion like it's the last bus of the night.*
> — TERRI GUILLEMETS

- Enjoy the day. Rest, do the things that are right for you to become "performance ready". Don't fixate on what has happened up to today or the pending performance. Go out for a walk or a run. Take your mind off of the performance itself. If you have done the work, you need to trust and allow yourself to be in the moment and it will take care of itself.

- Know how much time you will need prior to the performance at the theater to get ready and feel comfortable. Take into account traffic, weather, etc.

- By this time you should have figured out what and when to eat before a performance. It differs for everyone. However, do eat something. You will be using a lot of energy during the performance.

Bring what you need to be comfortable for the performance. Some suggestions of what should go to the theater with you:

- Your score.

- Cards, flowers for cast members and backstage personnel. It's not done much anymore in the USA, but it is a tradition to give opening-night cards to the conductor, stage director, and fellow colleagues. Write a short, personal note to each about how much you enjoyed working with them and wishing them good luck for this opening nights performance and you hope there will be an opportunity to do this all again in the future. It is a nice gesture at the last performance, to give your dressers, wig person, make-up artist and any others who have worked personally with you every night, a thank you note as well, with a small tip ($5–20, depending on their services), or if you prefer, a small gift, as a token of your appreciation.

- Robe

- Lotion/hairspray/shampoo/conditioner

- Washcloth, towel and soap

- Deodorant
- Toothbrush and toothpaste
- Something to replenish your energy between acts (grapes, protein bars, etc.)
- Water
- Pitch pipe for warming up (Make sure you are warmed up physically, mentally, and spiritually, as well as vocally.)
- A mint or similar to put in your mouth, to keep the saliva present, and out of courtesy for those "close" duets
- Appropriate dress clothes for men and women if you are going out after the performance, makeup for women

Additionally, here are a few other pre-performance items to consider:

- Check your costume each time. Make sure it is all there and does not require any repairs.
- Check that your props are in place.
- Go to the stage, if you can, and make your first entrance.
- Get into your make up, costume, and wig. If you are sharing your dressing space, always ask about using hairspray before apply it.
- Don't wear perfume or cologne. Many people are allergic to it.
- Always use deodorant and take the time to clean your teeth. It is a show of respect and courtesy to your colleagues.
- Look through your score, if you need to.
- Give yourself time to be by yourself to get centered—in the zone—and in character before you go onstage. If you don't have a private dressing room, ask if there is a room somewhere where you could be by yourself for a few minutes.

FINANCIAL PLANNING REMINDER:

• Keep all receipts related to this performance. All expenses incurred while on the road for this production are tax deductible.

• Take a manila envelope and put the name of the company, date (beginning to end) of your employment, and all your receipts in it. Make a habit of checking to see if you have the receipts from everything you purchase or eat.

• When you get home, process your expenses as suggested in the Taxes section. Do it right away before you forget what the expenses were for.

• Do this for each separate performance. At the end of the year it will be much easier to prepare your taxes.

> The one thing that matters is the effort. It continues, whereas the end to be attained is but an illusion of the climber, as he fares on and on from crest to crest; and once the goal is reached it has no meaning.
>
> – ANTOINE DE SAINT-EXUPÉRY

Things can go askew during a performance while you are doing your "job." That is one reason why it is of paramount importance that you are solid with your words, music, and staging. It has probably happened to nearly every singer during a performance, where a conductor unknowingly gives you a wrong musical cue to come in too early, or tries to hold you back though you know it's the proper time for a musical entrance. Or a piece of the set comes down unexpectedly, a prop is not there, someone steps on your dress, train, or cape as you start to move and it rips, your sword gets caught on something, someone forgets his or her entrance, etc. This is part of "show biz," and it does happen. Part of your job is to keep the opera running as smoothly as possible. So be prepared. If your music, words, and staging are solid, you will be better prepared to handle any peculiar incidents that might occur during the show.

Acknowledging Your Audience

Applause is the only way the audience—who have just gone through this emotional rollercoaster ride with you—has of expressing their thanks, and releasing their pent up energy. Taking a bow is the manner of acknowledging and accepting the audience's appreciation for what you have given them, and needs to be done well, otherwise they feel cheated—as if you don't feel what they are offering is valued. Learning how to feel their response is an intrinsic matter, and you must pay attention to how you accept their appreciation, and when is the precise time for you to take your leave.

For a company bow, women always enter and exit the stage first, then the men. This process starts with the smaller roles entering first and they also leave first when taking a company or group bow. The leading roles enter last and leave last. When you take a solo bow, take your time. Example: starting at your left, make a slow steady sweep with your eyes around the auditorium all the way to the right side. As you do this, try to pick out several people in the audience to very quickly make eye contact with, and never forget the balcony. Then, facing center, on a slow count of 1–2–3, take your bow, holding that position for another slow count of 1–2–3. Rise, and if warranted, bow again. You have to give the audience time to release all their energy for what they feel toward you. If you don't, they may become frustrated and insulted that you have not accepted what they want and need to give to you. As you can imagine, this, like every other process you have learned up to this point, takes lots of practice in order to make it seem seamless and get really good at it.

Remember that the show is never over until you return home or to your hotel room, so continue to represent your Personal Brand until you get home. You may have fans waiting outside the stage door that want autographs or want to talk to you after the performance, or you may have to go to a party given by a patron. Be generous and gracious to them. Never ever let anyone know your failings or what you could have done better during this particular or any other performance. That bursts their romantic fantasy bubble. They don't want you to be normal, human, or like them. They want you to remain that character they have created when they think about experiencing your performance. Apply your schmoozing and communication skills. These are the people who will become your fans, the ones who will buy your CDs and DVDs, support you in performance, and want to see you hired again, so be generous while presenting your Personal Brand.

After all the performances are over, and before you leave for home:

- Make sure you get all of your reviews, photos, CDs, and DVDs. If they are not yet ready, they may have to send them to you, so make sure they have your current mailing address and phone number.

- What payment arrangements have you made with the management of the company? Make sure they have your current address if they are mailing your payment or make sure you get paid before you leave.

- Always be networking. Get to know all the singers, conductors, pianist, choristers, artistic director, general director, etc. Hand out business cards and get them from others, and stay in touch via your "A" and "B" mailing lists.

- Leave a great impression behind by continuing to be consistent through your Personal Brand. Try making an appointment with the artistic and/or general director. Ask if they know what operas they are considering for the next couple of seasons. If there is a role that interests you, let them know it even if you have to re-audition. Tell them how much you have enjoyed working with everyone involved in this production. What a great opportunity this has been and would they be comfortable with your keeping them updated on your future performances. Also, if you seem to be in their favor, you might ask if you could use their name when introducing yourself to others in the industry. Be genuine. Represent and present your Personal Brand.

It would be pertinent to also have a private talk with the conductor and stage director to see if they have anything coming up that might be right for you. Or perhaps they might be willing to suggest you to some company, or symphony that they will be working with in the future. This is called doing business and it is your job. Again, ask if they would be comfortable with your keeping them updated with your future performances and if you could use their names as a means of introducing yourself to others in the industry when applying for future auditions.

When you get home:

- Write a hand written thank you note to the General Director, conductor, stage director, stage manager, patrons, and anyone else you think might be appropriate. Check and double-check spelling.

- Keep in touch with the other singers via the virtual world, by letting them know how much you enjoyed performing with them and what you have coming up. If the right occasion came up, they might recommend you for a job. And of course you would do likewise. Our profession is not about competition, but about community and helping one another.

- If necessary, give yourself perhaps a day or two to recuperate. Remember, there might be a period of feeling let down or depressed after a performance, especially if you do not have another performance coming up right away. This is normal. Do not give in to it. Remember to stand tall and be your Personal Brand. Getting back into to your personal and business routine right away will help alleviate that bump in the road. Move on to doing something each and every day to move you closer to you ultimate goal. Prepare for the next performance, competition, apprentice or summer program and keep looking for the next opportunity to perform.

The promises of this world are, for the most part, vain phantoms; and to confide in one's self, and become something of worth and value is the best and safest course.

— **MICHELANGELO**

You now can say that you are a professional performer. This is just the beginning.

Concert Performance

Presenting yourself in concert or a recital is a good way to help keep your name in front of the public and those on your "A" list.

If you're self-producing your concert, find the best venue you can afford to rent for this occasion. Be sure to check the acoustics and feedback in the hall from where you will be singing, to make sure they work for you. It's ideal if the venue is centrally located, with easy and available parking.

- Is the venue big or small enough to accommodate those you are inviting?

- Is there a room in the back where you can change into your performance outfit, and where you can wait before going on-stage?

Once you have found the right place, make your deposit. Contact your favorite accompanist to see if they are available for the for the rehearsal and performance dates for the event.

- Will you charge an entrance fee or will your program ask for donations.

- Do some of your pieces require a small instrumental ensemble? If so, hire them right away and have them secure your rehearsal and performance dates, and be sure to reconfirm prior to the performance.

- Will you have your CDs or DVDs available for sale during this event?

- Consider asking a friend to act as stage manager on the day of performance, to make sure everything runs smoothly, leaving you free to concentrate on your performance. Give them a checklist in advance of items that need attention.

- Is a page-turner needed for the performance?

Call a few days before the rehearsal and performance dates, to confirm the already agreed-upon times. Make certain that any advance arrangements you've made are in place, and that you have all the equipment needed like extra lighting, extension cords, a chair for the page turner, outlets for recording equipment, chairs and music stands for other musicians who will be performing with you, etc.

Being professional and prepared in this way gives you a feeling of great confidence in your ability to present yourself in performance. As you start this whole process of putting a recital or concert in place, mind map or list all the things you can think of that will need to be taken care of ahead of time so you will not have to spend your precious time, energy and money running around before a rehearsal or performance making sure things are in their place. Ask for help when and if you need it. Don't wait until the last minute. This is presenting a consistent Personal Brand in a professional manner and continues to build your self-condifence.

I'm not funny. What I am is brave.

– LUCILLE BALL

REHEARSAL

- Arrive early to double-check that all is in place. Check in with the onsite stage manager. Walk around the stage and get comfortable. Find the dressing rooms and see what you will need to bring to make yourself comfortable on the day/night of performance. Check the lighting. If you are wearing new shoes for the performance, make sure they are properly scuffed on the bottoms so you won't slip and be sure to wear them during rehearsals to get comfortable with them.

- Check everything you will be wearing and using several days before the performance. Make sure your outfit is pressed and clean, hems, snaps, buttons, hose, socks, shoes, etc. are ready. Put everything you are going to need to take with you for your performance out or in a cloths bag a couple of days before you perform. That way you will see very quickly if you need to fix or replace something. It will give you peace of mind and allow you to concentrate on what needs to be done next.

- Make sure your accompanist and any other musicians involved have their music and understand where they are going, what they are to wear and what time to be there.

- Often it is either too cold or too hot in the waiting space, so be prepared. Bring something extra to help keep you either cooler or warmer.

> *Of course I'm ambitious.
> What's wrong with that?
> Otherwise you sleep all day.*
>
> **— RINGO STARR**

- Never try new medications/vitamins, whether prescribed or over the counter on the day of rehearsal or performance. Try them a week or so before so you can see how they affect you physically and emotionally.

- Stick to your normal routine. Do not try something out of the ordinary the day of a performance, i.e. massage, hair coloring, food, chiropractor etc..

PERFORMANCE

Here is a great place to put all of your practiced skills and tools to use. Use your Magic Carpet to invite your audience into your space. After the performance it's time to use your networking skills: inner language tools, rapport and listening skills. Allow your "Brat" to help you stay on point.

- Be prepared for anything. Deal with things by staying in the moment and focusing on what needs your attention in that moment only.

- Get to the performance space in plenty of time to do makeup, dress, and warm up. Leave time to get centered before you step out on stage.

- When you perform in an oratorio or other orchestral solo work, don't cross your legs while sitting on stage waiting for your turn to sing. Men should have two feet on the floor or sit with one foot forward and one foot under their chair, as if about to stand up. Women should sit with ankles crossed and feet to the left or right. Do not bring water onto the stage.

- The only time it's appropriate for an artist to applaud while on stage is when the conductor acknowledges the chorus and orchestra.

Follow-Up

As you already know, follow-up is a very important part of the professional process. Here is where you will use many of the business systems, skills, and tools you have already learned and are already available and in place. Always be working toward the next performance, audition, or competition. Until that opportunity arises, settle back as quickly as you can into your regular daily routine of work, and begin setting up lessons, coachings, and performing the necessary business maintenance tasks as you continue to pursue your career.

Here are some additional reminders and follow-up suggestions:

- Organize, copy, and file the information from your recent performance.

- Scan and send your program, any reviews, and perhaps a sound bite to the contacts on your "A" list.

- Put any new business cards in your business card holder and add the information to either your "A" or "B" list.

- Using your receipt folder from your recent performance, fill out your weekly tax information sheet and staple the appropriate receipts to the back. File these.

- Post your current reviews, photos, and sound bites on your personal web site. You can also add these materials to any other appropriate outside web sites.

- Lastly, write a short handwritten thank you note to the General Director, conductor, and stage director, saying how much you enjoyed the experience and that you look forward to working with them in the future. Check all spelling.

- If any of your recent colleagues live in your immediate area, call and see if they would like to have lunch or coffee. When you talk with them share any information you have about upcoming auditions and ask them if they know of anything coming up that would be appropriate for you, upcoming auditions, local performance groups you might not have heard of

The more chance there is of stubbing your toe, the more chance you have of stepping into success.

– **AUTHOR UNKNOWN**

or a church job as substitute for a colleague who may be ill or out of town.

- Start setting up lessons and coachings for the next project. Bring reviews with you to show those you work with.

- If you don't have another singing job right away, get prepared to perform again.

> *The question isn't who is going to let me; it's who is going to stop me.*
>
> – AYN RAND

Auditioning offers you an opportunity to show your stuff. How you choose to present yourself is of paramount importance so go ready to do your job with an agenda, and represent and present your Personal Brand in every way: how you dress, your attitude, your preparedness, your flexibility. This lets those for whom you are auditioning get an idea of the consistency of who you are, your Personal Brand and how you can benefit their company. It is an opportunity to use many of the "Personal Tools and Skills" you have gained. And don't forget your partner, your accompanist in this event. Arrange enough in advance to secure the accompanist with whom you have the most personal and musical rapport. It helps give you confidence and assures you of giving a comfortable and well rehearsed performance; getting the job done. Sing what you do best first. Go the extra mile with a handwritten thank you note to those for whom you have sung. You will be remembered for you professionalism and charm.

Now it is time to land that job. When you are hired you must be familiar with the terms and language involved in a contract. Do your homework by researching other types of contracts becoming familiar with their terms and content, then ask any questions you need to help put you at ease when it comes time for you to sign on the dotted line. Or by having done this research, you can create your own contract when you are producing your own performance. It can be simple, but you need to know how to cover your bases.

Knowing what to expect once you are involved in professional rehearsals and performances will help relieve some of the fear and doubt that can accompany the first few performing jobs you have. And they can be daunting, but with the information you now have, you will not only appear more professional but will be considered as the new young professional representing your Personal Brand in every way with consistency. Watch how others handle themselves. Listen carefully and with attention so you can learn what you want to add to your own way of doing things and what things you definitely want to steer away from. During rehearsals, stay awake and present, not allowing your mind to wander, so that you don't miss any pertinent blocking or general information. Become a generous colleague during performances. That also extends to those backstage—the stage manager, stage hands, as well as those who worked on your costume, make-up, wigs, etc., and helped you into them each performance, facilitating your transformation into the character. You will be remembered for all the right reasons.

If you are feeling down and a bit depressed after getting home from a performance, know that this is normal. Don't let these feelings go on for more than a day. Getting back to your regular routine is one tried and true way to help avert those types of feelings. Start making that next "job" happen.

Once you are home, it's time to finish putting the business aspects of this particular project in order. That means making sure you have written those ever so important handwritten Thank You notes and checked the spellings, organized and recorded your financial expenditures from this project, sent out your current reviews to those on your "A" list and finally, updated your web site, your blog, uploaded any clips you might have of the performance to the appropriate web sites. When you have accomplished all of this, step back and enjoy the memory of a job well done.

For a long time it had seemed to me that life was about to begin—real life. But there was always some obstacle in the way. Something to be got through first, some unfinished business, time still to be served, a debt to be paid. Then life would begin. At last it dawned on me that these obstacles were my life.

– FR. ALFRED D'SOUZA

> I am often asked how one knows when it is time to look for a Management Company and a Manager. Here is the answer: When the business aspects of your career start taking too much of your time and energy away from the many performances you have, it is time to look for a manager.

> Adventure is what happens when you just did something stupid.
> — PROFESSOR BERNIE

Because you have made yourself familiar with what to expect and what you need to pay attention to throughout this whole process, you will feel more at ease. Each time you perform, your confidence will grow. All you need now is more experience.

SUMMARY

Becoming an entrepreneur and running your own business, for the most part, is not something you may have thought of as necessary in building a singing career. The concept may be touched upon in school, but the magnitude of its importance and the consequences of not knowing how to best pursue the business aspects of a singing career, can have devastating results. This information is not often clearly defined, talked about or taught and yet it consumes, once you are out in the real world, about 90% of your time, energy and money. You need to understand the process, have the skills, tools, and confidence that you are prepared and ready to enter into assembling your own successful business.

Yes, having innate talent and a solid vocal technique is of paramount importance if you are thinking of having a singing career, but equally or even more important is understand how our industry really works today so you can eventually enter into it with less uncertainty, and mystification. Knowledge is power so do your homework; explore and investigate for yourself what the requirements are out in the professional world of singing so you can make a clear and educated decision if this profession is for you. If the answer is yes, you need to acquire and understand the business skills and tools needed to move you steadily forward on your career path. And that demands that you develop and shape your own business. You need to have realistic goals that excite and motive you, then build the strategies and tactics to implement those goals. Once that is in place it is easier to do business each and every day.

It is no longer practical or wise to simply pretend you are doing the work by only playing at it. If you don't take it seriously by making a commitment and staying focused on what you want to achieve, it is not as likely to happen. It is often not fun, habitually mundane, requires many personal sacrifices and you may expect temporary failure along the way like every other successful business person. It's how you choose to deal with failure that makes the difference. Being prepared by having done your own research as to what is really required in our industry to be successful and a careful introspective search of what you are willing to commit to and sacrifice, is the real work required before you can even consider making the choice to pursue this type of career. Growth in every area of your life requires taking risks, stepping outside of your comfort zone as you develop your unique and authentic Personal Brand. As a result you start using parts of your mind, body, spirit, and soul that up until this time have remained untapped. There is an amazing world of creativity and connection to the Universe that can work for you when you allow this to happen. You quickly become more productive, responsible and proud of your own hard earned success. You will be better prepared for entering the professional world, and others will acknowledge and recognize your strong Personal Brand, by your consistency in all the many roles you play, and you may potentially be rewarded by getting the job. You will be moving from "aspiring artist" to "emerging professional singer."

The *most important and beneficial point* I want to make is this: when you go away from this experience, don't go back to where you were and how you *used* to do things. Start from where you are right now, from this fresh new viewpoint as you move forward, even if you feel insecure or fumble as you start. Don't fall back into your old habits and ways of thinking. That's the easy way out.

You have all the resources that you will ever need to

Procrastination is the fear of success. People procrastinate because they are afraid of the success that they know will result if they move ahead now. Because success is heavy, carries a responsibility with it, it is much easier to procrastinate and live on the "someday I'll" philosophy.

— DENIS WAITLEY

> *You have to leave the city of your comfort and go into the wilderness of your intuition. What you'll discover will be wonderful. What you'll discover will be yourself.*
>
> — ALAN ALDA

be successful *right now,* so don't put all that you have just learned and practiced away, until you think and feel that it is the appropriate, proper, or safe time to work on your career and life skills. Risk it all. Get off the emotional rollercoaster, so that you can clearly see, hear, and feel what the situation is—what the facts are—and choose to take action or not. Don't immediately think of or get caught up in—or worse yet, become attached to—the outcome, what might happen later, because you've made this decision. You can deal with that when the time comes.

This is how you continually come back to the process of refocusing your energy to create the positive results you want. You stay flexible and curious; you expect and welcome failure and mistakes, because this is how we learn and grow. So, start using your expanded skills, tools, and new information daily in all that you do—even those mundane chores you hate. Use them or lose them! Remember that when you are congruent on the inside, it is very easy to be consistent on the outside. And boy, does that feel good!

EPILOGUE

looking ahead

NOW THAT YOU HAVE completed, digested, and hopefully used the information, skills, and tools contained in this book, continue to refer to the sections that are pertinent to your needs as you move forward in your career. If you get stuck or lost along the way, using this as a reference book will help remind and refresh your thoughts and actions, giving you the opportunity to brush up on your new skills and tools. It will prompt you to get back on track. I have found through my own experience that my level of understanding of most things in life, once tried—whether it be career or personal—continues to improve and become more refined with each new experience. I know if I stay awake, present, flexible, and curious, my insight into how I do what I do also improves, so that I can present and represent my unique and authentic Personal Brand, my product, with panache. And that is cool!

Most of the information that has been presented to you in this book is from my own experiences as an international opera singer in this crazy industry. I hope, through your own research, understanding, and practice of the subjects, skills, tools, and objectives presented in this book, that you will have found new and fresh insight into the kind of further education and knowledge needed to not only make a

I know not what the future holds, but I know who holds the future.

– AUTHOR UNKNOWN

solid decision about pursuing singing as your vocation, but that it has also helped you realize how to better avoid some of the pitfalls that can occur along the way. It has been a very rewarding journey for me. I continue to travel this road with great respect and admiration for all those who have come before, and more importantly, to those right now that have the heart to follow. Now you are obligated to pass on what you have learned to those following in your footsteps. You must feel and experience the trip, and enjoy each and every moment along the way.

CAREER TRANSITION

So, what happens if you find, after a period of time, that you are no longer interested in committing to the work and sacrifices involved in pursuing a singing career? Are you willing to continue putting that much dedicated time, energy, and money into such an uncertain future?

Pursuing a singing career can be almost like an addiction, because you are always thinking that big break might be just around the corner and you have already sacrificed so much of your time, energy and money to chasing this dream, it's hard to know when to say enough is enough! How many years of trying are you willing to give in this kind of quest? Is that big break just around the corner for real or are you just kidding yourself? It's hard to look at making this kind of decision without it becoming emotionally charged. But, if you are having doubts or are just plain old tired of the chase, then maybe it's time to take one huge step back off that Inside Time line leaving the emotion over there, and look at facts and alternatives of choosing another avenue. Maybe you want to remain in the music business, and because of the work you've already done, and your level of understanding of this industry, decide to become involved with a different branch of the business, and enjoy *that* tremendously, leaving you time to enjoy and keep in balance the other parts

> *Liberty is the possibility of doubting, of making a mistake.... of searching and experimenting... of saying "no" to any authority—literary, artistic, philosophical, religious, social, and even political.*
>
> – IGNAZIO SILONE

of your life. Or maybe you are inspired by another aspect of your many talents. Here are some questions to consider:

- How will you know if what you are feeling is just one of those slumps you will eventually get over or if what you are feeling about changing career direction is the truth?
- How will you justify having spent all that time, energy and especially money, preparing for something you find now you really don't want to pursue?
- What if you find that a career as a singer is just not what you though it was going to be? As a result, you feel totally out of balance.
- What will others think of you if you make this decision?
- What will you think of yourself, if you make this decision?
- What will you do with your life now?
- Where should you go?
- How will you identify who you are now to the public, even though that doesn't change the core of your Personal Brand?

A bend in the road is not the end of the road... unless you fail to make the turn.

– **AUTHOR UNKNOWN**

    I want you to know that this section of my book was prompted by one of my own former student's career dilemmas. She was extremely talented, had a beautiful voice, interpreted and felt the music, was tall, slender, beautiful and very well liked by everyone. She was ready to step out and do some auditioning. In doing so and getting several jobs, performing several times, she decided she didn't really like the life style and didn't relate well with the business. She became depressed and finally after much coaxing, told me how she felt. She was so afraid of disappointing me and everyone else who had helped her. Even thought she knew that my philosophy is to do in life what makes you happy within yourself and with what you are doing, she found it difficult to admit she wanted to make a change.

> *Study anyone who's great, and you'll find that they apprenticed to a master, or several masters. Therefore, if you want to achieve greatness, renown, and superlative success, you must apprentice to a master.*
>
> **– ROBERT ALLEN**

It is a difficult choice for everyone, even for someone who has had the encouragement from the beginning to do what makes them happy. After discussing it, she decided to refocus. She transferred to a more appealing location out of New York City, but stayed in the same business she was currently involved in with her "day job." In addition, she is working toward an advanced degree in elementary education. She is much happier now, and still performs in semi- and professional community productions, but without all the pressure of pursuing a career. She is enjoying herself and her life, and feels much more in balance with who she is.

Change is inevitable! Life constantly revolves around the changes and transitions that happen and how we then choose to deal with them. If you don't believe me, think about the fashion industry, hair styles, cars, microchips, and the ever expanding virtual world. Think about relationships, leaving home, graduation from college, and finding a new apartment and roommate.

An ending is the beginning of change and transition. It is the time to consider what new opportunities out there might interest you. It is time for letting go of old obligations and priorities to make way for your new reality and experiences. It is always a chance for growth.

Don't be surprised if you notice you are experiencing a period of time when you feel distressed, uncomfortable and especially disassociated. Letting go of a dream is like experiencing and mourning the death of a loved one. The fact is, you are mourning a loss; that of an important, usually long held dream. This is a time for letting go of old beliefs; it is an opportunity to just let yourself be. This empty feeling allows room for you to experience self-reflection, recharging, and reorientation. Don't rush this process. It is a very important part of the transition.

This period is actually necessary to make these changes in your life possible. Transitions always conclude with a new beginning. Here are some points to consider if you are thinking about changing the direction of your life:

- Take your time. Change and transition are emotionally draining. You are, after all, mourning the death of something very real, the death of a dream. It is possible that this can affect you mentally, physically, spiritually and financially. Do not rush this process. There is no time line. It will take as long as it takes.

- Recognize why and how you are uncomfortable. Change can produce anxiety, anger and doubt. And those emotions can register strongly within your physical body. Become aware of where you are holding any tension and continually take that big step off your In Time Line leaving the emotion "over there" so you can breath and better center yourself during this process. Or conversely let yourself feel these powerful feelings. Study them. Know where and how they are affecting your physical body. Where in your body do you hold the tension? Is it in your lower abdomen or in your shoulders or jaw? Can you release it? Then every time you feel that tension, hold it for a minute and release. This is a great tool to use any time you are dealing with emotional issues in your life.

- You may feel like you're letting others down. You may feel like you are letting yourself down. You may feel guilty. You may feel like a "failure." These are the most common and limiting beliefs that can carry us far, far away. In reality, you know that our "failures" and "mistakes" are how we learn and grow, they are just feedback. What this feeling is saying is, if what you used to do is not getting the results you want, or is not giving you the outcome you were looking for, try something else instead, and use your new skills and tools, plus your past knowledge and experience, to help move you forward.

- Do not just react by running away from the hurt and pain. Know where you want to go. Always run toward something.

If you're going through hell, keep going.

— **WINSTON CHURCHILL**

> *Life is to be lived. If you have to support yourself, you had bloody well better find some way that is going to be interesting. And you don't do that by sitting around wondering about yourself.*
>
> **— KATHERINE HEPBURN**

Do not act for the sake of action. Doing something about your present situation may be tempting because you feel so uncomfortable where you are presently that you may want to do anything to escape it. Taking action for the sake of escape just prolongs or delays the process you have to go through to find a new beginning, a new dream. Recognize it for what it is and sit in it for a while. Be present and start observing your body, mind and spirit in this condition.

- Pamper yourself a little. Take really good care of yourself while you are in this limbo. Try to keep your personal routine going, that is key. Eat healthy, exercise and be with good company. Try to stay balanced. This will give you some stability.

- Find a good listener. Do you have a friend or family member who will listen and *not* give advice, unless you ask for it? You need a chance to spill everything that's on your mind, without getting any feedback, in a safe environment. This will most often give you the opportunity to find what you are looking for, all by yourself. Or if it is more comfortable, you may want to consider talking with a professional counselor.

What does your future hold? This is the time to start the process of figuring out what you really want to do next. Performers, being very organized, disciplined and focused, make good candidates for almost any job. This means you do have transferable and valuable skills. Some areas you might consider have to do with communication/interpersonal skills, managerial skills, and problem solving. Know your strengths and how you can best market yourself to a prospective employer. Do a serious self-evaluation:

- Find out what you are seriously interested in by volunteering, taking a college course or two, taking a career workshop, by giving yourself time to dream.

- What matters to you in your work environment? Is balancing

- your business, personal and financial life of importance to you? If it is, how do you want to make that happen?

- How much money do you have to make to live the life style you want? Can you downsize and be comfortable and content?

- Are you dissatisfied with your career or only with your job? In other words, do you like the field you are currently in overall? Perhaps there is another aspect of the current industry you are involved in that might really work for you.

- What is motivating you to make a change at this time?

- Write down your ideal job description. Create your dream job. Don't let reality rear its ugly head. Let your imagination go! Write down what you would like to do other than singing, how many hours you would like to work, with whom you would work (what type of personality), where and for how much money, etc. Let the sky be the limit. When you have finished, take a hard look at what you have recorded and see if there can be any truths to it. After evaluating it, if it makes sense and feels right, make it come true—*one step at a time*.

- Take your time to explore all avenues of employment. Finding what you love to do may show up in the most unlikely place. Don't discount anything in your search. Live your life to the fullest.

Regret for the things we did can be tempered by time; it is regret for the things we did not do that is inconsolable.

– SYDNEY J. HARRIS

    As I said before, change is inevitable because life is not static. Life is filled with the ever changing movement of living. Sometimes the change occurs without your participation, and sometimes you choose to make a change. What's important is how you choose to deal with that change, that transition and know it is not only within your power, but you now have the skills and tools to help make it happen in a more productive way . You can run away and bury your head in the sand and say, "woe is me." You can feel sorry

> *Some day, after we have mastered the winds, the waves, the tides, and gravity, we will harness for God the energies of love; and then for the second time in the history of the world, man will have discovered fire!*
>
> **– TEILHARD DE CHARDIN**

for yourself, get depressed and angry by becoming the victim of the circumstance, or you can make the choice to deal with it by stepping off your very emotionally charged Inside Time line, take a hard look at the facts and the situation for what it is, take action if needed, and do not become attached to the outcome or start worrying about what will happen. It's only feedback and an opportunity to grow and change. Here's a quote that says it all:

> "If you don't make the choice of how to live your life, someone else or some other circumstance will make it for you."

My choice is to participate in my life to the fullest extent, to get busy living. *Avanti!*

INNER LANGUAGE SYSTEMS SAMPLE WORDS

VISUAL	AUDITORY	KINESTHETIC
Look	Ring	Move
Picture	Sound	Impress
Bright	Say	Stir
Spectacle	Key	Throw
Delineate	Scream	Handle
Discern	Tone	Touch
Shortsighted	Sing	Stroke
Glimpse	Ask	Impact
Outlook	Note	Crush
Expose	Compose	Sharpen
Graphic	Hear	Feel
Reveal	Shout	Irritate
Preview	Tune	Tap
Paint	Voice	Crawl
See	Hear	Hit
Illustrate	Alarm	Strike

RECOMMENDED READING

Throughout this book I have woven together where possible the philosophy, concepts, insight, and inspiration of those that have come before, those out there now pushing the envelope, along with what I have learned from my own life and career experiences, so that you won't have to totally reinvent your career "wheel" from scratch.

If you are interested in further expanding your personal and business horizons, here are some interesting books that would be worth your time and energy. Enjoy!

Adams, James L. *Conceptual Blockbusting.* New York: Addison-Wesley, 1990.

Adler, Stella. *The Technique of Acting.* New York: Bantam Books, 1988.

Andreas, Steve, and Charles Faulkner, ed. *NLP: The New Technology of Achievement.* New York: William Morrow, 1994.

Bellantoni, Paul. *So You Wanna Sing In Germany? How to Dive into the Opera Smorgasbord of Central Europe.* Lulu.com, 2008.

Bing, Stanley. *Throwing the Elephant: Zen and the Art of Managing Up.* New York: Harper Collins, 2003.

Bly, Robert. *Iron John.* New York: Vintage, 1992.

Bykofsky, Sheree. *Me: Five Years From Now.* New York: Stonesong Press, 1999.

Cameron, Julia. *The Artist's Way.* New York: Putnam, 1992.

Cameron, Julia. *The Vein of Gold: A Journey to Your Creative Heart.* New York: Putnam, 1996.

Campbell, Don. *The Mozart Effect.* New York: Avon, 1997.

Caruso, Enrico, and Luisa Tetrazzini. *On the Art of Singing.* New York: Dover Publications, 1975.

Chopra, Deepak. *The Seven Spiritual Laws of Success.* New York: New World Library, 1994.

Cole, Toby, ed. *Acting: A Handbook of the Stanislavski Method.* New York: Crown Publishers, 1955.

Cornyn-Selby, Alyce P. *Procrastinator's Success Kit.* Portland: Beynch Press, 1987.

Covey, Steven R. *The 7 Habits of Highly Successful People.* New York: Simon and Schuster, 1990.

Craig, David. *A Performer Prepares.* New York: Applause Theatre Books, 1999.

Csikszentmihalyi, Mihaly. *Creativity.* New York: Harper Collins, 1996.

Dornemann, Joan, with Maria Ciaccia. *Complete Preperation: A Guide to Auditioning for Opera.* New York: Excalibur, 1992.

Dunkel, Stuart Edward. *The Audition Process: Anxiety Management and Coping Strategies.* New York: Pendragon Press, 1990.

Emmons, Shirlee, and Alma Thomas. *Power Performance for Singers.* New York: Oxford University Press, 1998.

George, Mike. *Discover Inner Peace: A Guide to Spiritual Well-Being.* San Francisco: Chronicle Books, 2000.

Godin, Seth. *Tribes: We Need You to Lead Us.* New York: Portfolio, 2008.

Gorrie, Jon. *Performing in the Zone.* Lulu.com, 2009.

Gray, John, Ph.D. *Men are from Mars, Women are from Venus.* New York: Harper Collins, 1992.

Green, Barry, and W. Timothy Gallwey. *The Inner Game of Music.* New York: Doubleday, 1986.

Greene, Don. *Audition Success.* New York: ProMind Music, 1998.

Hanff, Helene. *Underfoot in Show Business.* Boston: Little, Brown, and Co., 1980.

Helfgot, Daniel. *The Third Line.* New York: Schirmer Books, 1993.

Henri, Robert. *The Art Spirit.* New York: Harper and Row, 1923.

Highstein, Ellen. *Making Music in Looking Glass Land,* 3rd ed. New York: Concert Artists Guild, 1997.

Janis, Byron, with Maria Cooper Janis. *Chopin and Beyond: My Extraordinary Life in Music and the Paranormal.* New York: John Wiley and Sons, 2010.

Jeffers, Susan, Ph. D. *Feel the Fear and Do It Anyway.* New York: Fawcett Columbine, 1987.

Johnson, Robert. *He–She–We.* New York: Harper and Row, 1989.

Jourdain, R. *Music, The Brain, and Ecstacy: How Music Conquers the Imagination.* New York: Morrow Press, 1997.

Lehmann, Lilli. *How to Sing.* New York: Dover Publications, 1993.

Lamperti, Giovanni Battista, ed. by Wm. E. Brown and Lillian Strongin. *Vocal Wisdom: Maxims of Giovanni Battista Lamperti.* New York: Taplinger, 1957 (facsimile).

McTaggart, Lynne. *The Intention Experiment: Using Your Thoughts to Change Your Life and the World.* New York: The Free Press, 2008.

McWilliams, Peter. *Do It! Let's Get Off Our Buts.* New York: Prelude Press, 1994.

Menaker, Daniel. *A Good Talk: The Story and Skill of Communication.* New York: Twelve Books, 2010.

Miller, Richard. *Singing and Imagination.* New York: Oxford University Press, 1998.

Millman, Dan. *The Inner Athelete.* New Hampshire: Stillpoint Publishing, 1994.

Morris, Eric, and Joan Hotchkis. *No Acting Please.* New York: Spelling Publication, 1979.

Morris, Eric, *Acting from the Ultimate Consciousness and Being and Doing.* New York: Perigee Books, 1988.

Oliver, Donald. *How to Audition for the Musical Theater: A Step-by-Step Guide to Effective Preparation,* 2nd ed. New York: Smith and Kraus, 1998.

Ostwald, David F. *Acting for Singers.* New York: Oxford University Press, 2005.

Peck, M. Scott, M.D. *The Road Less Traveled.* New York: Simon and Schuster, 1978.

Ping, A.C., *Be.* New York: Da Capo Press, 2004.

Ping, A.C., *Do.* New York: Da Capo Press, 2004.

Pink, Daniel H. *The Adventures of Johnny Bunko: The Last Career Guide You'll Ever Need.* New York: Riverhead Trade, 2008.

Pollar, Odette. *365 Ways to Simplify Your Work Life.* Chicago: Dearborn Financial Publishing, 1996.

Ristad, Eloise. *A Soprano on Her Head.* New York: Real People Press, 1982.

Roam, Dan. *The Back of the Napkin.* New York: Penguin Group, 2008.

Robinson, Ken, Ph.D. *The Element: How Finding Your Passion Changes Everything.* New York: Penguin Group, 2009.

Robinson, Ken, Ph.D. *Out of Our Minds: Learning to be Creative.* New York: Capstone, 2011.

Rufus, Anneli S. *Stuck: Why We Can't (or Won't) Move On.* New York: Penguin Group, 2009.

Seabrook, John. *Nobrow: The Culture of Marketing, the Marketing of Culture.* New York: Vintage Books, 2001.

Silver, Fred. *Auditioning for the Musical Theater*. New York: Penguin Books, 1998.

Stanislavski, Constantin. *Stanislavski On Opera*. New York: Theatre Books, 1975.

Stanislavski, Constantin. *An Actor Prepares*. New York: Theatre Books, 1936, 1977.

Sullivan, Gail, and Dorthy Maddison. *Kein Angst Baby*. New York: New York Opera Newsletter Books, 1994.

Thomson, Robert Stuart. *Italian for the Opera*. Vancouver: Godwin Books, 1992.

Tolle, Eckhart. *The Power of Now*. Novato, California: New World Library, 1999.

Tolle, Eckhart. *A New Earth: Awakening to Your Life's Purpose*. New York: Penguin, 2008.

Tomatis, Al. *The Conscious Ear*. New York: Stanton Hill Press, 1991.

Ury, William. *Getting Past No*, New York: Bantam, 1991.

Walker, David J. *You Are Enough: Always Have Been... Always Will Be*. California: DeVorss Publications, 2007.

Wheatly, Margaret J., and Myron Kellner-Rogers. *A Simpler Way*. San Francisco: Berrett-Koehler Publishers, 1996.

Wilson, G.D. *Psychology for Performing Artists: Butterflies and Bouquets*. London: Jessica Kingsley, 1994.

Yanashita, Keith, and Sandra Spataro. *Unstuck*. New York: Portfolio, 2004.

Zander, Rosamund Stone, and Benjamin Zander. *The Art of Possibility*. New York: Penguin Group, 2002.

Zukav, Gary. *Seat of the Soul*. New York: Simon and Schuster, 1990.

WEEKLY PROFESSIONAL EXPENSES

	SUN	MON	TUES	WED	THUR	FRI	SAT	WEEKLY TOTAL
Professional Services								
Résumé Packet								
Equipment								
Dues								
Music/Books/Publications								
Performance/Audition Expenses								
Travel Expenses								
Car Expenses								
Recital Expenses								
Utilities								
Business Supplies								
Postage								
Miscellaneous								
DAILY TOTAL:								

TOTAL EXPENSES FOR THE WEEK:

AUDITION JOURNAL EXAMPLE FROM VELVET SINGER

© 2011 Bill Bennett, www.velvetsinger.com

Lyric Opera of Chicago, Ryan Opera Center

Category	Note	Poor	Below Average	Average	Good	Excellent
Overall Assessment	Went very well overall, I was happy with it.	-2	-1	0	●+1	+2
Health	A touch tired from rehearsal night before.	-2	●-1	0	+1	+2
Concentration	I took time to focus before and it worked well.	-2	-1	0	+1	●+2
Relaxation	I was a bit tense, but better than normal.	-2	-1	0	●+1	+2
Enjoyment	Enjoyed "performing."	-2	-1	0	●+1	+2
Warm-Up Session		-2	-1	0	+1	+2
Introduction		-2	-1	0	+1	+2
Accompanist	We achieved really good ensemble.	-2	-1	0	+1	●+2
Memory of Music		-2	-1	0	+1	+2
Vocal Security	Overall very solid. I committed to the	-2	-1	0	●+1	+2
Low Notes		-2	-1	0	+1	+2
High Notes		-2	-1	0	+1	+2
Breath	A little tight, forgot to release my belly before a	-2	●-1	0	+1	+2
Legato		-2	-1	0	+1	+2
Vibrato		-2	-1	0	+1	+2
Intonation		-2	-1	0	+1	+2
Diction		-2	-1	0	+1	+2
Coloratura	I was so happy with how the notes came out in the Mozart. I think it must have been that I finally started with it and so my breath was more activated -- REMEMBER that sensation!!	-2	-1	0	+1	●+2
Rhythmic Accuracy		-2	-1	0	+1	+2
Text Accuracy		-2	-1	0	+1	+2
Vowels		-2	-1	0	+1	+2
Onsets / Releases		-2	-1	0	+1	+2
Overall Expressiveness		-2	-1	0	+1	+2

GOAL FLOW CHART

GOAL:

	Obstacles to Goal	Solutions to Obstacles	Deadline Date	Rewards

Is It Worth It?	Ultimate Goal and Deadline Date

GOAL FLOW CHART EXAMPLE

	Perceived Problems	Solutions	Target Date	Pay-off	Ultimate Goal Was It Worth the Time and Effort?
	Who to ask?	Hometown support – contributors to local Opera Company, businesses, church, family, Opera guild	2 Months before audition	Possible monetary support now and in the future.	YES!!!! I have a realistic plan with an actual time line to help me accomplish my goal of getting these audition expenses. I have a lot of self-confidence and improve my chances of doing well in this audition. I also know how to prepare for the next time I need this kind of help.
	Ask for part or all of expenses?	Put a business plan together breaking into categories all the expenses so that those who are interested can choose a part of the plan or all of it.	6 months before audition.	Using my organizational skills and improving my presentation. Learning to network and schmooz.	
	Place to stay?	I have an aunt in a nearby city or maybe stay in hotel if the expenses are covered.	4 months before audition	Being comfortable before the audition.	
Audition Expenses	Find accompanist in the new city?	Call the local university and schools, ask Opera Company or auditions committee.	2 weeks before	Chance to setup a rehearsal before the audition.	
Goal	Help with finding the right look?	Consult a personal shopper at the major dept stores in town. Go to the make-up dept and do a make-over. I need to get used to the new me.	6 months before audition	I look and feel great. I have a lot of self-confidence. I like the new me.	

APPENDICES • 263

SAMPLE RÉSUMÉ

Jane Doe
MEZZO-SOPRANO

OPERA PERFORMANCE

ROLE	OPERA	COMPANY	CONDUCTOR/DIRECTOR	DATE
Rosina	*Barber of Seville*	Peters Opera, Millet, OH	Joe Smith	April 2010
Dorabella	*Cosí fan Tutte*	Tubac Opera, Ames, CO	Mark Doe/Sally Hart	Feb 2009
Orlofsky	*Die Fledermaus*	Smith Opera, Smith, NJ	Don Jones	Oct 2009
Flora Bervoix	*La Traviata*	Amis Opera, New York, NY	Bill Hole	Aug 2008
Inez	*Il Trovatore*	Book Opera, New York, NY	Sara Smart	May 2007

PERFORMANCE-READY ROLES

Siebel	*Faust*
Cherubino	*The Marriage of Figaro*

MUSICAL THEATER

ROLE	SHOW	COMPANY	CONDUCTOR/DIRECTOR	DATE
Cleo	*Most Happy Fella*	Musical Home, Wee, FL	John Marsh/Silva Horn	June 2006
Bloody Mary	*South Pacific*	Musical Home, Wee, FL	Sara Smart/Jane Kelly	May 2006

APPRENTICE/TRAINING PROGRAMS

Audition Workshop, 6 classes	Project Audition, New York, NY	Sue Mont	Fall 2008
Dance Royal, 8 classes	QRX Ballet Company, NY	Harry Potter	May 2008
Cherubino, *The Marriage of Figaro*	Meow Apprentice Program, NY	Mark Doe	July 208

EDUCATION

University of Maine	Bachelor of Music degree in Voice Performance	2000-2005

VOICE TEACHERS AND COACHES

NAME	AFFILIATION	AREA OF EXPERTISE	YEAR
Van Brande	Post Opera	Voice Teacher	2005-2010
Steve Jones	Ess Opera	Vocal Coach	2007
Jossie Dessen	School of Music	Diction Coach	2004-2005

AWARDS

Program Award	Amis Opera, New York, NY	2004
Miss Ohio	Miss Ohio Competition	2002
Ruffus Singing Award	Men's Club of New York, NY	2006

SPECIAL INTERESTS AND ACTIVITIES

I teach dance at the Yough Youth School. I am the accompanist for the Men and Boys Choir at St. Mark's Episcopal Church. I also take weekly classes in hatha yoga, and am an avid traveler.

45 W. 20 STREET, APT. #24, NEW YORK, NY 10001 | PHONE +1-212-679-9012 | JDOE@JANEDOE.COM

SHORT BIO SAMPLE

Jane Doe

MEZZO-SOPRANO

From her beginnings as a young performer growing up in a small, rural town in New Mexico, to winning audiences' rave reviews, Ms. Jane Doe has generated a loyal following with her persuasive acting and delicious voice.

At her most recent recital, Ms. Doe's innovative program and beautiful singing was not only enthusiastically appreciated by the audience, but she received a glowing review from the *Park Central Sun*. Jack Place said, "A beautiful program, beautiful voice, beautiful young woman."

Having recently won the prestigious Pit Award, Ms. Doe will next perform with the Major Chorale at Carnegie Hall in New York City. While there, she will coach with Maestro Tullio in preparation for her debut as Inez in *Il Trovatore* with the South Park Opera, in Cincinnati, Ohio, in March of this year.

You can follow Ms. Doe's career on Facebook and Twitter, or via her web site, www.janedoe.com.

45 W. 20 STREET, APT. #24, NEW YORK, NY 10001 | PHONE +1-212-679-9012 | JDOE@JANEDOE.COM

SAMPLE COVER LETTERS

JOHN DOE
LYRIC TENOR

August 31, 2011

Tomorrow Opera Company
Henry Smith, General Director
1234 Circle Street Suite 44
Everytown, NY 12345

Dear Mr. Smith,

Susan Williams, conductor for the Mean Opera Company's production of *The Elixir of Love,* in which I sang Nemorino, suggested that I send my materials to you.

She was most impressed with my performance, and knew this opera was scheduled for your upcoming season. She said she would be conducting that opera, and would very much like for you to consider me for your production.

Included you will find my résumé, photo, reviews, and a CD. I would very much like to sing for you; my schedule is fairly flexible. I look forward to hearing from you at your earliest convenience. If I have not heard from you by September 12, I will take the liberty of calling you. Thank you for your time and consideration.

Sincerely,

John Doe

---

200 W. 50 STREET, APT. #5G, NEW YORK, NY 10022 • +1-212-876-5432 • JOHN@JOHNDOE.COM

Jane Doe
MEZZO-SOPRANO

November 5, 2011

Wyatt Servian, General Director
Azmo Opera Company
Anytown, OH 80214

Dear Mr. Servian,

I understand that you will be in New York City in December, to audition prospective singers for your upcoming production of *Faust*. I would very much like to be included in the list of singers you will be hearing.

    I have not had much performance experience to date, but have had the pleasure of recently winning the prestigious Smith Award, for which I sang Siebel's Aria. I have performed many of the scenes from *Faust*, and it is a role that my coach, Maestro Zin, agrees is performance-ready. I would love the opportunity to sing it with your company.

    Enclosed you will find my résumé packet with all the pertinent information. If you have any questions, or need any additional information, please do not hesitate to call me. If I haven't heard from you by November 12, I will take the liberty of contacting you. Thank you for your time and attention.

Kindest regards,

Jane Doe

45 W. 20 STREET, APT. #24, NEW YORK, NY 10001 | PHONE +1-212-679-9012 | JDOE@JANEDOE.COM

HOW TO MARK YOUR MUSIC

This example shows a clear indication for the accompanist of where to start the piece. Note how the translation is written over the music, and the marks indicating the strong beats within a measure.

Here is an example of the traditional indication of a musical cut in a score, using the two syllables of the Latin word *vide* ("to see") to indicate the beginning and end of the cut. The lower example shows a small sketch illustrating the stage set, to easily indicate stage directions at that point in the music.

CHARACTER CHART

Name: _____

_____ Sex _____ Age _____ Birth Date _____

Birthplace _____ Nationality _____

Religion _____ Feelings About Religion _____

Languages Spoken _____

Political Party _____

Class in Society _____ Lower _____ Middle _____ Upper

Morals _____

Ambitions _____

Education _____ Date Graduated _____ Major _____

Name of School _____ Where _____

Married _____ Divorced _____ Single _____

Family:

Father _____ Profession _____ Living or Dead _____

Mother _____ Profession _____ Living or Dead _____

Divorced/Happily
Married _____

Brothers/Sisters
(names, ages) _____

Happy Home Life? _____

Interesting Information Regarding Family _____

Physical Appearance:

Height _____ Weight _____ Eyes _____ Hair _____ Mouth _____

Feet _____

Hands _____ Fingers _____ Shoulders _____

Limbs _____ Complexion _____ Face _____

Breasts _____ Waist _____ Hips _____

Neck _____ Ears _____ Nose _____ Teeth _____

Type of Body _____

Any Birthmarks or Scars _____

Posture _____ Appearance _____

Profession:

Type of Work _____

Quality of Work Performed _____ Reputation _____

Hours Worked _____ Income _____

Military Service:

Character Traits

Outstanding Qualities _____

Character Flaws _____

Habitual Expressions _____

Habitual Mannerisms _____

Fears _____ Frustrations _____

Temperament _____

Attitude Toward Life _____

Leader/Follower _____

Personal Information

Hobbies or Favorite Pastimes _____

Favorite Newspaper _____ Favorite Records _____

Favorite Books/Magazines _____

Favorite Colors _____

Type of Men Preferred _____

Type of Women Preferred _____

Favorite Entertainment _____

Favorite Foods/Drinks/Clothing/Jewelry _____

City Background _____ Country Background _____

House Type & Style _____

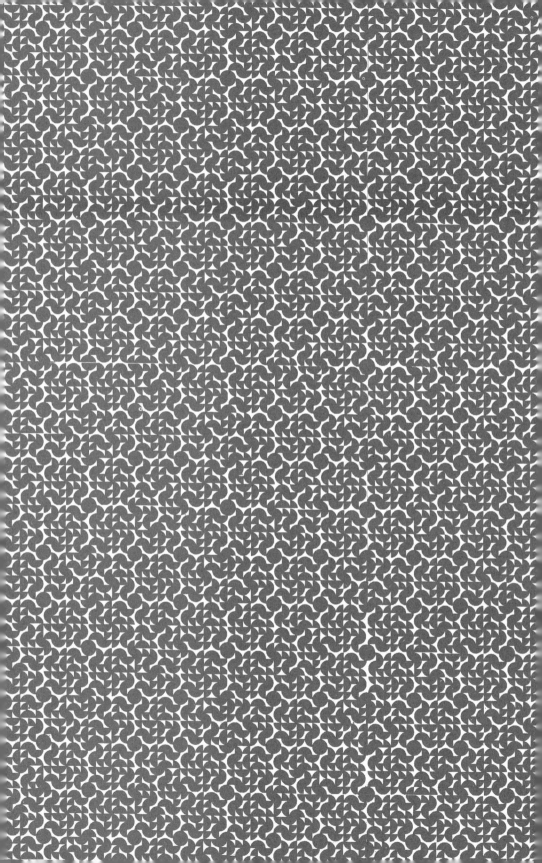

ABOUT THE AUTHOR

For as long as she can remember, singing and performing have always been in Carol Kirkpatrick's blood. From her beginnings in a small farming town in southeastern Arizona, through her early first-place triumph at the prestigious San Francisco Opera Auditions, and subsequent career on international stages, Ms. Kirkpatrick has thrilled audiences and critics alike. "A major voice, one worth the whole evening." (*The New York Times*) Since retiring from the stage, she continues to be in demand as a voice teacher, clinician, and adjudicator of competitions including the Metropolitan Opera National Council Auditions. Combining her knowledge of performance, business, and interpersonal skills, she has written the second edition of her highly regarded book, *Aria Ready: The Business of Singing*, a step-by-step career guide for the singer and teachers of singing. *Aria Ready* has been used by universities, music conservatories, and summer and apprentice programs throughout the world as a curriculum for teaching Ms. Kirkpatrick's process of career development, making her "the" expert in this area. She lives in Denver, Colorado.

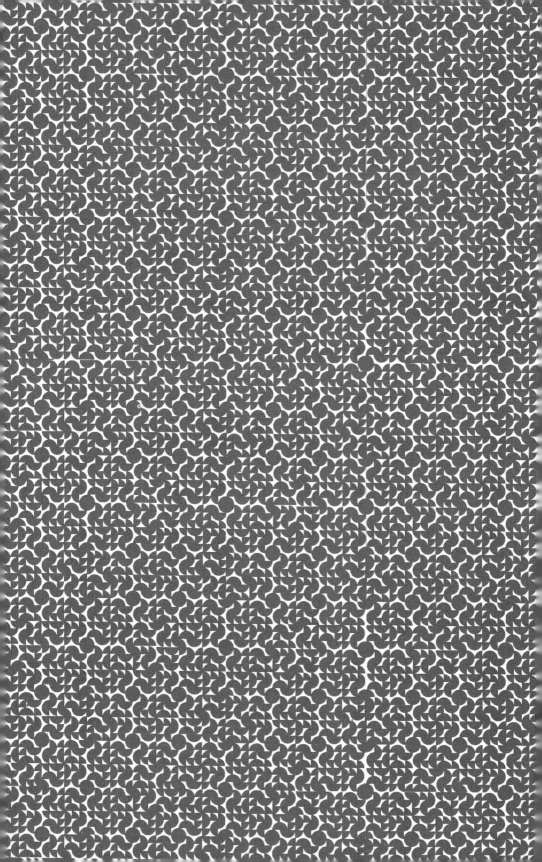

INDEX

A

A and B lists, 178, 179, 183, 221, 237, 241
accompanists. *See* répétiteurs/accompanists
acting, coaches and classes, 45–48
agents. *See* managers/agents
AGMA union contracts, 172–74
Alexander Technique, 15–17
application letters of recommendation, 164–65
audience, acknowledging, 234–35
auditions
    about: process overview, 210–11
    aria to begin, 216
    canceling, 213–14
    completing audition page, 217–18
    deductible expenses, 199
    dos and don'ts, 214–15
    dressing for, 211–13
    experiencing results in advance, 66–67
    first impressions and, 213–14, 218–19
    focusing in the moment, 215–16
    follow-up after, 167–69, 216–18
    getting, 50–52. *See also* marketing; networking; PR packets
    getting comfortable with, 214–16
    illness and, 213–14
    information sheet, 167–68
    journal, 261
    preparing for, 216
    reasons for not getting roles, 218–20
    researching decision-makers, 215
    resources for finding, 177–78
    second-guessing, 218–20
    tactics, 211–16
    unscheduled, 220–21
auditory inner language system, 96

B

Backstage, 177–78
belief systems, 63–71
    about: overview of, 63–64
    the Brat and. *See* "The Brat"
    changing, 68–71
    communication and, 103
    discovering, 64–68
    environment and, 64–65, 67
    events and, 65
    experiencing results in advance and, 66–67
    "failure" and, 63–64
    knowledge and, 65–66
    mind/body connection and, 67–68
    "mistakes" and, 64
    past results and, 66
    real vs. imaginary world and, 68
    releasing old limitations, 68–71
binders/notebooks
    for exercises, new ideas, 12, 20
    of music, 41–42, 214
bio, short, 159–60, 265. *See also* résumé
body language, 90–92
book list, 256
book overview, xviii–xix
books/publications expense, 199
bowing, 234–35
brand. *See* Personal Brand
"The Brat," 85–89
    dealing with, 69–70, 86–89, 215–16, 217. *See also* motivation
    defined, 46, 62
    getting to know, 85–89
    negative self-talk and, 46, 62, 69–71
    recognizing and acknowledging, 86
    reconnecting with, 86–88

"The Brat" (cont'd)
    self-discovery and, 62
    using productively, 88–89, 240
    as your friend, 86
    See also belief systems
breaths, marking, 29, 42
budget, crafting, 188–93. *See also* taxes
business cards, 51, 150, 186, 236
business plan package, 205–6
business skills and tools, 200
    about: overview of, 111–15
    audition/performance follow-up, 167–69
    contracts, 169–76
    filing system, 143–44
    gaining confidence in, 112
    mind mapping and, 113–15
    naming your company, 115
    questions to begin molding your business, 115
    time management systems, 145–46
    unfamiliarity with, 111–12
    web site, 145
    See also communication; goals; Inner Wiring Systems; job descriptions; marketing; PR packets; rapport
business supplies expenses, 200

C

car expenses, 198–99
career. *See* auditions; business skills and tools; job descriptions; jobs; marketing; performances; PR packets; singing career
CD, 160–63
    duplications, 162
    finding recording studio for, 161–62
    guidelines for, 160–61
    labels, 162–63
change
    difference pattern and, 83–84
    double pattern (sameness with exception and difference), 84
    internal timetable, 83–84
    sameness pattern and, 83
    sameness with exception and, 83
character(s)
    chart, 270
    connection with other characters, 35
    flexibility in approach, 224–25
    highlighting your lines, 30
    inspiration for, 34
    learning new roles, 30–32
    rehearsals, 224–31
    researching and understanding, 32–38
    similarities between you and, 34
    studying with famous interpreters of, 49
    translating words of. *See* translating
    See also working music
circle exercise, 17–18
Classical Singer magazine, 177
coaches
    conductors as, 44
    drama, classes and, 45–48, 224
    roles of, 42–43, 44–45
    specialists, 43
    tips for choosing/working with, 43–45
comfort zone
    change and, 83
    personal space and, 102, 103–6
    releasing old limitations and, 68–71
communication
    asking questions and, 100–101
    body language and, 90–92
    filtering systems, 103
    heartfelt, 102–3
    inner language systems and, 92–98
    listening and, 98, 99–101, 182
    paraphrasing and, 98, 100
    personal space and, 101–6
    prerequisite for, 89
    self-alignment and, 106–8
    understanding and, 98–99
    See also networking; schmoozing
company, naming yours, 115
concert performances, 237–41
contracts, 169–76
    AGMA union, 172–74
    creating your own, 175–76
    non-union, 171–72
    other information about, 174–75
    training/apprentice program, 169–71
cover letter, 151–54, 266–67

D

diction and pronunciation, 26–27, 28
drama, coach and classes, 45–48, 224
dressing
    for auditions, 211–13
    for concerts, 239
    for performances (and after), 230, 233
    for rehearsals, 226
dues expense, 199

E

equipment expenses, 198
expense chart, 260
expenses. *See* budget; taxes
experience, getting, 50–52. *See also* auditions; marketing; networking; PR packets

F

fachs (voice categories), 23–25
filing system, 143–44
finances
    affording lessons, 14
    crafting budget, 188–93
    fundraising, 201–6
    grants, 206–8
    See also taxes
financial officer job description, 188
first impressions, 176, 213–14, 218–19
folders
    filing system for, 143–44
    presentation, for PR packets, 166–67
following up
    after auditions/performances, 167–69, 216–18, 236–37, 240–42
    on leads/contacts, 183–84
fundraising, 201–6. *See also* grants

G

gate keeper. *See* "The Brat"
goals
    activation process, 131–32
    creating structure for, 138–39
    definition of terms related to, 128–29
    determining/establishing, 116–19
    example of process, 132–33
    fear inhibiting, 118
    finding appropriate goal, 130–31
    importance of, 116
    overlapping, 140
    prerequisites for starting process, 133–34
    proven tips for, 134–37
    questions to answer about, 117
    rehearsing your success and, 137–38
    setting process, 127–39
    short term, flow chart, 262–63
    strategies, tactics and, 128–30, 131, 138–39
    stumbling blocks to, 118–19

    timeline tools for. *See* Inner Wiring Systems
grants, 206–8

I

individual sound, discovering, 9
inner language systems, 92–98
    auditory (hearing) system, 96
    connecting with others and, 92–93, 94–95
    identifying your system, 93–94
    kinesthetic (feeling) system, 96–97
    listening and, 98, 99–101
    sample words, 255
    using all, 98
    visual (seeing) system, 95
inner systems and patterns
    about: overview of, 55–56, 62, 108–9
    negative self-talk and. *See* "The Brat"
    tools, skills for staying on path, 72–73. *See also* motivation
    See also belief systems; Personal Brand
Inner Timelines. *See* Inner Wiring Systems
Inner Wiring Systems
    benefits of using both Inner Timelines, 124–27
    exercise, 126–27
    goal determination and, 118–19
    goal-setting process and, 127–28
    Inner Timelines and, 118–19, 121–27
    Inside Time and, 122–23, 125–26, 127
    motivation styles and, 119
    motivational triggers and, 120–21
    Outside Time and, 122, 124, 127–28
Inside Time, 122–23, 125–26, 127
internal timetable for change, 83–84

J

job descriptions
    financial officer, 188. *See also* finances
    manager/agent, 147
    marketing/PR director, 176–79
    office manager, 140–42
    you, the client, 208–10
jobs
    auditioning for. *See* auditions
    considerations for taking, 221–24
    getting experience, 50–52
    main reasons for accepting, 223
    See also performances; rehearsals

INDEX • 277

K

kinesthetic inner language system, 96–97

L

language tools, 25–28
    diction and pronunciation, 26–27, 28
    pronouncing like a native, 26–27, 53
    resources, 25–26, 27–28
    translation/transcription resources, 27–28
learning
    languages, 25–28
    music. *See* working music
    new roles, 30–32. *See also* character(s)
lessons
    agenda for, 12
    asking questions during, 13
    financial considerations, 14
    finding voice teacher for, 9–12, 13–14
    hiatus from, 14
    open-mindedness toward, 13
    preparing for, 12, 14
    recording, 12–13
    trial, 10
    warning signs to heed, 13
letters
    cover, 151–54, 266–67
    of introduction, 152, 158, 167, 203–4
    of recommendation, 163–66
    See also following up
listening, 98, 99–101, 182
local/community performing organizations, 178

M

"magic carpet," 105, 185, 211, 216, 240
managers/agents
    finding/choosing, 147–48, 177, 178
    job description, 147
    questions to answer about, 147–48
marketing
    determining client entry level situation, 177–78
    job description for marketing/PR director, 176–79
    product sales, 176–79
    tracking contacts and mailing lists, 178–79
    web site, 145, 183
    See also networking; PR packets; schmoozing
memorizing, 21, 29, 31, 34, 95, 96, 97

mind mapping, 113–15
mind/body connection
    belief systems and, 67–68
    body language and, 91–92
    examples, 67, 91–92
    real vs. imaginary world and, 68
    releasing old limitations and, 68–71
motivation, 73–85
    about: overview of traits, patterns, systems, 73–74, 84–85
    activators, 80–81
    carrot *and* stick for, 73–74, 79, 119
    carrot-oriented, 74–76, 119
    external, 80–81
    internal, 80
    internal time clock for change and, 83–84
    maintaining balance and, 75–76, 77–79
    personal inner wiring and, 119–21
    reasoning process and, 81–83
    scenario, 79
    stick-oriented, 76–79, 119
    triggers, 120–21
Musical America, 177

N

negative self-talk. *See* "The Brat"
networking, 49–50, 179–87
    asking questions and, 182–83
    for auditions/jobs, 51
    creating/maintaining relationships, 112–13
    defined, 49, 180
    developing skills for, 98, 102, 104, 105
    following up and, 183–84
    getting comfortable with, 181–83
    keeping contacts informed, 49–50
    optimizing, 112–13, 147, 174, 181–84, 208, 211, 236, 240, 241–42
    schmoozing compared to, 179–80. *See also* schmoozing
non-union, 171–72

O

office manager
    filing system for, 143–44
    job description, 140–42
opera
    language tools, 25–28
    your job as singer, 9
Opera America, 177
Outside Time, 122, 124, 127–28

P

patrons, fundraising and, 201–6
performances
   acknowledging audience, 234–35
   approach to, 231–34
   checklist of things for, 232–33
   concert, 237–40
   day of, suggestions, 231–33
   deductible expenses, 199
   follow-up after, 167–69, 236–37, 240–42
   getting experience, 50–52
   handling the unexpected, 234
   higher expectations, 225
   networking after, 236, 241–42
   networking for, 49–50
   post-performance checklists, 235–37
   practicing/preparing for, 21–22. *See also* character(s); practice; working music
   pre-performance checklist, 233
   professional demeanor after, 235
   See also rehearsals
Personal Brand
   advantages of, 58–59
   defined, 57
   discovering, 59–62
   inner systems/patterns and, 55–56, 62, 108–9. *See also* belief systems; communication
   making right impression, 183–84, 242
   phrase completions for identifying, 59–62
   self-alignment and, 106–8
   your job description and, 208–10
personal space, 101–6
   comfort with others and, 102
   comfort zone and, 102, 103–6
   conscious use of, 101–2, 103–6
   heartfelt communication and, 102–3
photographs. *See* publicity photos
polishing/finishing touches, 49–50
postage expense, 200
PR packets
   about: overview of, 149
   CD, 160–63
   contents summary, 151
   cover letter, 151–54, 266–67
   deductible expenses, 198
   fundraising and, 201–6
   guidelines and guiding principles, 149–51
   letters of introduction, 152, 158, 167, 203–4
   letters of recommendation, 163–66
   presentation folders, 166–67
   publicity photos, 154–58
   resources for where to send, 177–78
   résumé, 158–59, 261
   reviews, 163
   sending, 177
   short bio, 159–60, 264
practice
   in apartments, 18
   approaching new piece, 20–21
   best system for you, 22
   circle exercise, 17–18
   fachs (voice categories) and, 23–25
   focus during, 19
   focusing on, exercise, 17–18
   goal of, 17
   language tools, 25–28
   listening to recorded sessions during, 19–20
   missing, noticing effects of, 22
   "on purpose," 18
   for performance, 21–22
   recording sessions, 19
   systems of, 17–21
   without using voice, 19
presentation folders, 166–67
professional service expenses, 197
profile, singer's, 1–5
publicity photos, 154–58
   finding/choosing photographers, 155–57
   importance of, 154
   mistakes to avoid, 154–55
   orientation of, 157–58
   reproducing, 157–58

R

rapport
   body language and, 90–92
   defined, 89–90
   See also communication; networking; schmoozing
reasoning process
   options and, 81–82
   procedures and, 82–83
   provoking motivation, 81–83
recital expenses, 199
recommendation letters, 163–66
recording
   CD for PR packet, 160–63

recording (cont'd)
   lessons, 12–13
   practice sessions, 19
recordings
   fachs (voice categories) and, 23–24
   listening to and analyzing, 19–20, 23–24, 31
   not relying on, 31
rehearsals, 224–31
   for concert performances, 237–41
   flexibility in approach, 224–25
   higher expectations and, 225
   points to consider (dos and don'ts), 226–27, 228–31
   preparing for, 224–26
   reviewing daily, 227–28
   stage direction and markings, 228
rehearsing success, 137–38
relationships
   audition/performance follow-up and, 167–69
   creating and maintaining, 112–13
   importance of, 169
   tracking contacts and mailing lists, 178–79
   See also networking
répétiteurs/accompanists, 39–42, 53, 76, 160–61, 214, 217, 220, 242
résumé, 158–59, 264. *See also* bio, short
reviews, 163
roles. *See* character(s)

S

schmoozing
   art of, tips and suggestions, 184–87
   defined, 180
   networking compared to, 179–80. *See also* networking
scores
   comparing recordings to, 31
   learning symbols, staging in, 21
   marking up, 20, 29–30, 227, 228, 266–67
   verifying editions of, 30, 32, 175
self-alignment, 106–8
short bio, 265
singing career
   about: overview of starting out, 7–8, 52–54
   discovering your unique sound, 9
   fachs (voice categories) and, 23–25
   knowing what lies ahead, xvii–xviii
   looking ahead, 247–54
   overview and summary, 242–46
   questions to answer about, 2–5
   transitioning from, 248–54
   transitioning from university to, 1–5
   your job description and, 208–10
   See also auditions; business skills and tools; job descriptions; jobs; marketing; performances; PR packets
singing technique
   anchoring, 15
   discovering your unique sound, 9
   fachs (voice categories) and, 23–25
   listening to yourself and, 13
sponsors, fundraising and, 201–6
stage direction and markings, 228
"startle response," 15. *See also* Alexander Technique
style of music, 38–39
success
   goals for. *See* goals
   rehearsing, 137–38
supportive letters of recommendation, 165–66

T

taxes, 193–97
   deduction/expense categories, 197–201
   expense chart, 260
   keeping records, 193, 195, 196–97
   requirements, responsibilities, and documents, 193–96
   self-employment considerations, 193, 194–95, 196
time management systems, 145–46
tracking contacts and mailing lists, 178–79
training/apprentice program contracts, 169–71
transitioning from university, 1–5
translating
   approaching new piece, 20, 28–29, 30
   language tools/resources, 25–28
   word for word, 28–29
travel expenses, 199

U

utilities expenses, 200

V

"Velvet Singer," 168, 261
visual inner language system, 95

voice categories (fachs), 23–25
voice teacher, 8–15
    attachment to, 14
    changing, 14
    discovering your unique sound, 9
    famous "name," 13
    financial considerations, 14
    finding, 9–12, 13–14
    importance of, 8–9
    observing teaching process, 10
    questions to answer about, 11
    roles of, 9–10
    styles of teaching, 9
    traits to avoid, 11–12, 13
    trial lessons, 10
    See also lessons; practice

W

web site, 145, 183
working music, 28–32
    accompanist for. *See* répétiteurs/accompanists
    approaching new piece, 20–21, 28–29
    deciphering rhythms, 20
    expressing words through music, 31
    knowing score edition, 30
    learning new roles, 30–32
    marking up music, 20, 29–30, 227, 228, 268–69
    memorizing, 21, 29, 31, 34, 95, 96, 97
    style of music and, 38–39
    translating words, 20, 28–29, 30
    understanding tempi, 29

FIND *ARIA READY* ON THE WEB:

FIND A HOST OF practical resources for your singing career, as well as access to Carol Kirkpatrick's free monthly *Aria Ready Newsletter,* on her website, *www.ariaready.net.* You can also follow Carol and *Aria Ready* on Facebook, *www.facebook.com/ariaready.*

*Set in Warnock and Cronos
Designed and composed by Kevin Hanek
Printed and bound by Sheridan Books,
Ann Arbor, Michigan*